Don't Ask Me What I Mean

Also by Don Paterson

Nil Nil

God's Gift to Women

The Eyes

Landing Light

AS EDITOR

101 Sonnets

Robert Burns: Selected Poems

Last Words
(with Jo Shapcott)

Don't Ask Me What I Mean

Poets in their Own Words

Edited by Clare Brown and Don Paterson

PICADOR

First published 2003 by Picador
an imprint of Pan Macmillan Ltd
Pan Macmillan, 20 New Wharf Road, London N1 9RR
Basingstoke and Oxford
Associated companies throughout the world
www.panmacmillan.com

ISBN 0 330 41282 5

1 3 5 7 9 8 6 4 2

A CIP catalogue record for this book is available from
the British Library.

Typeset by Intype Libra Ltd
Printed and bound in Great Britain by
Mackays of Chatham plc, Chatham, Kent

Contents

Introduction

Poets are mad. To which tired statement we would usually find ourselves obliged to append 'as the received wisdom goes'; sadly, we can now dispense with that obligation, at least in part. The evidence that poets belong to the most mentally unstable of professions is now statistical as well as anecdotal.* The systematic interrogation of one's own unconscious is dangerous and perhaps foolhardy work; but poets have no alternative, if they are to access those darker corridors of the memory and imagination from which they might recover the true poem. The doors to these rooms often open more easily than they close, and the consequent leakage between the two worlds is poetry's unique occupational hazard, like drummer's tinnitus or miner's emphysema. No surprise, then, that when it comes to that most delicately fraught of subjects – themselves – many poets are either legendarily reticent or evasive, both strategies deriving from a strongly and sensibly self-protective urge. So this book – a guide to the work of almost all the major poets published in the UK in the last fifty years, written by the poets themselves – would have been impossible either to commission or to edit; it had to be got by surreptitious means.

* To take one of several studies: Arnold M. Ludwig, 'Method and Madness in the Arts and Sciences', *Creativity Research Journal* (Vol. 11, No. 2, 1998). Ludwig took a large sample of eminent individuals from many different professions, concluding that men and women in 'artistic occupations' have higher rates of mental instability than the rest. Among the artists, writers had the highest lifetime rates of mental disorders, and among the writers . . . the poets.

And, truth told, largely fortuitous. We were working through the archive of the Poetry Book Society as it approached its fiftieth birthday, with the idea of taking some kind of nostalgic glance back through half a century of the organisation's quarterly *Bulletin*. We were – and here the lurch into cliché is unavoidable – quite unprepared for what we discovered. ('Goldmine' is a word too easily reached for in these circumstances, but we found it on our lips continually.) Here was the last piece Louis MacNeice wrote before his death; Ted Hughes writing both on his first book, *The Hawk in the Rain*, and on the publication of Sylvia Plath's *Ariel*; Paul Muldoon on the etymology of 'quoof'; Carol Ann Duffy on difficulties with gonks; Simon Armitage on his debut collection; and practically the only words Geoffrey Hill has written on his own work – to say nothing of rare and brilliant contributions from Seamus Heaney, Kingsley Amis, U. A. Fanthorpe, Theodore Roethke, Philip Larkin, Elizabeth Jennings, Michael Longley, and many more. Some of these pieces had featured in anthologies in the past, but to our amazement no attempt had been made to gather them together in any systematic way.

Founded by a group of poets and publishers led by T. S. Eliot and Stephen Spender in 1953, the PBS aimed to develop and expand the readership of contemporary poetry. We often like to indulge the fantasy that those poets who now form the twentieth-century canon were best-sellers in their time, but the poetry-book-buying public has long been a tiny minority. Eliot and his friends attempted to improve matters by setting up a panel of selectors to sift through a pile of manuscripts four times a year, and choose the best new collection for each quarter, with the winning book then being sold to subscribers. The company chugged away with modest success for more than twenty-five years until the late seventies, when, under the shrewd chairmanship of Philip Larkin (typically, the only poet with the prudence to copyright his *Bulletin* article) a wider selection of books was made – four Recommendations, as well as the Choice – and the company became an Arts Council-funded book club.

Selection as a Quarterly Choice doubles or triples the sales of most poetry books. Amongst poets, the Choice has long been a much-coveted accolade, and bagging a Recommendation a sort of bittersweet consolation. One condition of accepting either honour is that the poet is required to write a short piece for the *Bulletin*. When faced with this request many poets are deeply uncomfortable – or at least convincingly affect to be so. Once, when asked what a particular piece *meant*, Robert Schumann responded by merely playing it again; this would clearly have been the preferred strategy of most poets posed the same question. In the past fifty years, then, the PBS has been squeezing blood from stones. But stone-blood is remarkable stuff; the glittering and gritty ichor that thumps through this book represents words as hard-won as any in the literature.

No specific remit was ever given to the poets. They could write on any aspect of themselves or their writing they liked. Some embarked on a poem-by-poem exposition of the work in their new book, which in many cases, with the benefit of hindsight, we can read now as almost an inventory of its shortcomings. Some treated it as a confessional, and there is some painfully candid reading here; many others forced themselves, for the first time, to articulate their personal philosophy or ars poetica.

It's almost horrific to note how soon posterity's ugly sister, the tumbrel of oblivion, grinds into action to deliver the less talented to their fate. Some poets, the cat's pyjamas through some three-year stretch of the late fifties or mid-sixties, have disappeared without a trace. While we had desperately hoped to unearth some unfairly neglected genius, it seemed that no great injustices had been done. What did provide the occasional shock was the great good sense and wisdom sometimes spoken by poets of average gifts – and nonsense by men and women of indisputable genius; though it should have been no surprise to find that the method is one thing, the ability to say something intelligent about it another.

And we wouldn't claim that the taste of the selectors has been unerring. It was annoying, looking back from this end of fifty years, to see some latter-day Fredegond Shove or Annabella Plumptre occasionally win out over Auden and MacNeice – and thoroughly chastening: we must assume that our own contemporary perspective is just as woefully foreshortened, and we're getting the pecking-order as badly wrong now as ever. But given that our only criteria were a) that a piece be well written and b) that it aspire to more than a list of contents, we were delighted at how comprehensive the selection turned out to be. The postmoderns will gripe at the omission of their stars, but the PBS was always aimed at a general (i.e. non-academic and non-practising) readership, one which the *ampersandeurs* neither possess nor actively seek. Some terrific live performers have also emerged over the last twenty years, but the selectors reasonably tended to take the view that their books were largely mementoes of the live show. This leaves that broad swathe in the middle, so often dismissed as the 'mainstream', a word which nonetheless accurately designates those poets engaged with the English lyric tradition. Within that group there are, we think, no more than a small handful of significant omissions. We have also included a few non-British poets who have been particularly influential on the British scene.

There are several poets represented here by more than one piece. Whilst these are all brilliant writers, this was not meant to indicate any opinion on our part of their seniority – they just happened to write more entertainingly than anyone else. We could happily have filled a book with Douglas Dunn's, Thom Gunn's or Hugo Williams's articles. There was a dishearteningly long stretch, beginning in the mid-seventies and extending into the eighties, when everyone bar a handful of poets forgot how to write a sentence, and chatty half-formed adumbration was the order of the day. (The alphabetised contents was one way of disguising this.) It seemed to take another hippie legacy – Thatcherism – to provoke the crew into literary seriousness again.

The little collection of *aperçu* and aphorism apart, these pieces have been as lightly edited as possible. All we removed were the courteous / begrudged / genuinely delighted / radiantly insincere thank-yous to the PBS selectors, references to specific poems that would be meaningless to the general reader, and in one or two instances a rogue paragraph of incontestable dullness. We have dispensed with dutiful and unenlightening ellipses, since this is not a reference book.

So there we have it. The cry of 'Don't ask me what I mean' – uttered in arrogance, in anger, in forlorn desperation, and all points between – has been perhaps the most common response to the request for an article (though that particular formulation belongs to the Scottish poet Kathleen Jamie). With a gun held to their heads, though, nearly all the poets find something quite remarkable to say on their subject. We believe these mini-essays form a unique alternative account of a turbulent and fascinating period of our literary history, and offer the reader a rare glimpse of the inspiration, method, fear and love that lie behind this literary form so often left to mumble darkly behind its own hand. We hope that readers will find it as startling and illuminating an experience as we did. So dip in anywhere, and see what these astonishing minds – so often spoken for, in both senses, by critics, academics, interviewers, publicists, biographers, detractors and champions – have to say for themselves.

Clare Brown **Don Paterson**

Kingsley Amis

A poet ought to feel complimented when somebody invites him to talk about his poetry, but he is more likely to behave as if he had suddenly been hauled to his feet to reply to a toast. Rather in the tone of one declaring himself unaccustomed to public speaking, he will mutter something about preferring to think that his poems tell their own story, about finding his work too personal a thing to discuss it in front of his readers, or about being 'too busy writing poems' to decide on his attitude to what he is doing – a favourite get-out, this, and one that should indicate an enviably high output. What he would probably like to say, if he is honest, is that he will see his readers or anyone else damned before he will reveal his almost total ignorance of what on earth he is up to as a poet. If he did try to formulate his ideas on the question, he knows how trite and/or pretentious they will sound. He is uneasily aware – and often actually announces – that many of his poems are not as good as he would like them to be, and that, since being a poet means he is almost certain to suffer from pathological laziness, some of them are not even as good as he could make them – this he announces less often. No wonder he will fight hard not to reveal any personal standard against which his readers can estimate his work.

Since this attitude is one I hold myself, I am inclined to judge it healthy. I reinforce it with the view that it is most difficult, given all the fluency and self-centredness in the world, for a poet to generalise accurately about his own work, inasmuch as every poem is an attempt at solving a completely new problem, so new that there cannot be many poets who finish one poem without some tiny apprehension that they will never be able to write another. But something positive must, I suppose, be said. Many of the poems in my book seem to me to be about morals: they are supposed to put some sort of moral question and sometimes to state or hint at an answer. This does not mean that I expect other people to find the questions relevant or the answers satisfying, or that poetry of my kind strikes me as better or more serious or what-have-you than any other kind, or that I consider myself in some special way qualified to make moral pronouncements. The poems are not meant to exhort or convince, but to interest, and for this reason they are designed to be as straightforward and entertaining as possible. This, again, does not mean that they may not all turn out to be both unintelligible and glum. Who am I to say what they are like or what they mean? That is the reader's job.

A Case of Samples: Poems 1946–1956 1956

Simon Armitage

I'd figured on constructing some snappy A to Z account of myself and the book, beginning A for Armitage and ending Z for *Zoom!*, but after failing to assign any significance to the other twenty-four letters, I've decided to stick with the A and the Z, the bookends of the alphabet, the extremities.

A for Armitage, born 1963, Marsden, Huddersfield, where I resettled after graduating then postgraduating from Portsmouth and Manchester. From the word go I've indulged in all the wrong subjects: Geography, Politics, Sociology, Psychology, even Oceanography, and although I couldn't have written half of *Zoom!* without such a broad skim of knowledge, I can't help thinking there are greater things to know about; better books to have read. On weekdays I'm a probation officer. I'm always on the look-out for some Chekhov-like analogy, such as probation being a wife and poetry being a mistress, but the infidelity goes deeper than that. The reality of such an occupation is this: it's frequently depressing, sometimes frightening and occasionally completely crushing. I'm permanently open to offers, so if there are any would-be employers looking to recruit an over-qualified, under-utilised and highly versatile body to excel in any capacity whatsoever . . . M for modesty. That would have fitted.

Zoom! the collection is sixty-one poems arranged almost chronologically, covering the period 1985 to early 1989. Five quid for three and a bit years' work, in my book, is a bargain. It's hard to express with any conviction just what the sixty-one poems are about, but certain themes, as they say, are recurrent. That's not giving much away, except to suggest that the subjects, although not unimportant, are often nodes around which a voice or a language can cluster. It's often a narrative or yarn, a build-up of images and links pebble-dashed with a mix of idiom, slang and cliché. Cliché, someone said, is anathema to poetry since it represents a bias against the truth. The notion that poetry owns the franchise on Truth has come as a great shock to me. Also, on that note, although real life is the main ingredient of these poems, they are seasoned with a generous pinch of verisimilitude. Let's call it the binding, the small egg-white lies that hold the pieces together, or the preservative by which they might last.

'Zoom' the poem is another story, a cartoon actually shown on TV some years ago. Graphically, it dived in through skin and blood, right to the limit of science: ions, atoms, quarks, whatever there is fizzing about in there. Then it zoomed out, past the Earth and the universe, out to black holes, supernovas, other galaxies. The point was, both ends of the spectrum looked exactly the same, and to a sixteen-year-old bunking off school with a pretend headache, that was highly poignant. Ten years later, when I remembered it, it seemed to fit nicely, seemed to embody the idea of similarity, which is one of the cornerstones of poetry. It represented likeness between apparently unlike extremities: small and big, loss and gain, obscurity and notoriety; even A and Z. It made everything in between worth thinking about.

Zoom! 1989

A couple of years ago I was invited to Jerusalem, and, as a part of the package, driven in a broken-down Mercedes-Benz around the West Bank of the River Jordan, and finally to Qumran, where the Dead Sea Scrolls were unearthed in the 1940s. Straight away, and not for any obvious reason, I was very taken with the story of their discovery – in earthenware pots in a cave – and wrote a poem in the car on the way back to the hotel. I realised as I was writing it that it was part of something new – a new beginning or a new book – so in the poem, it's me who finds the pots in the cave, and inside them a manuscript of my own work, the first page of which is a poem, describing me finding the pots in the cave, and inside them a manuscript of my own work, the first page of which is a poem, describing me finding the pots in the cave . . .

Going to the Holy Land was like going to Narnia. It had only ever existed as a never-never place, a map in the front of a book with a sheet of grease-proof paper to protect it, and since that visit I've become more interested in the overlap between fact and fable, and therefore in mythology, beginning with Christian mythology, having a head start in that field. Many of the poems in the book employ the image of the Cross, seen from different angles, such as the mast of a ship, or as a scarecrow or gallows, and there are various reworkings of passages and parables, most of them transferred to a twentieth century setting somewhere in the West Riding. I've also become a little bit interested in magic, or specifically in associative magic – like producing like – which is why metaphor and image and simile continue to be not just at the root of what I do, but my reason for doing it.

What else? There are several dog poems, on account of me becoming the legal guardian of a bitch Hungarian Vizsia, and a couple of translations, one again from Samuel Laycock, who was born in the village where I live, and wrote in Pennine dialect. As for the long poem that takes up over half of the book, I don't feel like saying much about it apart from the obvious, such as the fact that it describes a bonfire at the end of the century, and that it took me ages to write. I always thought that producing something of that size would put me in hospital, but the actual experience was different – not being troubled by the problem of closure, not looking for the pot of gold at the bottom of the page, just picking the thing up like a length of knitting and adding a few more rows every now and again. Also, I remembered last week that when I was younger, I promised myself that

I'd write a book about bonfires, believing myself a world expert in their construction and the art of lighting them. As a kid, 5 November rated alongside birthdays and Christmas, although the last bonfire I took any active part in ended in tears, when a five-inch nail went through my boot and straight through my foot as well. I watched the blaze from my bedroom window, lapped in bandages, coming to terms with it.

The Dead Sea Poems **1995**

John Ash

The Goodbyes is divided into three parts containing twenty-seven poems in all. Its themes are more urban than pastoral, even, to some extent, historical and architectural, since there are obviously more buildings and streets than trees or hills. There are images drawn from cinema, television, opera and science fiction. There are fake ruins, nostalgic nocturnes and modernised fairy-tales. The idea of musical structure is also important to the book, and I regard the title poem as a set of variations with an extended, adagio finale. This doesn't mean that I use the words for their sound values alone without reference to their generally accepted meanings but it does mean that, like aesthetes and Symbolists before me, I sometimes feel that I am aiming at effects that are easier for a composer to achieve. For me, poetry is not 'a spiritual exercise, a state of the soul or a placing of oneself in a situation' ('I' is not a word that occurs with any frequency), but more of an attempt to reproduce 'the splendour and freshness of a dream language'. For this reason the words aren't always expected to behave like responsible citizens earnestly in search of moral uplift: they are allowed, on occasion, to stand on their heads, thumb their noses, or suddenly burst into tears over nothing. Set subjects are suitable only for school exercises (the kind favoured by unimaginative teachers) but I distrust the kind of poetry that is never about anything but itself, and readers have a right to expect to find something they can grasp at once, if it is only the surface colours of objects and their reflections (those 'crumpled party dresses and grapefruit segments' or 'blue cranes of the container-depot'); however, I draw the line at homely, moralising anecdotage, lurid autobiographical 'revelations' (if I were to divorce a wife or lose a lover, a smiling censor would step between these events and the poems), or description of the leadenly 'realistic' sort that endows every scene it encounters with a familiarity deadening as chloroform. After all, who wants to read the world as a mediocre novel-in-verse? (Quite a number of people, as it happens: it would be foolish to imagine that there isn't a ready market for the kind of writing that induces a comfortable stupor.)

It should go without saying that the language of the poems must be an immediate pleasure in itself. If they have anything to say it has to do with the gulf between the limited and repressed nature of life as we live it, and the life we are able to imagine. The poems express this gulf. They also imply that there should exist some mechanism whereby the transforming power we call artistic imagination could act directly on life (on 'society' if you like). Such a mechanism does not exist, and this may account for a recurring note of bitterness and loss in a book designed as an elaborate *divertissement* for readers to enjoy as much as they would a very good party. Indeed, many of the poems were written to the accompaniment of the kind of music you might hear at parties or good nightclubs, that is to say, modern dance music, most of it originating in New York, the songs of August Darnell, Ashford and Simpson or the Chic Organisation, and on occasion the words of these songs have found their way into the poems.

The Goodbyes 1982

George Barker

I'll do my best, in spite of the fact that I haven't got anything at all to say about these poems that the poems themselves don't – or ought not to – say. Of course it's the vast division between that 'don't' and 'ought not' that causes all my trouble. Since I really do not know what these poems are supposed to say, apart from the things that they do in fact say, it's a little difficult to speak. I've never been able to believe that poets invented or made up or created poems: it has always seemed to me that the poem allowed the poet to discover it much as a water diviner is permitted to come upon water. For this reason I don't see how the poet can have much to say about his own poems except in such terms as: 'This one is muddy but it's got a lot of iron in it' or 'I think I left part of this one still lying in the ground' or 'If you look closely at this poem you will see right the way down to Hell.'

I can, though, if you should wish it, give a few facts about the circumstances in which I discovered some of these poems. The first and longest, 'Goodman Jacksin and the Angel', derives its topography or setting from the situation of the old cottage in which I live here on the border of Sussex and Surrey. This cottage is set half a mile up an old public right of way through deep woods; and halfway along this lane, dividing Surrey from Sussex, stands the five-barred gate at which this dialogue of a farmer and an angel is supposed to happen. (There is a stud farm for racehorses on one side of this lane; I think that the figure of Goodman Jacksin is somewhat like the remarkable farmer who runs this stable. I think he is remarkable because I never met before a man who, if he set his mind to it, could breed a horse with wings or a unicorn.) This poem was written in six weeks of the winter of 1953 and was originally subtitled 'A Theological Eclogue' but this was scrapped because it's really pretty obvious.

There is a poem called 'Calendar Thoughts for the Month of the Dead' which was originally entitled 'Calendar Thoughts for February 1953'. I believe it was the Greeks who called February the Month of the Dead: I was born in it, and I know how right they were, so I changed it. Forgive the frivolity and futility of this note, which I cannot imagine being of service to anyone.

A Vision of Beasts and Gods 1954

Nearly all the poems in this book got themselves written in ten weeks during the spring of 1961. I could hope that they are a bit simpler in style and a bit better in character and a bit less blowzy than their predecessors. Rome seems to me an extraordinarily good place for poems, just as some spots are good for mushrooms. When I came here I knew that I had simply to get up in the morning and collect the verses. I was continually reminded of John Clare's remark when they asked him where he got his poems. He said: 'I went out into the fields and found them there.' And so, for what they are, I found the poems in this book skulking among the fallen masonry of Trajan's Forum, or growing out of the Altar of Cassar, or lifting their hind legs against the pillars of Apollo. Now I wonder if it might not be simply a question of finding out where poems are, for surely it would be misguided to look for the Lyre Bird in a museum (that specimen in the Natural History Museum in South Kensington is dead) or for the Muse herself in the London Library? But however that may be (what the hell, Mehitabel) I was grateful for being given these poems (that is, the good ones; the dud ones I stole, but that's that) because, like all other poets, as I believe, who have sat around for far too long with their faculties furled, I had thought never again to be revisited by the donative powers, if, indeed, I have ever been visited by them. I may not have honoured their gifts; but I think I was visited. And if these terms of speech seem pretentious, and I suppose that they are, for one is hinting of a matter about which no one knows anything, I cannot think that these terms are much more pretentious than any others in which one might speak. Even Valéry's image of the white-coated poet as scientist appears now to be a claim of transcendental and even apocalyptic proportions. What can one say? A man does not invent poems; they discover him.

The View from a Blind I 1962

If I could put into five hundred words what these poems are about I would certainly not have wasted my time and paper elaborating those five hundred words into a lot of verses. And so I can't truly say: 'These poems are about love or death or money and they try to do this or that or the other.' They are about what they are about. Nor do I think it irresponsible to remark that they got written for two reasons: first to get them out of my head and second in the hope that they might give some people some pleasure. It is rather as though one removed with a pen-knife an abscessed tooth in the conviction that its roots might be shaped like Rodin's *Kiss* or a Japanese netsuke or the soul of the prophet Job. Or anything else that a poem might be said to look like before it gets written.

In the versification of some of these poems I have tried to avoid the gallumphing or galloping or thumping mechanics of much formal metre by evolving a line in which the emphases have been elided or ironed out as in telegrams. This metrical telegraphese represents an effort to enter the region of rhythms that exist in between classical prosody and common prose, and it differs from sprung rhythm in that I have tried to take the spring out of it. This kind of verse I have tried and am trying to construct out of a conviction that the rhetoric of metre has become almost as meretricious as the rhetoric of grammar. English verse has, in my opinion, reached such a condition of elaborate decadence on the one hand and crude banality on the other that it could be compared with the internal combustion engine just before the invention of Whittle's jet. In this sense I have tried, in some of these poems, to eliminate the Otto Cycle of classical scansion and to invent a kind of verse from which, as in telegrams, almost all the rhodomontade of rhetorical emphases has been eliminated.

Dialogues Etc. 1976

James K. Baxter

Coming out of the difficult thirties, into the rock and pumice lands of the forties, a more or less established New Zealand poet in the position of untidy solitude that this entails, I felt the need to speak personally and clearly to my fellow countrymen – and out of this need came the title sequence of my book, *Pig Island Letters*. For some time the obsession with a tight formal structure had seemed a danger to me. One could so easily be building magnificent bird cages with no birds inside them. So I wrote the sequence with the minimum of formal control and what was for me at the time the maximum of social content: there was a price in doing this of course, but I think it was well worth it. Twenty years ago I decided which side of the road I would travel on – whether as a man of letters, hoping for a cosmopolitan reputation, or as a Pig Island poet, desiring mainly to understand and converse with my fellow countrymen and the land itself. My instinct led me to the second position; perhaps through a deep loathing and horror for the UNESCO civilisation in which so many creative minds are swallowed up without a trace. But it seems to me perfectly reasonable that overseas readers should listen in, if they so wish, to a Pig Island poet conversing with his dead and living fellows.

Here, if you break wind at the Bluff it can be heard north of Auckland, a matter of a few hundred miles away. This may subject one's personal motives and attitudes to the glare of a tribal scrutiny which is hard to endure; but enduring it, one learns a little more about the tribe. The Pig Island tribe does not make me happy. Many of my poems have proceeded from a rock-bottom grief and rage; but grief is the other side of love, and rage, as Yeats has told us, can spur a poet to keep moving in the middle years.

The mystery of identity is always regional, I think – a matter of a few loves and friendships, a few well-known places, and an eventual particular death. Through my poems I seem at times on the verge of discovering my own identity; but this may be a delusion, a slight touch of megalomania. Why should one expect to be more integrated than one's fellow monads of the Western world, who watch their TV sets and wait to hurl projectiles at one another? In the meantime there is the experience of conquest and defeat on a white page, struggling to make the symbols carry the secret weight of one's own experience and the experience of the tribe. As somebody said (Auden, I think), the rest is silence – one cannot write about silence; but one can learn to trust it, as I do indeed, in terms of the Catholic cosmology I believe in. The words are in my books. I trust the Pig Island critics will break their teeth on them. The critics can only tell me, quite often incorrectly, what I have done; they cannot tell me what to do next. But one can learn from fellow poets anywhere. I learned from reading Thom Gunn how to use the syllabic forms that predominate towards the end of *Pig Island Letters*. And one thing I share with the Marxists – for me, the social and poetic impulse are never separate and distinct. Partly, at least, one writes in order to be of use.

Pig Island Letters 1966

John Betjeman

I have written verse for as long as I can remember. I have always preferred reading poetry to reading prose, which is why I have found reviewing such an odious task – I read out loud to myself and cannot skip and this causes me to read slowly.

If we are influenced by the first poetry we read after the nursery rhymes we all know, I was influenced by W. E. Henley's *Lyra Heroica*, which I was given at the age of about six or seven. I would not read blank verse in those days, as I considered not using rhyme was cheating. I used to think then that you merely had to have the same number of syllables in each successive line to make correct scansion. I didn't find out about stress till I was about thirteen.

I have never thought one subject more 'poetical' than another, but have delighted in the niceties of rhyme and rhythm and choosing certain metres and rhyming schemes to suit certain subjects. A place or a moment recalls a mood I want to put down. A line comes to me. It gives me the beginnings of the rhythm for the poem. I put down the line on the nearest available bit of paper – the back of a cigarette packet or a letter (which consequently doesn't get answered) and think about the rest of the poem in trains, driving a motor car, bicycling or walking – wherever I can be alone and recite the words out loud until they seem to be the right ones in the right order. I write very slowly and copy the completed draft out five or six times before I am contented with it. Once this process is over, I am no longer interested in the verse.

I think everyone is a poet when young and that hearing

and reading so much prose drive the poetry in most people underground. It then wells up again in the vast public memory for the words of popular songs. Much of my own verse has been written to the tunes of *The English Hymnal* and *Hymns A. & M.*, which are part of my heritage. The fact that my verse has sold so well strikes me as lucky and miraculous, for I think many living poets are better than I am.

Summoned by Bells **1960**

Eavan Boland

When I came back to Dublin in my early teens, after a childhood away, my first real emotive encounter wasn't with family or friends. It was with the city itself. I tried to read myself – a complete outsider, or at least I felt I was – into its uncertain, unreadable history. I found a series of broken, fractured clues of what it meant to be this sea-coast city, endlessly over-written by power and style. And in those first years when I was trying to understand my own background, the idea of colony became a fascinating presence. Not so much threatening as intimate: I could find myself in it.

This book is three parts speculative, but one part at least is rooted in this physical landscape. The sequence of poems called 'Colony' looks back to that time. Some of the excitement and resistance of my discoveries turn up in it.

But it wasn't just the long-ago breakages that got into that relationship with the city, and which find their way into this book. I was at boarding school in Ireland in my late teens. I used to go back at weekends to stay with my sisters in Dublin. It was an hour or so by bus, trundling and swinging along the beautiful coastal edge of the city. Sometimes I changed buses in Dun Laoghaire. The old colonial harbour looked strange to me on those weekend twilights or winter darknesses. It was chunked up with granite and its long pier wandered out towards the Irish Sea. It was often foggy and mysterious when I got there.

But it wasn't the harbour as such that stayed with me. It was the mailboat. A huge crate of lights and steam and iron, it would remain each night by the pier, ready for its evening departure.

Sometimes I saw it go. Sometimes I saw it halfway out. Sometimes it was a twinkling, disappearing figment out on the horizon by the time I got there. Occasionally I got there just before it left. One evening I saw a young woman saying goodbye to her family. She wore a winter coat, and her suitcase was beside her. There were all the hungry, wretched signs of a leave-taking. Then I went around the corner, got my bus and went into the city. And she went to another place.

This book is about the many things for which the last sight of a land – the last curve of the horizon, the last possible white glimpse of a face or a hand – is a true sign. The growing up and away of children, the changing of a familiar neighbourhood and the sheer, brute physical distance from the things and people you love. But it is also about the fact that the lost land of the title – some territory that can never be claimed, held, kept – has, for me, become more enduring than any of the places I've called home.

The Lost Land **1998**

Charles Boyle

He was short and fat and bald; he had a string of love affairs but never slept with the woman he most adored; his military career was inglorious (though he once claimed to have saved the lives of two German prisoners and a flock of merino sheep), and as a civil servant he was bored and incompetent (in a letter in code sent to his superiors he included the key to the code in the same envelope); he craved fame as a dramatist, became a novelist, and never made enough money from his writing to live off (*De l'amour*, he reckoned, sold seventeen copies in eleven years).

Stendhal was a comic figure of genius, so close to the bone that laughter is painful, and he has hovered above my desk for some time (there are a couple of Stendhal poems in my 1993 collection, *The Very Man*). Roughly a quarter of the poems in *The Age of Cardboard* 'take their cue', as the blurb says, from Stendhal, but not in any programmatic way: any Stendhalian project is by definition a matter of spontaneous detours, a muddling of dates and places and a laying of false trails. As an example from the master of the latter, take the first chapter of his longest autobiographical work, *La Vie de Henri Brulard*: on the opening page Stendhal casually refers to his experiences as a colonel in Napoleon's army at the battle of Wagram in 1809; by the end of the chapter he has admitted he wasn't a colonel, but a civilian commissioner looking after supplies; in actual fact he wasn't at Wagram at all, but ill with syphilis in Vienna. This kind of extravagance with the truth is, besides being very funny, a surprisingly effective autobiographical method: for all the liberties taken, the baseline is fidelity to the self, to the writer's frustration with the facts as they stand, and to his impulse to be unfaithful. In retrospect, I think a similar impatience is evident in many of the non-Stendhal poems in my book – which deal with, among other things, flying children, yawning, a lost earring, quasi-religious rites involving parked cars, and misprints and other errors.

Stendhal wrote fast (*Souvenirs d'égotisme* in two weeks, *La Chartreuse de Parme* in fifty-three days) and sometimes on automatic pilot, but at his best with an immediacy and directness I envy. A year or so back a colleague told me on the phone that he'd seen some of the poems from this book in a magazine and that they'd made his wife laugh in bed. That's the kind of lit crit I like.

The Age of Cardboard and String **2001**

Edward Braithwaite

Peter Laslett tells the story of how one day during the war he went up the stairway of the Library of Congress and there, at the top, with fixed bayonets and generally heavily armoured, were two splendid United States Marines in front of illuminated cases containing the Declaration of Independence and a copy of Magna Carta. They were, he said amidst laughter, 'guarding our mythology'. There was, he added, a profound irony in the situation. For me, a West Indian, ascending those same stairs, there would have been an even deeper and quite different kind of irony. I am heir (I suppose) to much of what that 'mythology' represents, but the Marines – and I myself – would have been uncertain of my exact relationship to it. In fact, I may well have been more concerned with the bayonets than with the precious scripts they were protecting. Once, for instance, travelling by train in Germany, where the Army of Occupation was still very much in evidence, I was challenged by two Marines to produce my 'card'. I did my best to explain that not only was I not a soldier in disguise; I was not even an American. The more looming of my two inquisitors hitched up his belt (he had two heavy revolvers on it, so it kept slipping down), and demanded again to see my 'card'. Reluctantly, because I thought I had read somewhere that it should be surrendered for inspection only to those in 'constituted authority', I surrendered my British passport. The Marines had a good long doubting look at it and then, not really satisfied but thwarted by those crowns and lions, they threw it back in my face.

But mythologies are necessary. The American negro has moved (or at any rate is moving) from Civil Rights to the darker neighbourhood of Black Power. Even before this, Aimé Cesaire in the Francophone West Indies, had enunciated his liberating concept of negritude.

In the English-speaking West Indies we have not (yet) developed anything similar. Some see the failure to do so as very parlous indeed: the persistence of a 'slave mentality'. Others see it as an honest stance: the refusal to create new shibboleths for old. Yet others regard the whole question as painfully neurotic: the expression of a basic inferiority complex. *Rights of Passage* reflects this triple view. It is based on my own experience of that old triple journey: in my case, from the Caribbean to Europe, to West Africa and back home again; and through its various rhythms attempts to illustrate what home – or lack of home – means to those who up to now have been unable to afford the luxury of a mythology.

Rights of Passage **1966**

John Burnside

Many of the poems in *The Asylum Dance* arose from conversations – from a casual chat over morning coffee with a neighbour, or passing encounters 'on the way' in Greece, or Norway, or Indiana, to longer, hopefully lifelong, exchanges with people I like to think of as 'soul friends' (perhaps most of all, those conversations I have had with people who live at the edge of great spaces, men and women who dwell near the sea, the desert, the prairie, or the Arctic Circle). If anything could have served, for me, as a reminder that poetry is a shared practice, arising out of exchange, inspired by the pauses in conversation and the sounds and silences of habitat, it was the writing of this book, where so much arose from the relationship between the making of a poem and the act of listening, not only to other humans, but – in a hopelessly clumsy way – to the land and the water and the air. Or not so much a relationship, perhaps, as a continuity: I have come to feel that the poems I write are not so much made, or composed (by me), as heard.

It's a reminder that lyric poetry, at least, is one of the few remaining (but I think, against all the odds, vital) traces of an essentially oral (or perhaps aural) culture – because in essence a (lyric) poem is not written, but spoken: not read, but heard. I believe that the two poets to whom this book is an unacknowledged tribute, Octavio Paz and William Carlos Williams, would have agreed. What I have learned from them is the extent to which the poem is a participatory event; that the traditions of poetry are wider than the dominant models or modes of thinking would lead us to imagine; that inspiration has some kind of meaning, if it refers purely to the air we breathe and the earth with which we dwell.

This question of dwelling is one that haunted the making of this book. I have no desire – and do not presume – to write openly polemical poetry 'about' the environment, first because I tend to dislike, as a matter of personal taste, poetry that is 'about' anything (no matter how worthwhile the subject matter); second, because the poetry I most value tells, as it were, in an oblique way, rather than directly: it is concerned with image and cadence and – I cannot avoid saying it – a form of magical (that is, invocative) thinking, as opposed to the factual and the descriptive. Nevertheless, I do consider the poetry in this book meaningfully political (amongst other things), in that it tells – obliquely – some stories about dwelling, and about estrangement – which are, I believe, vital questions with regard to our participation and survival in the life-world as a whole.

The Asylum Dance 2000

Ciaran Carson

The genesis of *Opera Et Cetera* lay in my writing a poem, in July 1994, and my difficulty in finding a name for it: sometimes, a poem begins with a title; sometimes, one suggests itself in the course of writing or at the point at which the poem is abandoned to the world; but in this case, I drew a blank. Being loath to call it 'Untitled' – as in those readings of the sixties and early seventies where, as I remember it, the poet would follow that one up with 'Untitled 2' – I eventually decided on 'X' with its attractive hints of anonymity and cancellation. It then occurred to me that other letters of the alphabet might be essayed. 'X' had taken the form of five long-lined (up to twenty syllables, or the equivalent of two iambic pentameters) rhyming couplets, and this seemed a handy matrix, where one could play with propositions and conclusions in much the same way as a sonnet form. The alphabet is an arbitrary sequence, but the skeletons of stories, as in a child's primer, lie behind it, while, at the same time, monkeys with typewriters spring to mind. I've just noticed that several half-rhymes or assonances happened in that last sentence, and I now remember how rhyme was a powerful springboard from which to launch oneself into the unknown. For, each time that I sat down to try another letter, I had no idea what I would write; nor would I have any clue about the outcome. But the accident of rhyme, once I hit on one, would provide a narrative thread, and by about the third couplet, one would have some idea as to its direction.

At any rate, I was pleasantly surprised when, in a month to the day, the sequence was completed. It was published as *Letters from the Alphabet* by Gallery Press on 6 February 1995. Throughout its writing, thesauruses and dictionaries had been constant companions. I am especially fond of the 1983 edition of *Chambers 20th Century Dictionary*, and its appendix of 'Quotations from Latin, Greek and Modern Foreign Languages' next seemed an attractive area to dissect: this came out as a sequence of eleven poems based on Latin tags. It seemed logical to call it *Et Cetera*.

Looking back at *Letters* and *Et Cetera*, it seemed that many of the poems were concerned with surveillance, or code, or disguise, though I had been largely unconscious of it at the time. In Northern Ireland, as in any troubled state, you have to watch what you say and how you say it. I remembered, at the height of the Troubles, listening to the police short-wave radio and its spelling out of salient names in code: Alpha, Bravo, Charlie, and one imagined, or tried to visualise, what incidents were happening in that aural landscape of dark static. So I began *Opera* – the works, the business, the things which are made, the covert operations. I am pretty ignorant of opera as a musical genre, beyond the received plots and arias; but I think it is to some extent dependent on cliché, and the sequence plays around with hand-me-down, sometimes histrionic ideas of narrative: Romeo and Juliet, Holmes and Watson, Keats and Cortez, Robin Hood and the Sheriff, Montagues and Capulets, all held together by various musical motifs. Concurrently to writing *Opera*, I was commissioned to translate, or make versions of, poems by the Romanian Stefan Augustin Doinas. These works, in their investigation of language and its place within a mysterious internecine state, seemed germane to my concerns, and, again, seemed to form a sequence, which I called 'Alibi', thinking of its Latin meaning of 'elsewhere'. And, of course, 'elsewhere' is often a lie; elsewhere can be here, or there, wherever the crime took place. Poems can be such versions of reality.

So, the whole enterprise of *Opera Et Cetera* was partly willed and mechanical, partly arbitrary and given. But I can truthfully say that I never knew what I was writing until it was written, or what was coming next. Poems are written for many reasons: one of them must be enjoyable surprise.

Opera Et Cetera 1996

For many years, some fragments of the work of the great French poets Baudelaire, Mallarmé and Rimbaud, half-remembered from schooldays, had been hanging around in my mind; and those bits of music led me, in 1997, to try and translate the original scores. I ended up with seventeen sonnets by Baudelaire, nine by Mallarmé, and eight by Rimbaud, which were published in 1998 as *The Alexandrine Plan*, by the Gallery Press.

Rather than be dutifully literal, I thought it a more interesting obligation to be bound by the rhyme-schemes and scansion – the alexandrine line – of the originals: and such was the pleasurable difficulty of this undertaking that I thought I'd try some sonnets of my own in the same format. The spark for the first sonnet, 'The Poppy Battle', which I completed on Guy Fawkes Day, 1997, was the debate as to whether the newly elected President of Ireland, Mary McAleese (like myself, a Northern Irish Catholic educated at Queen's University, Belfast) should – or should not – wear a poppy for the annual commemoration of the battle of the Somme. This led me to explore the pharmaceutical and emblematic ramifications of the poppy, and before long I found myself embarked on the sequence of seventy-seven sonnets which makes up *The Twelfth of Never*.

I discovered that the French stuff – Baudelaire's realm of the senses, Rimbaud's ironic commentaries on war, Mallarmé's syntactical subterfuges, all of them concerned with notions of *liberté*, both political and aesthetic – was not that far removed from the issues of contemporary Ireland, the ongoing struggle between idealism and pragmatic reality. I finished the book in 1998, two hundred years after the failed Irish rebellion of 1798, which had been inspired by the French. So the songs of '98 were very much in my mind; the French alexandrine line, with its extended foot, seemed not that far removed from Irish ballad metre; and the sonnet, to my mind, can perform some of the functions of song. It also has great anecdotal possibilities.

Orange lilies, green shamrocks, flags, emblems, badges, disguises, fairies, metamorphoses, drugs, war and peace, among others, came into the picture. I began to think of the poems as woodcuts populated by stark interrogating figures. Indeed, our assumed rights are often questionable. I was brought up between the Irish and English languages, and still wonder about the way to say a thing. Poetry does not offer any answers; the fun is in the investigation.

The Twelfth of Never 1999

Charles Causley

For me, the central problem in writing is the age-old one of communication. There's not much point in talking on a dead line. 'Simplify, simplify,' wrote Thoreau. But at just what point does one stop, and allow suggestibility to take over? Every poem is a venture along a knife-edge towards that exact degree of simplification.

The effect of a poem (but not necessarily its 'meaning', whatever that implies) should be instantaneous. At the same time, the poem should conceal certain properties that may only reveal themselves very gradually. It's not the business of the poet to allow a poem, at a first reading, to burn itself out in one brilliant flash. The poem must have something in reserve; it must be capable of showing fresh aspects of its nature to reader as well as to writer, perhaps over a period of years of reading and re-reading.

Poetry, to me, has always been a special kind of autobiography. In the process of writing it, something highly personal has – somehow – to be universalised. I'd hope that the poems in *Underneath the Water* together form a unity, and aren't merely a lot of fragments. This hope may very well be forlorn, for the poet is the last man on earth to judge the total effect of a new collection of his own work: he is too near, and already too far, from what he has written.

Apart from the years 1940–1947, I have lived all my life in Launceston, a small Cornish market-town. Since 1947, I have worked as a teacher (all subjects from religious education to disorganised games), mainly with children under the age of twelve. As a child, I went to the same school where I now work: a rather grim-looking building put up in 1840 on the rim of the borough allotments.

It's not surprising, then, that several poems in *Underneath the Water* are concerned with childhood: my own, and of those I try to 'teach' – always conscious of Bernard Shaw's maxim that he who attempts to 'mould' a child's character is the worst type of abortionist. I am also concerned to examine, and re-examine, the mythology of my own town, whose stones I sometimes think I know too well for comfort. Two other obsessive themes I hope I shall now never escape are those of the war and the sea. It was Brendan Behan who described his neuroses as the 'nails and saucepans' of his trade, and expressed not the slightest wish to be free of them. I share the sentiment.

I think I became a working poet the day I joined the destroyer *Eclipse* at Scapa Flow in August 1940. Though I wrote only fragmentary notes for the next three years, the wartime experience was a catalytic one. I knew that at last I had found my first subject, as well as a form. Living and working on the lower-deck meant that if I was to write anything at all, then it would have to be in the kind of shorthand of experience (to use a horrible phrase) poetry happens to be.

I've tried to go on doing this. I write my poems slowly, at about the speed of coral; and I recognise that this slowness of pace may be equally as dangerous as writing quickly. But I feel that one of the poet's greatest dangers is the impatience that Goethe warns against: 'We must be right by nature so that good thoughts may come before us like free children of God, and cry "Here we are!" '

Underneath the Water **1968**

Kate Clanchy

I've just got my first review. It's from *The Big Issue* and it says Kate Clancy (*sic*); poems about blokes. Well, really. I always had an uneasy feeling that my poems about men would preoccupy the critics, but that strikes me as reductive. In the circumstances, though, it seems coy to insist that my poems are really about the power of the imagined life, or to point out that there's a very good poem purely about rain on page 29 – so I've decided to write about gender.

Ages ago, at university, I got an A– for Feminist Theory. I could, and would, have told you all about women writing in hysterical voices, the endless deferral of meaning, gaps in texts, the (absent) iconography of breast milk, and the real, terrible difficulties that women have had in writing. It was a lot of fun, and very productive as a critic – at one point, I remember, I had an original thought about *Jane Eyre* – but it didn't help me to think that I might write, and seemed to censor my restless, preoccupying desires for the arrogant young men camped just outside the seminar room, with their leather jackets and their certainty.

I couldn't fit my life into the life of the women writers I admired; line up my loving, domestic father who carried me to nursery school on his shoulders, my remarkable mother, who insisted I should have all the education and space she had fought for and more, with bullying Barrens or gruesome Plaths. I was offered, instead, and have led, the life that women writers have always dreamed of. I have earned my own money, found my room of my own, controlled my fertility, chosen my friends –

I have lived like a man. Interestingly illegitimate to say, but mostly I was still struggling with the wish, not to write, but to be the object of someone else's writing – to be a martyr, a victim, a muse, an object of desire. I was, unsurprisingly, hopeless at this – muses are silent.

My road to Damascus was reading Carol Ann Duffy's *The Other Country* in a dusty school stockroom. I went around for weeks clutching the book and reading the poems to anyone I met. I transformed my thinking – here was a woman writing about desire, anger, loss, and not in disguise, through the mirrors and refractions that I had been taught to look for, but directly, in full colour, with music, with smells. I thought – perhaps I can do that.

So I started, writing about desire just as men always have – for that is all I think the muse is, desire – proclaiming, seducing, reproaching, all of it out loud, all of it in the most accurate language I know, the language that does not seem to me to defer meaning, but to fix it – poetry.

There is a line in *Much Ado About Nothing* that has always haunted me: 'O God, that I were a man, I would eat his heart in the marketplace.' I am allowed, by freakish grace of history and family, into the marketplace, and I'll stand there and proclaim my poems about blokes, and there will be laughter and some blood, but no one will try to cart me off to the asylum. I can hardly believe my luck.

Slattern **1996**

Austin Clarke

I cannot claim to have seen Queen Victoria on her last visit to Ireland, owing to lack of interest. My father lifted me up in the middle of the Dublin crowd but my attention was held by the decorations at the city boundaries.

I had not even heard of the Irish literary revival or the Abbey Theatre till my first year as an undergraduate. I was fortunate, therefore, in catching a last glimpse of an exciting period and in meeting Yeats, Æ, Lady Gregory and others. When my first poem was published in a local periodical, a friend brought me to one of Æ's literary gatherings in a Sunday evening. Æ said a few encouraging words and made me sit beside him. I was bewildered to find that everyone was discussing politics. Suddenly the poet turned and introduced me to a queer-looking little man on my left. This was James Stephens, and I was delighted for I had been reading his *Hill of Vision.* He glanced up at me sharply and said, 'That was very good verse of yours but I hope you don't think it was poetry.' Undaunted by this reproof, I came again on the following Sunday. On my way home, I found myself in the tram beside James Stephens. This was too much for me and I did not venture back to Æ's house until several years later, when I had written my first book. I had learned my lesson and realised how firmly the poetic privileges and rules were guarded.

I saw most of the early plays of Yeats at the Abbey Theatre and, when the curtain fell, the author always appeared outside it, a dim figure against the footlights. He was still the Poet of the

Celtic Twilight, swaying, waving his arms rhythmically, telling us in a chanting voice about his 'little play'. I was determined to write verse plays, despite the fact that the small size of the Abbey audience on these occasions indicated that it was not a popular pursuit. Eventually I sent a verse comedy to Yeats, asking respectfully for advice. It came back after six months with a badly typed note, in which the poet quoted a few lines in very free rhythm to show that I 'should have written the play in prose'. When I settled down in London in the early twenties, I met George Moore, whose later Greek and Irish romances I admired very much. He, too, was a strict Victorian. One evening, after dinner, he read out a lyric of mine which he liked. When he came to the second stanza, he stopped and said severely, 'There are two syllables missing in the first two lines.' I pointed out that I wanted to suggest the effect of an otter suddenly diving. 'No, no,' exclaimed Moore, 'the lines in every stanza should match.' The master of the most subtle rhythm in modern prose would permit no liberty to verse! Today young poets can do what they wish and need not feel that they are committed to any particular movement.

Few critics realise how powerful was the influence of the Irish literary movement. This was due not only to the rediscovery of Gaelic mythology and poetry, but also to the fact that it was one of the last phases of the great Romantic Movement. I found myself writing long poems about our heroic period without knowing very clearly why I was doing so. I climbed into upper glens to find the right setting for them. Once, however, on a sunny morning, I trespassed into the Seven Woods at Coole, where Yeats and Æ.

Have seen immortal, mild, proud shadows walk.

Suddenly I saw a rich blue gleam dart through the distant leaves. Was I to see a vision too? A moment later I saw the blue flash again. Wondering if it were a peacock, I crept closer and peeped between the branches. Crossing a lawn towards a

Georgian mansion, I saw a tall fisherman wearing a raincoat of sky-blue watered silk. To my astonishment, I recognised Yeats. He had become the ideal Fisherman of the poem he was to write many years later.

Despite my sceptical temperament, I found it difficult to avoid the visional intensity of my elders, especially when the temptation towards superstition took the form of woman. Ella Young, pale, ethereal, dressed in grey flowing silks, looked like an ancient priestess and when she lit a joss stick and spoke of ancient gods, I found it hard to resist. Maud Gonne was as fascinating when she spoke of her awareness of the Invisible Land. She had drawn Yeats into revolutionary politics but he had lured her even farther into the visionary past. It was not until 1938, when I published *Night and Morning*, that I found myself back in the present.

The title poem of *Old-Fashioned Pilgrimage* is a description of a visit I paid to America to see places associated with writers whom I read when I was adolescent: Emerson and Thoreau had had much influence in the early days of the Irish revival. Professor Edward Dowden was one of the first to praise Whitman, and T. W. Rolleston translated *Leaves of Grass* into German. Among other subjects dealt with in the book are Vietnam, the Pill and Ecumenism, grave and gay.

Old-Fashioned Pilgrimage 1967

Billy Collins

Performing an act of literary criticism on your own writing is a little like do-it-yourself dentistry: a sloppy affair at best, not to mention the pain involved for writer and reader alike. But in the interests of experimentation and in a mood of gratitude after having my book picked as a Poetry Book Society selection, I will open wide and reach for the drill.

The title was drawn from a poem I wrote about an art work that my wife gave me for my birthday a couple of years ago – a piece which served, conveniently enough, as the cover art for the book. The work is composed of nine squares of black Carrara marble onto which has been printed, by some mysterious process of emulsion, a detail from one of Eadweard Muybridge's motion-study photographs of horses. Muybridge, by tripping a sequence of camera shutters along the perimeter of a race track, was the first to provide a definitive answer to the vexing, age-old question of whether all four hooves of a galloping horse leave the ground at once (they do).

The work was hung (and continues to hang) in the largest room in our house, and the haunting demeanor of the horses, plus the question of why my wife would purchase such a thing for me, prompted the poem that became the book's title. Some bookstore browsers might be misled and assume the book is about horses, but I only see that as an opportunity to attract new readers. I have long appreciated the gentle deception involved in such perversely misleading titles as Richard Brautigan's *Trout Fishing in America*, which is not really about trout fishing, and

Henry Taylor's brilliantly titled recent collection of poems, *An Introduction to Fiction.*

Someone once remarked that many young poets want to write a book of poetry, but they don't want to write any poems. I am one of those poets who writes poems one at a time, not books of poems. A book occurs when enough decent work piles up to constitute a book. At this point in my so-called career, I have certain rituals I follow in organising a book. For example, I like to place at the book's outset a poem which addresses the reader directly. I have read a lot of poetry that seems to be oblivious to the presence of a reader, and I place a poem in the beginning to assure readers that I am not only aware of their existence but determined to engage and maintain their attention – shamelessly. In *Nine Horses,* it's a poem called 'Night Letter to the Reader'.

As for the order of the poems, I am also ritual-bound. What I do to order a manuscript is to spread all the poems out on the floor and then walk around them, like Jackson Pollock over a canvas, looking for a poem to tell me that it would rather be next to a poem other than its current neighbor. I keep listening for the poems to tell me what other poems they want to be with. Gradually, like people at a party, smaller groups are formed. It's not that these groups are thematically or tonally similar. I couldn't articulate exactly what they have in common. I just try to put them in the kind of company they might be at ease with. This requires a light, Ouija-board sort of touch. I often have to interrupt this occult process by walking around the house a few times to clear my head.

As for the poems themselves, what can I say except that every one is a failed attempt. That each fails in its own special way might be as much uniqueness as I can claim for them. Think of it this way: the ideal poem for me is one in which the reader could never be sure at any given point if the poem were serious or trifling, earnest or playful. Poetry provides a safe home for ambiguity and ambivalence. Any poem which sets out to be merely amusing or merely sincere fails to take advantage of poetry's strange duplicity. What keeps me writing poems – besides the sheer self-entertainment value of playing with language – is the impossible hope that one day I will produce that perfect poem, the one that is balanced precisely on the knife-edge between comedy and tragedy, or at least between silliness and sincerity. As it is, every poem I have ever written loses its balance and falls to one or the other side. No wonder there are only the two cartoonish masks of drama: tragedy's grimace and comedy's rictus smile. Never the fleeting face of irony.

But enough of this dentistry. And anyway, my theory of writing poetry is like Ron Padgett's philosophy of life: just cook well, then butter and serve. Butter and serve.

Nine Horses 2003

Wendy Cope

A perceptive reviewer of my last collection, *Serious Concerns*, observed that it was written 'out of deep despair'. This one wasn't. Life got better, and I became even less prolific than I used to be. In 1999 someone told the *Sunday Times* that I had stopped writing. They printed this information without bothering to check it and I didn't really mind, but it wasn't true. Most years since 1991, when my last book went to press, I've produced a handful of poems. There were times, admittedly, when I thought I was just too contented and boring to write any more. One day, when I had been feeling entirely convinced of this, I was surprised to find myself writing the poem I've called 'Being Boring'.

It occurred to me that *Being Boring* would make an eye-catching and daring title for the whole book. My publishers said it was too daring, and they were probably right. Anyway, although the idea amused me, I decided that an amusing title might be a mixed blessing this time round. It's difficult enough to get the world to notice that my poems don't all have jokes in them. So I settled for *If I Don't Know*, the title of a poem about wandering around the garden on a beautiful evening in June.

The garden comes into half a dozen other poems in the book. Here I have paused for a long time, trying to think of some more generalisations to make about the contents. There are a few love poems, one or two humorous items about the opposite sex, and three poems about paintings – two poems I quite like and one I dislike intensely. As in my earlier books, there are some poems about poetry and poets, none of them, this time, by Jason Strugnell. There's a sequence of short poems called 'Traditional Prize County Pigs'. These are not about poets or about men. They are about pigs. There's a poem about socks. There's a poem about a confirmation present. And some others, about this and that. You will have gathered that this is not a book with a theme.

The last poem is a twenty-two-page narrative called 'The Teacher's Tale'. It is fiction but it draws on my experience as a London teacher. I began teaching in 1967, when my central character would have been six years old, and continued until the 1980s. The story is in rhyming couplets, which turned out to be more difficult than I expected, and the going was sometimes very slow. I cheered up when someone told me that Milton only managed twelve to fifteen lines a day when he was working on *Paradise Lost.* And he didn't have to think of rhymes.

If I Don't Know **2001**

Frances Cornford

I have written verses all my life, but very rarely a poem that goes on to the next page, and if it does it is generally one of my worst poems.

I am rather more satisfied with my late work than with my earlier, because on the whole it is simpler and more detached; though when I have been especially moved I think I have always written fairly simply. Nevertheless, to start writing in the Edwardian era was certainly a handicap for any minor poet, since at the back of our minds we carried a heavy cargo of affectations and half-dead poeticisms. On the other hand I am glad that a good deal of skill in manipulating words was expected from us as a matter of course, though any that I myself managed to acquire alas did not come from a classical education, which my scientific family had not considered necessary. It came chiefly, I believe, from the endless poetry games I played as a child, above all with my brother Bernard Darwin, who was nine years older than me, and at that time an inspired writer of light verse. Our poetry game consisted in choosing six or eight words at random, and then having to fit these into a coherent verse or two, within ten minutes. I remember feeling quite sick sometimes with the effort to be worthy of my brother's ready and delightful praise, as well as my shame, when, although time was up, I had not been able to work in, say, the word 'hippopotamus'.

My mother read me Elizabethan and seventeenth-century lyrics when I was quite young, and I remember learning by heart, very early because I liked it so much, Sir Thomas Wyatt's

Forget not yet the tried intent
Of such a truth as I have meant . . .

and delighting in Suckling's

If of herself she will not love,
Nothing can make her:
The devil take her!

This last seemed wonderfully daring to me. When I was about fourteen, my father introduced me to some of the poems of Swinburne and Browning. I was allergic to Swinburne, which rather puzzled me, because I had thought I should naturally always like the same things that he did, but Browning was a revelation to me. The line about the blue spurt of a lighted match made a small thunderclap in my mind. I suddenly saw that ordinary every-day experiences, such as I thought nobody but myself noticed, could become real poetry in a book. Later I used to sleep with a volume of Browning under my pillow, though the book sometimes seemed to have a great many corners in the middle of the night.

I gave no consideration to the verses I found myself writing from time to time, because the whole ambition of my youth was to be a painter, a career for which I was remarkedly ungifted.

The painter William Rothenstein was a friend of my parents, always very kind to me, interested and helpful, though at the same time he was never for one moment falsely encouraging. When I was a grown-up young woman I used sometimes to sit and draw with him in his studio, and he would talk to me about anything that came into his head. One day, agreeing with something or other he had said, I added: 'I've written a poem about that.' Afterwards he made me produce a few youthful lyrics from the bottom of my writing case, and then said: 'But this is what you ought to do.' Those eight words opened my eyes. Though I realised that he had overpraised what I had actually shown him, I saw from then on that verses came naturally to me and that painting did not.

Rothenstein persuaded my father to print privately my first volume of poems. Roger Fry reviewed it very kindly in the *Times Literary Supplement*, and it had a small *succès d'estime*.

By then I was married, and very glad to have found my own medium, since for a woman wanting to lead a usual domestic life, there is no form of creation so feasible as scribbling spontaneously on the backs of envelopes, and then struggling hard with the scribbles during quiet interludes of time.

Collected Poems 1954

Patrick Creagh

When you invite a poet to write about himself and his work, you are asking him to tell you his secrets. If he is a young poet, and does so, then he is young and foolish, because his secrets are as like as not his only possession. A secret is the only kind of information which, when given away, is never set eyes on again. It is not like a funny story, which only comes to life when it is told. So a poet's secrets are his hoard of treasure, and nothing short of a dragon is a worthy guardian for them, not even St Peter.

What I mean by secrets, of course, is the personal experience from which poems are made. This is usually a mess of half-formed, malformed, misunderstood, obscure and perverse data which can only be completed, reformed, grasped or clarified by being made into works of art. That a successful poem is a work of art is sometimes forgotten. It is a joy kissed as it flies. Elucidation, however perceptive, bends the joy to itself and destroys the winged life. And in terms of what came before the poem, which is all the explanation a poet can give, it is a step back into the darkness, if the poem is successful.

The 'experience' in a successful poem is seen on the point of emerging from incomprehensibility, and one step further would stretch it on a cold white table in the morgue of over-simplification. As it becomes intelligible, thought ceases to be personal. Everything that is truly ours is baffling, and in understanding something we lose it without regret.

Is there no such thing as a personal poem? In the strict sense, there is not. There is only a poem made from the delirium of personal experience. When the excitement or suffering of that experience affects the reader, this is due not to the experience, but to art. Perseus took the measure of Medusa by looking in the polished shield Athene gave him, but the myrmidons of common-sense were turned to stone.

A poem is a work of fiction, and totally unreal. As he handles experience and wrenches it into art, a poet takes the real and from it creates something imaginary. He 'leaves a metaphor where there was once a man'. Metaphors are hard and durable, but the fragments of experience, like men, are complex, incomplete and mortal. 'Never seek to tell thy love.'

A Row of Pharaohs **1962**

Fred D'Aguiar

1963. The beginning of the severest winter in living memory. A telegram from Guyana answers my parents' prayers – POST THE CHILDREN. Sent by either pair of my grandparents, it agrees to take my two brothers and me under its wing. Mummy accompanies us, leaving Daddy to take care of the house in snowbound Catford.

After thirteen days of an extremely rough crossing the liner reaches Trinidad. We fly the rest of the hop-over journey to Georgetown. We are victims of the widely held belief, rampant in the late fifties and dying a slow death in the early sixties, that only an upbringing like the one my parents had could save us and the children of my generation from certain moral decay, induced by growing up in England.

The rationale went something like this: hadn't they seen with their own eyes and heard with their own ears those force-ripe English kids giving their parents hell, making V-signs in their parents' faces when asked by them to do or not to do something or other, telling them to eff-off even, and worse didn't the parents just laugh, seeing in it a sign of precocity – a good thing! What so-an-so would-a do if such-an-such a thing was or was not said or done right away. How that damn pickney would-a get box into next week. An'y'u rememba de time Wynstan open he mout against he fadder? Rememba wha' 'appen? Before he finish he sentence – I mean before he could-a get out de first word – is nah flat-out he end-up flat-out fram a back-hander?

The voyage left Greg, Patrick and myself with a permanent need to rock, either in order to fall asleep or in our sleep. My four other brothers, Andrew, John, Godfrey and James, none of whom have sailed, do not exhibit this phenomenon. I am watching Patrick's recently born son, Ashley, for any sign of the genetic transmission of what we have come to call rocking.

In the house at Airy Hall, occupied by upwards of twenty children belonging to various aunts and uncles, we are warned (by the children) not to proceed in a path crossed by a black cat (in town a black cat is good luck), to never visit places where there is no pinch of salt handy to throw over the shoulders or no wood to touch for luck in case of bad talk, or no garlic, horseshoe or cross over the threshold, never look into the evil eyes of certain people who stare you out long enough to deposit a curse on your head, never pee on fire if you don't want to wet your bed into adulthood, never break a spider's web with your face (it's unpleasant), and never, never, never steal a penny weighting the lids of a dead person's eyes or he will haunt you, unable to leave this world for the next until you do.

We are also warned about a range of nocturnal spirits. The Buckoo is a male dwarf. He roams the yard and fields near the house at night in search of stray children. A Buckoo's victim is found lifeless but without a scratch. This is because the Buckoo is only interested in the child's spirit.

The Jumby is another spirit, this time returned from the dead for the sole purpose of haunting the living. They can appear in human form or else are known to the sensitive as a sensation: hairs on the back of the neck stand on end; the skin goose-pimples in the warmest of weathers; the sudden, involuntary shudder, the cold sweat. On the stillest days they shake bushes, bang doors and windows. They are the figures seen from the outside of the house crossing a window; when you rush indoors there is no one to be found. They make the noises in a room you are sure is empty.

As for Ol' Higue, the most vicious spirit of all since she turns into a ball of fire and sucks the blood out of babies, that's another story, except to say we are introduced in my book to a woman who is so tall she has to duck through doors, who is said to be clairvoyant, telepathic and an insomniac, who's called Mama Dot.

Mama Dot 1985

Donald Davie

A poet writes, not what he wants to write, but what he finds he can write; he writes, or at any rate he prints, only what is left after the spirit of the age and his own incapacities have ravaged and pared down his own more ambitious intentions. And so the image of himself and his own world which emerges from his poems is as disconcerting to him as to anyone else; the poems in print give back to him the image of a stranger, a stranger whom he may even, quite heatedly, dislike. And yet it is no accident that some things and some attitudes turn out to lend themselves to his pen, certain others to resist him; for this means that those intractable themes are things he has not felt with the sincerity that poetry demands. It is this which makes the writing of poetry for the poet a process of self-discovery; this image which emerges from his poems considered together, this stranger, is a person whom he has to recognise as more truly himself than the person he had always supposed himself to be.

This poem I call mine, *The Forests of Lithuania*, has revealed to me some new sides of this poet who bears my name. I am glad to see, for instance (what I had almost despaired of), that he is capable of breaking out of the circle of his private agonies and dilemmas, in order to acknowledge that there are other people in the world besides himself, very different but just as interesting. It turns out that he is capable of responding to trees and animals and clouds and flowers as good and beautiful in themselves, not just as symbols of his own inward world, images by which that inward world may be made outward and manifest. He seems to have learned how to be more straightforward and lucid than ever before, at least on some subjects. And I think he has learned some new tunes to play, in the music of verse. In other ways he still disappoints me; I suspect there are yet other sides to him which may be revealed in the future, when he has found out how to be sincere about them.

Of course it's easier to see why I am interested in this mysterious person than to know why others should be interested. That must depend, I suppose, on how far they can recognise in him not a wholly special case but someone representative of his nation and his generation. And although his poem is set in a foreign country and a past age, I think it can be seen to come out of England in the 1950s, if less directly than the poems of Philip Larkin or John Betjeman, just as certainly – if only because he is himself, consciously and fervently, an Englishman of the present time. I hope you will like his poem.

The Forests of Lithuania 1959

Peter Didsbury

The majesty of language. We get exposed to a 'bracelet of bright hair about the bone', or 'aspens dear whose airy cages quell', and poetry perpetuates itself. No problem. The poet can give the same answer to the question Why? as the mountaineer: Because it's there. But also, and unlike the climber, and far more importantly indeed: So that it should continue to be there.

For me, the excitement of language itself, with its literally infinite possibilities, and the conviction that in writing a poem one is exemplifying, in however small a measure, the creative processes and hunger at the heart of the universe, are the *sine qua non.* These are premises which do nothing to constrain. They also, incidentally, help me to formulate my distaste at being described as a postmodernist. To make no other objection, I believe I'm engaged in tasks and duties and pleasures which are nothing if not ancient.

That Old-Time Religion is not a thematic collection, and nor did it set out to be. One of the main reasons for writing, and then collecting, poems still seems to me to be to discover what's been going on in the heart and mind, and I've never been particularly interested in using them simply to express something I'm already clear about. Certain themes do emerge, though, and I'd be quite happy about describing some of these as 'religious' in orientation.

The opening poem, entitled 'The Shore', describes an epiphanic experience of the Void, or Emptiness, which occurred to me while carrying out archaeological fieldwork one freezing February day on the Humber foreshore. Other short lyrical pieces arising out of related Zenic perceptions occur throughout the book, and may be seen as counterpointing the darkly comic absurdities of some more rigorously confident cosmologies. The title poem portrays God Himself in the process of discovering the frustrations of omnipotence, his sophistries exposed as He's given the run-around by a suavely urbane Satan.

Rather nastier versions of the Foremost Among the Angels and his Creator make their appearance in 'The Devil on Holiday', the longest poem I've published to date and one which takes as its starting point the Deity's instruction to Satan, recorded in the Old Testament, to walk abroad on the Earth and see whom he can tempt. The particular part of the Earth in question in my version of the story turns out to be a rather luxuriant analogue of the city of Duluth, which Satan doesn't recognise because, of course, *he's never been to America.*

The protagonist of 'The Devil on Holiday' proves to be seriously wrong in his perceptions of what's going on, and so, I'm interested to realise as I write this, are several others of my characters in this book, from the bear who confidently expects to be transmuted into a sofa at the moment of death to a poet who, while writing to an editor, unwittingly betrays his interest in achieving a lasting relationship with money . . . and a poet can't get much more mistaken than *that.*

That Old-Time Religion **1994**

Michael Donaghy

It's embarrassing to discuss your own poems in print. You come across as either an awestruck fan of your own genius or a tedious explainer of jokes. Might as well save time and submit your effort directly to Pseuds Corner.

First off, my apologies for the title of this book. God knows I resisted it – too hieratic, I thought, too romantic, too dry ice. And I appreciate the valiant efforts of all those wiser friends who fought on my side, even the one who suggested I call it *Grimoire*. But we lost. In the end these poems insisted on banding together under a word that could easily appear on a perfume bottle or a computer game. But let me list a few reasons in *Conjure*'s defence.

First, it's an imperative, a command to perform magic – a word which in turn could mean anything along a scale that runs from Jesus to Tommy Cooper. I mean by such blasphemy to suggest that all the trickery of art, the hours spent practising the deception, perfecting the sleight of hand or calculated ineptitude, is a necessary distraction for both the illusionist and the audience so that some genuine transformation can take place in our heads. The ritual gesture wherein I hold the Jack of diamonds up for your scrutiny before changing it into the very card you picked earlier is hocus-pocus, a corruption of *hoc est corpus*, wherein I elevate a sliver of bread and change nothing of its appearance, though, as Aquinas tells us, the species of the Eucharist has been sanctified. The poetry readings I attend are sometimes like in-house performances at the Magic Circle. An audience of fellow professionals sits back taking notes or wondering where the performer bought his rabbit. My aim in writing these poems, however, was to address the initiates of poetry's Magic Circle as well as a broader congregation.

Secondly, 'conjure' derives from the Latin *conjurare*, to swear together, suggesting a ritual performed by two or more celebrants, not a solitary act. I tried to avoid talking to myself in the reader's presence because it's rude. But I invite my readers to play the role of eavesdroppers and hope they won't insist on knowing precisely who I'm talking to (even if it's them). I fancy I'm bound by the sanctity of the confessional – not as in 'confessional poetry', mind, but the box where the sacrament is conducted. It's pointless to speculate, and I'm not about to say whether any given poem in this collection is a fable or an indiscreet disclosure slipped in to satisfy some readers' appetites for 'intensity'. The facts of my little life are beside the point. I tried to tell the truth by working truly. One morning in my devout childhood when I was queuing to confess that week's lies it struck me that the adults queuing with me were likely guilty of an unperceived sin of arrogance, of assuming it was they and not the massed total of their experience that had sinned. Such spells of vertigo have led me to experiment with different voices.

Thirdly, I'm struck with a peculiar connotation this verb once enjoyed in its long history. '*Nay, I'll conjure too,*' says Mercutio, lampooning Romeo's new role as love-sick erotic poet.

Romeo! humours! madman! passion! lover!
Appear thou in the likeness of a sigh:
Speak but one rhyme, and I am satisfied;
Cry but 'Ay me!' pronounce but 'love' and 'dove;' . . .
I conjure thee by Rosaline's bright eyes,
By her high forehead and her scarlet lip,
By her fine foot, straight leg and quivering thigh
And the demesnes that there adjacent lie,
That in thy likeness thou appear to us! . . .

'Twould anger him
To raise a spirit in his mistress' circle
Of some strange nature, letting it there stand
Till she had laid it and conjured it down;
That were some spite: my invocation
Is fair and honest, and in his mistress' name
I conjure only but to raise up him.

The meaning of raising a spirit in his mistress's circle is echoed in an anonymous eighteenth-century song sent me recently by a friend in which a young man can't sleep because he's troubled by a common complaint of youth:

So vigorously the spirit stood,
Let him do what he can,
Sure then he said it must be laid,
By woman not by man.

A handsome maid is enlisted,

She having such a guardian care,
her office to discharge;
She opened wide her conjuring book,
And laid the leaves at large.

Little in these poems is designed to conjure such frisky spirits up or down, but I admit to returning to the MS again and again over the past seven years, often in the dead of night, with an obsession comparable only to my more goatish impulses. Nevertheless, I hope *Conjure* lives up to its Latin origins, a ritual performed by two or more celebrants, not the solitary act.

Finally it's *Conjure* because it's dedicated to that master conjuror whose assistance in writing these poems has been invaluable. He was only four last April, but someday he'll be able to read both this apology for writing him such a gloomy, rainy and sometimes brutal book. And I hope he'll read these thanks, too, for forcing me to improvise so many fables when we were both half asleep, and recalling me, whenever necessary, to that world where, in the hour it took to write this report, two blue Lego blocks have conversed gently and consoled one another with kisses before barking and flying away.

Conjure 2000

Maura Dooley

When finally I arrived at the title of this book (*Kissing a Bone*) and phoned Neil Astley at Bloodaxe to tell him, he said it was fine. Ten minutes later he called me back amused and slightly anxious to ask whether I was aware of the ambiguity in it. Did I know the American expression 'a boner'? Dimly. I knew it dimly. An erection, a hard-on, a tumescence. Dear, dear, the frustrated inventiveness of the male vocabulary. The bone in this instance is the relic of a saint, hallowed, revered, behind glass – but certainly there are other bones creaking in this book, not many of them holy, not all of them dead. So I welcomed a little of that ambiguity.

People seem to feel this collection was a long time coming: five years. Well, sometimes life gets in the way. My father died, my daughter was born, I lived in another country for nearly a year, I moved house, I began to work freelance and changed jobs more often than shoes. Mostly these poems are far from being autobiographical or confessional, yet, between and because of these shifts, the poems began to assemble themselves. Darker poems than before and less biddable.

I wanted to write about loss in love and life with its embarrassments, and wry messiness, as well as its griefs. I wanted to write about memory and photography, their symbolic relationship, their devouring of each other and their eventual translation into 'history', which is, after all, only another kind of fiction.

Two parts of the book are gathered into brief sequences. One, 'The Future Memory' concerning the image, whether held in the mind or on film, and the other, 'Suburban Myths', describing the dissolution of a marriage. I hope these sequences can be plundered at will, that they will be dipped into and out of as much as read in strict order. The difficulty of making any order of such chaotic subject matter is part of the point. Other poems travel across very different worlds, emotional and geographical, via train, bus and Concorde – that extraordinary machine, a triumph of imagination over common sense, whose development and noisy adolescence ran pretty much in tandem with my own.

Now I have to see where the journey takes me next. U. A. Fanthorpe once told me always to keep back a few favourites, 'don't rob the nest'. Good advice, I think to myself as I look in my all but empty folder and try to remember how to write a poem.

Kissing a Bone **1996**

Mark Doty

I've been stunned – and deeply gratified – by readers' responses to *My Alexandria*, in part because this collection of poems grew out of a personal struggle that has been at the center of the last six years of my life. It is remarkably affirming to a writer when something forged in privacy, out of the need to give shape to difficult experience, becomes a text in which readers seem to find their own experiences reflected.

My writing has always been concerned with questions of mortality – how the evanescent world slips away from us, how time rewrites our experiences – but in 1989 these matters took on a new urgency when my partner of eight years learned that he was HIV-positive. This knowledge seemed to split the world apart; it seemed that almost everything about our lives had to be rethought, reconsidered. How much time did we have? How did we want to use that time? How could we live in the present, in the moment, when our sense of the future was so deeply compromised?

Of course we all know that our lives and the lives of those we love will end, but most of us are able to keep this knowledge at a comfortable distance. HIV infection changes that; the sword that hangs over all our heads suddenly looms a great deal closer. *My Alexandria* was written in the strange, anxious period between Wally's diagnosis and the onset of AIDS – a time of great anxiety, but a time that also offered, unlike illness itself, a kind of terrible leisure of contemplation, time to think.

This is not a book of 'documentary poems'. I think of it, rather, as a text and artifact of spiritual struggle. How does one learn to live in the grip of contingency? How might we be educated by anticipatory grief? And how, finally, do we love a world that's always disappearing?

The act of writing poems, of course, doesn't really answer these questions. A poem is more an embodiment of a question, a way of giving it form. When we give something a shape, when we hammer feeling into song, that act of making is in itself a consolation, a way of making the difficult bearable.

Writing these poems was one way of surviving; the work helped me to live. But poems don't exist just for their maker, if they really are poems; it's the act of shaping an experience in language for the reader which takes a poem beyond the realm of the therapeutic or self-expressive, which makes a poem a gift. The gift is given to the reader. But the writer is also rewarded, by feeling less alone, by connecting to other lives.

The warm responses of readers have demonstrated to me that HIV disease is not some separate war zone, but a part of the continuum of human struggle. Grief, it seems to me, is an education in both beauty and sorrow. The only response I can imagine to an admixture as difficult as the world's is some complicated counterpoint of praise and lament, and that is what these poems attempt to sing.

My Alexandria 1995

Carol Ann Duffy

At a poetry reading somewhere in England last year, I read the first poem in *Mean Time*; a poem whose longish title gave me A Certain Quiet Pride – 'The Captain of the 1964 *Top of the Form* Team'. I had, unquestionably, made this up. The poem is about a person – in this case, a man – who has never recovered from not being fourteen any more. During the interval of the reading, a middle-aged woman approached me in a friendly way. 'Do you know,' she said with a recognisable glee, 'you've really upset my husband.' Her husband, she went on to tell me over a glass of Regional Arts Association Red, had actually been the real-life captain of a *Top of the Form* team in the sixties. What's more, she reckoned that he was just like the poem. He was its eponymous hero. One of the lines in the poem tells how the boy owned a Gonk which he kept as a lucky mascot. After the reading, I got to meet the man in question. 'Now then,' he said keenly, 'I don't think we had Gonks in 1964.'

The poems in *Mean Time* are about the different ways in which time brings about change or loss. In the collection, I mean to write about time. The effects of time can be mean. Mean can mean average. The events in the poems can happen to the average woman or man. The dwindling of childhood. Ageing. The distance of history. The tricks of memory and the renewal of language. The end of love. Divorce. New love. Luck. And so on. In the last book I published with Anvil, *The Other Country*, I had begun to write more personal, autobiographical poems; and this switch from the dramatic-monologue-dominated stance of earlier collections is intensified in *Mean Time*; the techniques stumbled across and refined in writing in 'Other Voices' helped me to pitch my own voices – for we all have several – particularly when finding language for the painful areas dealt with in the poems 'Adultery' and 'Disgrace'.

Lastly, I have tried to order the poems in *Mean Time* in such a way that the collection shares the coherence of a record album; that it reads with some kind of emotional, not literal, narrative. Opening as it does with Manfred Mann's 'Do Wah Diddy Diddy' and closing with the quieter place-names of the shipping forecast – 'Rockall, Malin, Dogger, Finisterre' – *Mean Time* tries to record the brief words we hear and speak under the clock. In that effort, at least, I hope it is optimistic. Gonk.

Mean Time **1993**

Ian Duhig

Borders (and they're plural round here) always exhilarate me; the psychiatrist Babineau has written of those he termed 'compulsive border crossers' among his clients, who did so 'to be rid of one psychological state and catapulted into a new and better one'. Here, new and better states might be Scotland or the Roman Empire, but eventually attrition blurred their edges. A name for part of these borders which has sometimes been used for them all is 'the debatable land' where any ground is ground for an argument. With this country so subject to words, poetic traditions are layered and various – Seamus Heaney was drawn to the religious visionary poetry of Caedmon, while very different things appealed to Walter Scott. Poets also came on trading or raiding dragon ships, but the region has always attracted immigrants as well as invaders, notably from Ireland and China – nowadays dragon boats race on the Tyne and the Wear in honour of Qu Yan, 'the People's Poet' of the second century BCE. But the area's cultural richness has been achieved against a background of violence with local, national and international dimensions. Of here and its reiver warlords, A. L. Lloyd in *Folk Song in England* wrote that it was 'for a long time the territory of men who spoke English but had the outlook of Afghan tribesmen; they prized a poem as much as plunder'. Scott thought the more savage the society, the more violent the impulse it received from its poetry and music, and the indigenous border ballad has a filmic immediacy with each stanza like a frame, to borrow Charles Causley's analogy.

More than millennial violence was in the air when I wrote

the book, as it is now. Heightened conditions of military activity are visible in the north-east, where all the services have important bases. But a significant part of my book's imagery developed from a commission by Durham City Arts to write something connecting the landscape and literature of the region, which it was proposed would be inscribed on vellum itself to provide the link; it was central to the religious heritage of the region – '*the* writing medium for the new religion of Christianity', as Fischer puts it in his recent *A History of Writing*. Cattle were historically the gold standard, with such herds as the Chillingham Whites bred to be aggressive towards humans so reivers couldn't run them off easily. However, the commission came during the height of the foot-and-mouth crisis, when small farms everywhere were filling with silence. Researching the commission, another image that has struck me was from the dissolution of the monasteries, when illuminated vellum pages were torn from old gospels to re-skin drumheads.

Other aspects of regional traditions impacted on me, such as the images of 'kern-babies' in christening gowns, an explosion of corn where the child's face should have been; hare myths, especially Easington's, the Lambton and Laidley Worms (dragons). However, I saw the real strength of tradition on the regional reaction to 9/11. The appeal song chosen was Tommy ('the Pitman Poet') Armstrong's verses about the 1882 mining disaster, which he set to the tune of the contemporary parlour ballad 'Go and Leave Me if You Wish It', and called 'The Trimdon Grange Explosion'. (I believe this moving song was the one Philip Larkin mentions somewhere that he heard, which inspired his poem 'The Explosion'). But empathy and solidarity were achieved in terms of natural catastrophe rather than war.

Related reading brought me into contact with the intriguing case of the Saracens in the thirteenth-century romance *King Horn*; intriguing because, as Diane Speed has argued, they were pretty clearly still Vikings. But since they had converted to Christianity, new baddies were required. Millennial gleanings also included this from the eleventh-century blind Syrian poet Al-Ma'arri: 'The Jews, the Moslems, the Christians; they've all got it wrong. The World's peoples divide only into two kinds: those with religion and no brains, and those with brains and no religion.'

The Lammas Hireling 2003

Helen Dunmore

For several years I shared an attic flat in Bristol with a research scientist whose field was protein crystallography. People from the lab would often visit. We would sit around the kitchen table after a meal. Our kitchen window gave onto an open, magnificent view down to the Cumberland Basin, where ships belonging to Bristol merchants used to sail in from the West Indies. Beyond there were the round, Marie-Antoinette sheep pastures of Ashton Court. My formal scientific education had ended at fifteen, but gradually I came to absorb a little of the language and preoccupations of these scientists, and to become fascinated by their research into the molecular basis of life, and by the idea that this could be understood by working out the structures of the molecules. Words such as 'DNA', fuzzily overheard years back, sprang into focus. I looked at a picture of its double helix structure and began to grasp what a combination of laboriousness, creativity and luck must have led to its discovery.

Then I'd look out of the window. Away down the hill there was the dock landscape, knit up with the history of slavery. To the right there was the former private estate which now belonged to the council and ensured an anomalously pastoral landscape one mile from the city centre. There were many ways of looking at these landscapes, and so many structures embodied within them: first one would leap to the eye, then another.

Over the years I kept finding parallels between this branch of research science with which I'd happened to come into day-to-day contact and some aspects of poetic creativity. There's the same craft apprenticeship, the accumulation, conscious and unconscious, of a mass of data and a solid base of technique, and then, overlying this, a play of intuition and experimentation which struggles to apprehend patterns while at the same time it tries to break through them.

It took me a long time to come to grips with any of this in my own writing. In the summer of 1987, after I'd been writing very concentratedly for several months, I began to see how the twenty or so new poems I'd written were beginning to fit together, closely and solidly, and how they would relate to poems I had written over the previous year. A structure was emerging, and although I still had to write and rewrite many times, I knew I was working towards this structure, and not at random. This was very apparent to me technically – I found that there were echoes of rhythm, verbal correspondences, and many other formal connections between one poem and another. For me this was a very exciting way to work, and it began to feel as if the book itself was becoming a landscape, with each poem in turn picked out, floodlit, as I worked on it, then dropping into its natural place as the focus went off it. Except that I've become increasingly wary about the way they use the word 'natural' . . .

The Raw Garden 1988

Since I began to write novels I have often been asked whether I 'still' write poetry. I react strongly, and I don't quite know why this is. Perhaps it is partly alarm. The ability to write poetry can be withdrawn as easily as it is given. To be suddenly empty of poetry is a frightening thought, like an abandonment. It makes me think of Larkin's painful remark that he had not given up poetry: poetry had given him up. But there is also something comic in the idea that any poet with another source of income can be expected to snap shut that notebook, put a rubber band around it for the last time, and teach the computer to delete anything under eighty thousand words.

If writing fiction has affected my poetry, it has probably done so in a paradoxical way, by making my poems shorter and more lyrical. I hope there is a sense of compression in these poems. What I wanted to do was reduce them, so that the flavour would be as intense as possible. I get to like cutting more and more, the longer I write. It's exhilarating, because it has everything to do with the requirements of the poem, and nothing to do with the way each writer falls in love with his or her good lines. The sixteen-line poem 'At the Emporium' was originally a much longer narrative poem about a small shop in a seedy Brighton back-street. Stanza after stanza fell away. In the end, all that was needed was the proprietor 'lounging vested in his doorway' in the stupefying heat of afternoon. It could be any afternoon, but it is about to be hauled into notoriety by crime.

I called this collection *Bestiary*, but a bestiary says as much about human beings as it does about animals. The creation of beasts by the human imagination seems to be a necessary thing, and so does our involvement with them. We pour ourselves into dragons, gryphons and laidly worms; we line the Clyde to mourn the stranding of a whale. The most dangerous sexual offenders become beasts in tabloid headlines, and the tradition goes back to the Greek myth of the satyr, which blended man and goat. The beast is the unknown made flesh, fearful but fascinating, sometimes enchanting. To make a bestiary is to get under the guard of received ideas about beauty and cruelty. On opening a bestiary we stare at what is strange, and see ourselves looking back.

Bestiary **1997**

Douglas Dunn

Yeats wrote in a letter of reply to a young woman who had sent him poems: '. . . one should love best what is nearest and most interwoven with one's life'. Although I have only just discovered this beautiful piece of advice in Hone's biography of Yeats, it is something that I think I have always known. Yeats was of course advising that girl to continue writing about her native Ireland, but with a Scotsman's effrontery and recklessness I choose to be blind to the real significance the advice should have for me. Scotland is what I most want to write about and what I am least able to. The only way I can try to describe the poetry I have written so far, and it is not really for me to do this, is to suggest that I have tried to understand the familiar and the ordinary, and that locality has little to do with this.

This, I hope, is at least true of the poems I wrote in the second of the two years I lived in a terrace off Terry Street in Hull. It was never my intention that the poems be read as social or any other kind of protest, nor was I recommending Terry Street as a better because simpler way of life. My experience of the place made it impossible for me to want to do either of these things. The poems are not slum-pastorals.

Terry Street became for me a place of sad sanity. It was an alternative to the gaudy shams everywhere, a cave under a waterfall. But in thinking of Terry Street like this I was probably kidding myself into believing there could be a place not entirely of the age and yet handy enough to it for purposes of observation. Poverty makes men look foolish as well as their lives uncomfortable and I was no exception. I began to feel strange and lost, as though I was trying to inflict loneliness on myself, and I came to dislike Terry Street, and left it, although I still live in Hull. 'We free ourselves from obsession that we may be nothing. The last kiss is given to the void.'

Terry Street 1969

Four poems excepted, *Elegies* was written between April 1981 and the same month a year later, with subsequent deletions and alterations. A large number of other poems, written on the same subject and within that same year, were abandoned, unfinished, discarded or lost.

For me that represents an exceptional rate and intensity of work. But the circumstances were exceptional also. In retrospect I feel that during the year I worked hardest on *Elegies* it was only within each poem as I wrote it that my life had any meaning. That sounds melodramatic and I feel almost as if I should withdraw it. It seems to say more for poetry than my experience of it cares to admit. But I'll stand by it. It's true.

Among the received notions of criticism is the belief that there should be a distance of time between a grievous personal event and writing which reflects it. Never having believed that true of modest or remote calamities, it seemed timid to accept it of one appallingly intimate and close. There is more honour in discovering maturity of feeling by digging through the sentimental or overblown anguish which grief promotes. Such a subject is in any case resistant. Struggling with technicalities – metre, cadence, rhyme and so on – was very helpful, a mimesis of the real contest, which was with feeling.

Elegies 1985

Almost everyone faced with this task says the same thing: I don't like writing about my work; or, I never know what to say about my poetry. So I feel in good company – the companionship of the embarrassed. It's even worse when some of your poems are personal and sore. Much of poetry, though, depends on the exposure of the heart, and I'm not embarrassed by that, not in the slightest (although I think I would be were all of poetry so dependent). My declaration on that subject is contained in my poem 'Leopardi'. I hope it's exemplified in all my poems. In poetry, there should be no holding back. To trim, to under-say, and to over-say, to trade in the pusillanimous or the boastful, contradicts a principle of poetry; and if you do these things then you'll be found out. Or (or is it 'and'?) there's the most hellish event of all, when you find out for yourself just who and what you are in your work.

Obviously, my title adapts a phrase by John Donne in his poem about the shortest day of the year, where he writes of 'the year's midnight'. That I should call my book (and my poem of the same title) *The Year's Afternoon* doesn't mean that I'm more optimistic or less pessimistic than the Great Metaphysical. Indeed, I don't have the cheek to enter into even the most tentative of comparisons, because none exist, as I'm all too aware. The title, I suppose, suggests middle life as well as a turning point.

The poems were written between 1993 and 1999. For much of that period I was working on my long poem 'The Donkey's Ears'. It was a relief to have other writings to work on as an alternative to a poem that struck me many times as unfinishable. Writing is a curiously obsessive activity. Even after a day's work at a time-consuming and tiring day job, somehow or other you manage to invent a few hours at your private desk after the last memorandum of the day has been typed up, or a tedious report, or piles of essays have been marked, or a lecture written. During the twenty years when I was freelance, my routine was to work on poetry in the morning, and then reviewing, fiction or other literary jobs in the afternoon. I could get by financially, but only just. For almost ten years, my routine has been very different: I write whenever I can or whenever I have to, and it's almost always at night. It's like a bad habit; but perhaps that's what writing poetry is, or can become. I may have cured myself of it: I've written two poems in the past year, and during most of that time I was on sabbatical leave. I seem to need conditions that amount to those of adversity before I can put pen to paper. *Maudit?* No. Foolish, maybe.

A great deal of self-serving and arrogant nonsense is written and spoken about poetry. For me, it's enough for a poet to do what he or she does and get on with being true to what they ask of themselves and of their work. Although many of my poems are metrical, and rhyme, I don't see myself as a 'formalist'. In fact, I don't see myself as any kind of -ist.

The Year's Afternoon **2000**

Lawrence Durrell

It is an interesting business to try and write about one's own work, though I fear that the opinionations of creative people about the creative act cannot be fully trusted; besides, they lead one away from the work rather than towards it.

*

Who, for example, am I?

*

I have said nearly all I could say about poetry in my volume of lectures *A Key to Modern Poetry.* As far as my own practice of it goes (which is getting increasingly watchful and hesitant as I get older) the following phrase sums the matter up: 'Poetry, like life, is altogether too serious not to be taken lightly.'

*

I have been writing since childhood and have as yet not completely conquered a desire for fame (so hard is it to face the possibility that one is among the second-rate). If I should ever achieve the disinterested automatism for which I am searching in life, I don't doubt but that my technical grasp of the job would let me rise into the front rank. But this cannot be done by trying. One can only sit like a fisherman on a bank and watch the bloody float.

*

He who captures truth must first
Have conquered for the truth his thirst

The Tree of Idleness **1955**

T. S. Eliot

Poetry and the Schools

I have never been very much in favour of introducing the work of living authors into school curricula of the study of English literature, for two reasons. First, I think that schoolboys and girls should be given a background of the classic authors of our language whose work is part of history and can be taught as such. Second, I think that all growing boys and girls should have an area of literature which they're not taught anything about, on which they don't have to pass any examinations, in which they can make their own discoveries, their own errors, and learn for themselves. If every secondary school in the country joined the Poetry Book Society and had a shelf in its library exhibiting the books of new poetry, this year and last year and several years, and just left them there for the boys and girls in the upper forms to discover for themselves and find out what they liked, we would be doing a very great service, because it is in the years between fourteen and eighteen if ever that people become readers of poetry and lovers of poetry, and also amongst those readers will be the poets of that generation. I think every poet has been a reader of poetry before he has been inflamed with the desire to become a writer of poetry, and it is a good thing also that boys and girls of that age should learn to think of poetry as a living art, as something which is still being written and which will be written in their own generation. I have always held firmly that a nation which ceases to produce poetry will in the long run cease to be able to enjoy and even understand the great poetry of its own past.

D. J. Enright

A word about the title . . . Some of the poems in this collection are sad, a few are angry, others mingle sadness with ire. This latter combination, whatever etymologists may have to say, surely accounts for the literary mode known as 'satire'. Perhaps it isn't difficult to write satire, but (as the Roman poet remarked) it is certainly difficult not to write satire. Many of these items have to do, in a sombrely humorous way, either with first things, or with middle things (Adam has come a long way since he named the animals), or with last things – including (because it is there) death. There are a few nostalgic sideways glances in an Eastern direction, where life's ironies and paradoxes tend to be just a little more sharply focused than in the West, and a sequence which takes an apprehensive look at recent advances in poetry, prying and the processes of Public Personage. Elsewhere subjects are drawn from the mundane existence of metropolitan commuters and the more exotic life-style of mechanical computers; from the domestication of political issues, the spoilsport behaviour of sociologists, and the naturalness of the supernatural. Also touched on are the drawbacks attendant on supping with the devil, and the difficulty of getting into heaven; some ways in which the damned may choose to pass their time in eternity; the relative merits of freedom and fresh oysters, and of academic fellowship and artistic solitariness; the deep-rooted whimsicality in man's nature, his crying need for fantasy, and the ingenious and sometimes comic fortitude with which he faces adversity, mischance and himself.

As this prospectus suggests, the book may be felt to have a

certain unity of tone and preoccupation. It must be admitted, though, that the true derivation of 'satire' is from a Latin word meaning 'hotch-potch' or (which sounds rather nicer) 'medley' . . .

Sad Ires and Others 1975

Gavin Ewart

Two thoughts come into the mind of an Old Age Pensioner poet who has recently published his *Collected Poems.* First, that his next book runs the risk of coming as an anticlimax. Second, that there may not be much of his working life left.

For both these reasons, I've made this a large collection. Perhaps some of the poems repeat themselves, dealing with similar subjects; but I hope they're all sufficiently different to prevent the reader feeling that he or she has seen it all before.

Another, secondary, thought is that the reader might get tired of the forms in which I write. I do try to make the form fit the subject. One poem here, for instance, being about a 'Classical' headmaster, is in hexameters and pentameters (like Latin elegiacs); but even then, stanzaic poems, rough-and-ready sonnets, lyrics, songs, free verse – the number of ways is not inexhaustible. Because of this I have written some pieces as Patience Stronglets and some as 'prose poems'. I don't despise doggerel, either. It's very well adapted for some purposes. The roughnesses of many of Donne's poems, for example, don't do them any harm. 'Straight' parody is also represented here (a burlesque of Auden's forties Lyrical style and John Cowper Powys's *A Glastonbury Romance*). My poetic philosophy is, roughly, that poetry should entertain. It can do this in various ways (*King Lear* is entertainment) but the one thing it shouldn't be is dull. However worthy the sentiments, prosiness and lack of imagination kill poems. Wordsworth is a good example. He was an inspired describer of the physical world and his philosophy made sense (at least to him – which is the important thing for a poet); but the Muse deserted him and in his late work the marvellous original poems become boring ones. Perhaps too many people worshipped him, and his faults went uncorrected. Also, Wordsworth had no sense of humour. Humour is valuable. It makes a poet realise that he's not as important as he thinks he is.

In old age, one must expect some falling-off. My hope is that this hasn't yet started to happen. Although I expect it will. All one can do is fight back, with all the means at one's disposal. Artists are lucky in that their activities don't depend on physical strength. Unlike athletes, they can be as good – or better – at the age of eighty.

The New Ewart: Poems 1980–1982 **1982**

U. A. Fanthorpe

As usual, when they're together, and bound, I feel ashamed of them. Individually, they had a way of convincing me of their right to exist. But when they gape out at me, cheek by jowl, I feel like a mother with a whole clutch of unsatisfactory children.

There's this lass called Irritable Receptionist. Poor dear, she has much to put up with. But not everyone shares her obsession with hospitals and neurologists, epilepsy, EEG machines and doctor's handwriting. How to break it to her? And her younger brother, Ingenuous Naturalist. It's not as if he knows anything about nature; he just likes to write down what he sees. And we all know how dangerous that is.

Then the baby, Safety Pin. Unfortunately Safety has been asked to write about her childhood (I ask you! She's still in it!). In my view, to write about that sort of thing without even the suspect gift of charm, or at least of Adrian Mole-ishness, is to be heading straight for the Third Murderer's pillow.

No, I've not finished yet. There's Mad Photographer. At least he doesn't write about his own work, poor kid. What with overexposure, underexposure, and five fat fingers on the lens, it's kinder to draw a veil. No, what he writes about is his feelings when being photographed by other people. I find this very twisted.

Lastly, my eldest, the Logocrat (she's reached the grandiose stage). I wouldn't mind a love of words – it seems quite a civilized thing to have – but Loggy is a Logomaniac, which is uncivilised. She thinks words are our way of staying alive. Honestly! And what that has to do with a Tyneside mum in the twenties whose baby has died, or, come to that, with the early days of the *Daily Telegraph* crossword puzzle, I can't begin to imagine. And then, apparently, it all has something to do with the 51st psalm.

There's also the poor little lad Tristis. We never mention him.

I try to write about the hard things, as a way of making them endurable; but I see that a lot of the bright things have wormed their way in too: familiar upholders of sanity like Shakespeare, Quakers, Bristol patients, gardens, books, love. I wish I had thought in time of writing a poem to my publisher, Harry Chambers of Peterloo Poets, whose logo of a man reading in his bath while, above his umbrella, the plumbing or possibly the whole universe is in disarray, reveals him as another upholder.

I've tried to speak of them with a father's fondness, a mother's stern regard for the truth. But in the end they walk into the world on their own feet, and all one can do is rely on luck and the kindness of other people.

Neck Verse **1992**

James Fenton

The purpose of publishing *The Memory of War*, a collection of all the poems I wish to keep in print, is experimental. When my brother founded the Salamander Press as a garage enterprise, we wanted to see whether a small publisher of poetry could possibly do worse than the average well-known, established London firm. Most books of poetry are conceived in terms of a dreary formula (the slim vol of thirty short lyrics); they are badly printed, badly produced, seldom marketed, and now quite often remaindered. The standard of reviewing is primitive. The potential sales are in any case not gigantic. There was hardly a great deal to be lost if one turned one's back on the traditional methods, and went for an approach which suited the individual requirements of each poem or collection of poems.

I had published, in Quarto, an elegy written in Berlin. It had intrigued but baffled my friends, and I wanted to give it another chance in a different format. The revised work, published in a large pamphlet as *A German Requiem*, soon found its audience. The format confused the odd critic, who imagined the work to be a collection of poems rather than a single piece given space to breathe, but the revision had obviously made the thing more comprehensible. The work was reprinted, and in the meantime the garage enterprise hit lucky with an interim collection by Craig Raine, *A Free Translation.*

By now we could see the possibility of entering a more ambitious project, and since we had taken over from Seekers the remaining stock of my first collection, which we have now sold, together with a previous pamphlet originally put out by the

New Review, it seemed appropriate to gather together a collected poems. This is not as large an enterprise as it would be with most of the poets of my age and acquaintance. I write very little and have suffered long periods of muselessness. I am never short of ideas for poems, but between the idea and the execution there falls that famous shadow. *A German Requiem*, for instance, began life as a prose piece, and only received its present shape after a year's intermittent work and the accidental discovery, during a lecture, of a theory which made sense of two quite disparate elements which I had been unable to bring together. That the poem should have been thought obscure in England is due to the accidental circumstance that I was writing in a country where, I feared, what I was saying would be blindingly obvious.

Another new poem, 'Chosun', owes its existence to a chance reporting assignment in South Korea, and a misunderstanding over which room I was supposed to meet a contact in. By accident, I came across a wealth of material which I could plunder, verbatim, for a found poem compose. At the time of writing, I had no idea for the piece, only a large supply of curious lore. The method of working reminded me of an old notebook in which I had gathered, over ten years before, some material towards a practical ars poetica. Some of this I have included in this new volume.

The Memory of War **1982**

I hope, at least, that the reader will find variety: there are poems here in the very simplest of lyric metres, songs and ballads based on a musical beat, contemplative things and other things which I admit are somewhat foolish but which I couldn't bear to throw away. Some of the work seems to have taken years. Some of it was written in the thick of things.

For instance, there's a what-I-did-in-the-hols poem, 'The Milkfish Gatherers', written in a beach hut in the Philippines, at the very moment when the things I was describing were happening. Some fishermen landed a shark nearby. I went out, looked at it, and popped it straight into the poem. An insect hatched, was immediately eaten by ants, and, well before the ants had finished, I'd eaten it as well. And so on and so forth. There's a political poem, written during the first anniversary of the intifada in Jerusalem, and designed to appear in the Christmas issue of the *Independent* magazine. I'd been asked to write something as an accompaniment to a set of photographs which, time being short, I wasn't actually going to be able to see. I solved the problem by jotting down as many impressions of the city as I could, but casting them in the form of Milton's 'Nativity Ode'.

Another poem with a strange origin is 'The Ballad of the Shrieking Man', whose rhythms and story came to me, apparently complete, in a dream, in Paris, the day after a visit to the Café des Deux Magots. The nonsense poem, 'Here Come the Drum Majorettes!', was begun on the night of the revolution which forced the Marcoses to flee Manila. I was far too busy at the time to do anything more than jot down a few of the lines that had come to me, and compose an *aide-mémoire* to preserve the rhythms that were pounding in my head. The rest was completed several months later, on afternoon strolls around Quezon City, my home for three years.

The section called 'Out of the East' includes things written at that period, or things with an Eastern flavour – all of them designed as musical numbers. I wanted to write a pocket musical – it would have wildly extravagant words, exorbitant music and some first-rate dance (the essentials) but nothing else. No sets. No lavish costumes. No plot or book. The music was written by Dominic Muldowney, and we've performed it on three occasions, in varying stages of completeness. The only thing we haven't got round to yet is the dance numbers – a fact I regret, since the original working theory was that words, music and gesture were part of the original Big Bang that produced poetry itself. People used sometimes to say: poetry readings are all right, as long as the poets don't start to write for performance. That, they considered, would be selling art down the river. I go to the opposite extreme. I like to write for performance, but I end up doing things which are somewhat beyond my capacities as a performer. I couldn't sing you Dominic's settings, and I certainly couldn't dance the dance which the Shrieking Men perform, and which turns a whole town mad. I can't dance for toffee. Not for toffee. What I can do, at a poetry reading, is give you an impression of what a piece would sound like if it were performed by somebody else more competent than myself. So that's the solution I settle for, shamelessly. I've spent a long time in barrios where you're expected to sing for your supper, and that has knocked the inhibitions out of me.

My favourite poet is currently Herbert, that's George, not Zbigniew. My favourite singer is Tom Waits. I nick a lot of ideas from other poets. But I don't nick quite as much from Auden as I used to. So that must be progress, I think.

Out of Danger **1993**

Roy Fuller

Being asked to write about 'yourself and your poetry', I have to try to restrain myself from confidences that would be as embarrassing as superfluous. Like ordinary people, poets long to be loved. But all that is necessary is that they should be understood.

Whatever the value or success, or lack of them, of each individual poem, some intellectual effort has gone into all my verse, and I would beg a reader who has failed to get or be struck with (favourably or otherwise) anything I say to puzzle a little longer. I believe strongly in the virtue of poetry's allusive power. When Donne's readers saw 'snorted we in the seven sleepers den' it was not only the alliteration and vowel sounds of the phrase that made it poetry but also the fact that they knew precisely who the 'sleepers' were. So a line of mine about 'living through wars of wanting neither side to win' is intended to pin down an aspect of this post-Second World War epoch, when the progressive forces have so often been tainted with dictatorship or terrorism. Again, I would like readers to wring the last ounce out of lines like:

Why the short sword of Brutus dealt
A thrust at its beloved thing.

The symbolism of 'short sword' (cf. 'short arm'); the physical envy and love-hatred of son for father in the Oedipus relation; the tradition that Brutus was Caesar's natural son – such things, as well as the situation of Shakespeare's play, are what I want the lines to convey.

Analysis can never harm a poem. My ideal reader would challenge every adjective, even in the most 'poetic' passage.

Far from the scarlet and sustaining lung.

'Scarlet' because one's experience in a butcher's shop or in drawing poultry has made one realise that lights are the vividest red of any part of the body; and if the reader objects that the urban lung is soot-coloured, then I hope he will go on to realise that the lung of my poem belongs to a rural animal and is all the brighter for that. Above all, perhaps, the word suggests the lung as a generalised and idealised conception, the lung of the book on anatomy, for the pig of my poem is symbolical.

I have not meant to give the impression that my verse is difficult. It certainly does not set out to be. But in reading poetry, like listening to the monologue of a good comedian, nothing must be taken for granted:

The car in the lane that circumvents
The archipelagos of dung

(if I may choose a rather homely instance) – cow dung, obviously, because of its island shape; 'archipelagos' because of the tendency of a group of islands to consist of smaller and smaller islands at its extremity.

Collected Poems **1962**

John Glenday

I once had a friend who couldn't enjoy television in case something relatively insignificant happened on the periphery, such as a mouse running up the edge of the screen. It didn't matter whether it was *Panorama* or *Robin Hood*, he would be searching for that mouse in the shadows.

I'm not sure why light and darkness turn up so persistently in *Undark*. I was quite surprised myself when I was drawing the manuscript together and noticed the recurrences. Before that I had told folk, only half jesting, that the theme of my second book would be everything I'd written since the first one.

Undark was the trade name for the original luminous paint, invented by Sabin von Sochocky in 1915. At first radium was thought to have restorative powers, even make women more sexually attractive, so the factory workers would happily lick their brushtips to a point, or gloss their teeth so they would shine. It was only when they began falling ill that its real power was understood. I was fascinated by the contrast between that beauty and the deadliness of the stuff. Sometimes it seems to be the darkness that hurts us and sometimes the light. *Undark* begins and ends with the darkness being compromised in one way or another and in that respect it's a darkly optimistic book, if such books exist.

Spinoza described perception as 'that wherein the essence of one thing is concluded from the essence of another, but not adequately'. The manner in which we perceive things is a metaphor in itself. The way we view things in a strictly physiological sense, that is.

For instance, there are a number of unconscious eye movements going on all the time – minute tremors and slow drifts that keep the world centred in the mind. If the eye were to remain completely motionless, whether focused on light or on shadow, it would see nothing. You see, it's only change that the eye feels, as is also the case with the heart.

Likewise, when we look at an object of low luminosity, such as a faint star, we need to focus its light on the most sensitive part of the retina – the macula lutea. This is positioned just off-centre of the optic nerve, so to view that star as clearly as possible, we have to look slightly to one side. In poetry, we 'tell all the truth, but tell it slant'. That's the purpose of metaphor, of course, it's the lowest uncommon denominator on which we focus so that we can see something else.

I remember coming across a print of the American Civil War – I think it may have been Gettysburg after Pickett's charge – a scattering of plump corpses on a slope of field, caught in all their ragged detail. But behind them, behind them there were upright columns of half shadow and shadow – more shortages of light than anything else, which were of course soldiers moving through the background too quickly for the camera to catch clearly. In their world the dead were quite distinct and the living resembled ghosts and if I hadn't known better, I'd have tried to read something into that.

Undark **1995**

W. S. GRAHAM

MALCOLM MOONEY'S LAND (Facts)

1 Malcolm Mooney's Land is as real as Franz Josef Land.
2 Grammarsow is a Cornish dialect word for a Woodlouse. But its habitat is language also.
3 Telephones have not been installed in crevasses yet.
4 Nansen conceived the Fram which served him well. He knew when to allow himself to be drifted and when to act.
5 In The Constructed Space I tried to not allow any sensual imagery. Why? I don't know.
6 Dingdong is the name of an old tin-mine five miles from where I live.
7 Malcolm Mooney is not a real person. Robert MacBryde, Peter Lanyon, Roger Hilton, Elizabeth, Alfred Wallis, Europa, Bryan Wynter, King William IV, Tony O'Malley, Brigit, Don Brown, Johann Joachim Quantz, Nessie Dunsmuir, Nansen, and W. S. Graham are all real persons.
8 In The Dark Dialogues the place is Scotland.

MALCOLM MOONEY'S LAND (Observations)

1. Thoughts of the process of making poetry are often the subject of my poems although I hope the poem is left standing in its own right apart from any take awayable message the reader might discover.
2. I happen to feel most alive when I am trying to write poetry

So here I am battering against the door in case there might be somebody behind it.

3. I am always very aware that my poem is not a telephone call. The poet only speaks one way. He hears nothing back. His words as he utters them are not conditioned by a real ear replying from the other side. That is why he has to make the poem stand stationary as an art object. He never knows who will collide with it and maybe even use it as a different utensil from what he intended. Yet because I am only human, I hope I am in it somewhere.

Malcolm Mooney's Land 1970

I am pleased about the physical book. I like the feel of it and its cobalt cover. I even know (I almost know) what goes on inside it. The first poem begins with 'What' and the last poem ends with 'you'. Twenty-six poems. Twenty-six objects of fairly measured verse.

In *Implements in Their Places* I can discern maybe an effort somewhere to try to be more simple or, if you will, less confused by the English language. But the word 'simple' is difficult either applied to lines of words on the page or to the thought which provoked them. Maybe this book is going to be more entertaining to more people. Is that what I want? After speaking to myself I suppose I want to speak to the best, whoever they are, alive or dead.

Let us pretend you are my friend, Malcolm, staying the night here, and we are sitting at the writing table sipping a special malt with *Implements in Their Places* lying there innocently before us fresh from the press. Well, Willie or Sydney, you say as the name strikes you, what do you think of your book? I almost say, Well, there are bits I am not ashamed of, but before I can say that you reach out and open it up and crease it with your palm open at the first of the Implements.

Somewhere our belonging particles
Believe in us. If we could only find them.

The title poem, 'Implements in Their Places', is intended as a single, stationary object. The Implements are in their places and I expect the reader to maybe grow affectionate towards their order as well as to the Implements themselves. In 'Implement number 40' I invite you to pen in (neatly) some words of your own. I give you four lines. How lucky you are to have four lines of space to do what you like in.

Well, Willie or Sydney, what do you think of your new book? Malcolm, I don't know. I read it with interest. It seems to say some new things which couldn't have come from me.

Implements in Their Places 1977

Robert Graves

I have been publishing poems since the year 1909, since when I have watched a great many changes in fashion – names suddenly made and suddenly lost again, with here and there a real poet writing whom nobody pays much attention to, but who doesn't care because he's not competing with anyone but himself. It will always be that way.

The history of English poetry is traced in textbooks as a succession of movements or schools – the School of Chaucer, the Allegorical School, the early Tudor Dramatists, the Euphuists and so on, past the Anti-Jacobins, the Lake School, the mid-Victorian Romantics, until one reaches the Georgians, the Imagists and the Modernist Movement, for which the bell is now tolling. But schools and movements are fictions. If a school, meaning the disciples and imitators of a particular verse-craftsman or technician, achieves newspaper renown, this is a grave criticism of his sincerity. A poet should be inimitable. When two real poets recognise each other as true to their common vocation, this will only accentuate the difference between them in rhythm, diction and the rest. Any talk of a 'school' means that someone is peddling a new technique of verbal conjuring; as in commercial schools that teach writers of advertising copy how to make easily hypnotisable subjects believe what they themselves never believe in. Craftsmanship is self-taught by the poet's service to the Muse, who is unpossessable and never satisfied.

New Poems 1962 **1962**

Geoffrey Grigson

The right place for writers of poems to appear, in relation to themselves as poem-writers, is in their poems.

Exegi monumentum is acceptable, if rash, in a poem.

Five paragraphs or one paragraph about oneself as confector of poems beginning I believe, I do not wish, I write because, I am, should be considered indecent and should be unacceptable.

Statements that Poetry is, Poetry will become, are presumptuous.

The pronouncements I play in a mountain corner on a scrannel pipe and I play with myself in a confessional box without a curtain so that everyone can see the spasm on my face are self-advertising equally.

No astrology, no playing witch or warlock.

Attaching to oneself a proletarian form of a Christian name is writing one's advertisement or wearing one's Order of Merit at an art auction of one's own pictures.

At a Poetry Festival or a writers' conference Coleridge and Hesiod are unlikely to be encountered.

Poetry, poem – each word inclines to presumption, in relation to oneself. Even more so poet.

I regret a certain snobbery in these sentences.

If I could concisely explain I myself or poems or my poems or writing them, I should try not to write them.

Ingestion of Ice-Cream **1969**

Thom Gunn

I find the book difficult to speak about. I sent it off confidently, but by the time I got the proofs a certain revulsion had set in, and my main feeling by now is that, after six years, it doesn't really add up to very much. On the one hand, an indirection so delicate that subject matter seems to have been left behind with the crudities of earlier drafts; on the other, the strands of a sequence not braiding, as they were meant to do, but ending in a bulky and rather desperate knot of didacticism: in either case, a point is largely lost.

I do not want to be apologetic, though, so I'll try to say a few things about my intentions, which at least I can be fairly sure about. I think *Touch* does show a kind of development in attitudes from those of my earlier books. The point of the title must be obvious, as it is directly relevant to most of the poems in the book: the touch is not physical only, it is meant to be an allegory for the touch of sympathy that should be the aim of human intercourse. The man in the long poem called 'Misanthropes' at last discovers it, though he has in the past substituted for it the predatory bite of the animal. Against this poem I would put 'Confessions of the Life Artist', which owes a great deal to Mann's Joseph books. The Life Artist is the man who achieves a fair amount of control over his consciousness and his circumstances, but in doing so comes to realise that for this fullness of control he has to pay by certain lacks of feeling and of spontaneity. This poem is meant to summarise the nightmare of any civilised man, as the end of 'Misanthropes' is meant to summarise his dream, because one has to seek the fullness of control if one wants to avoid sloth; but it seems that the more controlled one is the more unfit one becomes for the spontaneity of 'touch', which is the only real proof, in a human anyway, of unslothfulness. The celebration of instinct in the first poem, 'The Goddess', is all very well, but instinct is ultimately self-protective and predatory and it defeats the exercise of sympathy just as much as the over-self-consciousness of the Life Artist. There remains the possibility that one can deliberately and consciously attempt to create in oneself a field which will be spontaneously fertile for the tests of sympathy, that one can form habits that are so readily available that they can seem like instincts. I do not mean that one can simply love everybody because one wants to, but that one can try to avoid all the situations in which love is impossible. And here I'm getting beyond the book into a subject that could be a proper exploration for several lifetimes of books.

Touch 1967

Most simply, *Jack Straw's Castle* consists of the poems I wrote between mid 1970 and mid-1975. Except for the group called 'The Geysers' and for the narrative which is the title poem, I wrote them one by one, without seeing much connection between individual poems, rather aware at times that they seemed to have nothing in common at all. Then, let's say in 1974, I noticed that there were certain patterns in what I had written. It turns out that if you write consistently about what is most important to you, you do end up with an organic consistency to a collection of poetry written within a certain span of time. So a five-year chunk of your life produces not merely an anthology of random observations: the sum of reflection and perception makes a design probably more honestly worked out than if you had originally planned it that way.

The design in this collection connects such matters as self-destructiveness, solipsism in the aspects of both freedom and imprisonment, the strategies of inconsistency and self-rescue, but perhaps I have said too much already, it is not for a poet to try reproducing in prose the ideas he discovers in his poetry. I had much better go on to say something about the sound of the poems.

There was a journalistic cliché a few years ago about 'voice'. So and so has at last found his voice or, conversely, so and so has failed to find a distinctive voice. I have never felt easy about the kind of stress implied. Distinctiveness can look after itself, what I want is the kind of voice that can speak about anything at all, that can deal with the perceptions and concerns as they come up. I do not court impersonality so much as try to avoid personality, which I'd prefer to leave to the newspapers. Of course a personality of sorts must emerge in anybody's poetry, but it's not the main thing I'm after; and I admit that for at least one of the speakers in the book, a Newfoundland dog, I did have to invent a specific voice. But mostly I have aimed for my people – a new-born baby, a hitchhiker, a speed junky called Faustus, an Orphic character in the hot baths, and Jack Straw himself – to speak with much the same voice as the 'I' does in 'The Outdoor Concert' and 'The Idea of Trust'. It is not an anonymous voice, but I hope that when you hear it you will be inclined to listen to what it is saying before you start noticing its mannerisms.

Jack Straw's Castle 1976

David Harsent

Pierre Bonnard first saw Marthe de Meligny as she stepped off a Parisian tram. He followed her to her place of work where she was employed to sew pearls onto funeral decorations and simply talked her into going away with him.

Or else he first saw her as she left the studio of Alberto Giacometti where she had been modelling. It was raining. Bonnard helped her across the street and, by the time they had reached the far pavement, they were in love.

Or else it didn't happen either way. No one knows for sure. But the fact is that, however they met, and whatever passed between them at that first meeting, Bonnard and Marthe spent the rest of their lives together. She was his constant subject and his constant companion.

After they had been living together for some thirty years, they decided to marry. Bonnard had not been the most faithful of partners and a recent, serious, affair had resulted in the near collapse of their relationship; it had also led to the suicide of Bonnard's lover. Maybe that had something to do with their decision.

Now, since they were to marry, Marthe had no choice but to reveal to Bonnard that her name was not Marthe de Meligny. Bonnard, it seems, had been living for more than three decades with a woman whose name he didn't know. Not Marthe but Maria. Maria Boursin.

Why had Marthe (as everyone continues to call her) practised this deception? Perhaps she had thought the name she'd chosen was classier; perhaps she had thought it right for an artists' model: more exotic, better for business. Was Bonnard outraged, intrigued, puzzled, indifferent? Again, no one really knows. They married and lived together until Marthe died in 1942.

That's the back story. It was never my intention to give an accurate or full account of Bonnard's and Marthe's relationship, but there were things I wanted to pilfer. The first was the indelible mystery of otherness – Marthe / Maria; Martha / Mary – a notion that admits people as, ultimately, unknowable even if (maybe especially if) they are 'known' over half a lifetime.

The second concerns Bonnard's painting, about which I've written before: not least a quality in his work that I refer to as 'the mysteries of domesticity'. It suggests that in the domestic quotidian can be found answers to questions we mostly ignore; that its rhythms and rituals go deep; that its images are limitlessly potent; that (as it were) all food is a sacrament.

The third bit of pelf was certain aspects of painting: compositions, hardware, techniques, subjects. There was also the notion of looking; of seeing; of the unblinking, unscrupulous and conscienceless gaze of the painter.

Out of all this, I wrote a sequence of poems that trades off a free interpretation of the Bonnard / Marthe story in order to arrive at a cumulative narrative of its own. It's an improvisation. Only the barest bones of the original story survive, but without it I couldn't have got started.

'Marriage' is one of two sequences in the book. The second is 'Lepus' – the hare. Bonnard's images have found their way into my work before, and so has the hare, most recently in a piece I wrote for Harrison Birtwistle and the Nash Ensemble. (In fact, I was working on 'Marriage' but also thinking about 'Lepus' when Birtwistle called me to talk about a project for the Nash. (I said, 'I can do the Martha / Mary dichotomy in women or I can do the hare.' He chose the hare.)

The witchiness of the hare, the hare as trickster, the creature's intense sexuality and its strong totemic presence in the world's mythologies has intrigued me for years. When I was in my teens,

I found a copy of John Layard's book, *The Lady of the Hare.* Its initial section is a psychoanalytical study of a woman who was having hare-dreams. Its second is a history of the hare in culture and myth: as trickster-hero, as a moon totem, as witch's familiar, as folklorists' darling, as orgiast. It struck an immediate and strong chord with me: like something I'd always known but had kept secret from myself. From then on, the hare was always around, using sharp elbows to clamber into my work, her gappy grin starting to crop up in my dreams just as it had in those of Layard's analysand.

I'd been reading the book on and off for years; then I suddenly saw that Layard's section headings were titles for poems. Now the hare was centre stage, just where she had always wanted to be. One section is called 'The hare used as a hieroglyph for the auxiliary verb "to be" ', and describes how the hare-sign in Egyptian hieroglyphic writing represents the sound 'wn'; the only instance of its solo appearance – that is, as a picture of a hare – is in the verb 'to be'; it never actually means hare. In fact 'hare' is represented by another hieroglyph altogether. It's this tricky, elusive, shape-shifting, nose-thumbing hare that continues to fascinate me.

Marriage 2002

Seamus Heaney

The poems in *Door into the Dark* are more dramatic than those in *Death of a Naturalist.* Many of the poems in that book said quite directly 'I remember.' And while much of the initial energy of these later poems still derives from images and situations I knew in the past, I believe that the recollected emotion now tends to be contained rather than confessed in the poem. For example, 'The Wife's Tale' began as an irrational desire to write about a woman bringing tea to a harvest field. Earlier I might have set down the picture and trusted that it was redolent of the emotion which it evoked for me. But this time the initial memory began to coordinate with questions about the balance between man and woman in marriage and the poem turned into a dramatic monologue that ended with a reference to Brueghel's painting of the cornfield.

The early part of the book looks back to the kind of work in *Death of a Naturalist* and leads into a series of poems on love and marriage. These I regard as the heart of the book. Then comes 'A Lough Neagh Sequence', seven short poems inspired by the mysterious life-cycle of the eel and the compulsive work-cycles in the eel-fishermen's life. I envisaged this sequence as a kind of Celtic pattern: the basic structural image is the circle – the circle of the eel's journey, the fishermen's year, the boats' wakes, the coiled lines, the coiled catch, and much else; and in places the connotations of the language are meant to relate the compulsions and confrontation of fish and fishermen to sexual compulsions and confrontations that occur beyond Lough Neagh. The book ends with a number of meditative landscape poems, some of which are meant to encompass notions about history and nationality – 'Shoreline' and 'Borland', for example.

The title of the book comes from the first line of 'The Forge', a poem that uses the dark, active centre of the blacksmith's shed as an emblem for the instinctive, blurred stirring and shaping of some kinds of art. And I was happy to discover after I had chosen the title that it follows directly from the last line in my first book. That line suggested that the two directions of my poetry were 'to see myself, to set the darkness echoing'. I hope some echoes have been set up.

Door Into The Dark 1969

Perhaps the first function of a poem is to assuage the poet's need for it to exist. For a while I found my needs satisfying themselves in images drawn from Anglo-Saxon kennings, Icelandic sagas, Viking excavations, and Danish and Irish bogs, and the result is the bulk of the poems in the first section of *North.* The second section is the result of a need to be explicit about pressures and prejudices watermarked into the psyche of anyone born and bred in Northern Ireland.

The title of the book, therefore, gestures towards the north of Ireland and the north of Europe. The first poems are set in Mossbawn, my earliest home, the last one in Wicklow, where I moved in 1972. Both place names have Norse elements. In fact, the language and landscape of Ireland, as the poem set on the archaeological site at Belderg insinuates, can be regarded as information retrieval systems for their own history: the bog bank is a memory bank.

The word 'bog' itself is one of the few borrowings in English from the Irish language. It means 'soft' in Irish, soft and wet, and one of its usages survives in the Hiberno-English expression 'a soft day'. But in our part of the country we called the bog the 'moss', a word with Norse origins probably carried there by the Scots planters in the early seventeenth century. So in the bog/moss syndrome, one can diagnose a past of invasion, colonisation and language shift, a past which, as Seamus Deane has pointed out, 'the Irish are conscious of as a process which is evidently unfulfilled'.

I cannot say why I should be possessed by past language and landscape, but many of the poems wrought themselves out of that nexus; as Robert Frost put it, 'a poem begins as a lump in the throat, a homesickness, a lovesickness. It finds the thought and the thought finds the words.'

During the last few years there has been considerable expectation that poets from Northern Ireland should 'say' something about 'the situation', but in the end they will only be worth listening to if they are saying something about and to themselves. The truest poetry may be the most feigning but there are contexts, and Northern Ireland is one of them, where to feign a passion is as reprehensible as to feign its absence.

North 1975

For a long time I couldn't decide what to call the collection. At first it seemed that it should be *The Real Names*, because the names of so many real people appear in its pages and because what happens in the poem of that title is what's happening throughout the book. Incidents from childhood and adolescence and the recent past swim up into memory: moments that were radiant or distressful at the time come back in the light of a more distanced and more informed consciousness.

'Informed consciousness'? Well, in the writing of any poem, there's usually a line being cast from the circumference of your whole understanding towards intuitions and images down there in the memory pool. If you're lucky, you feel life moving at the other end of the line; the remembered thing starts off a chain reaction of words and associations, and at that point what you need is the whole of your acquired knowledge and understanding, your cultural memory and literary awareness. You need them to come to your aid and throw a shape that will match and make sense of your excitement.

In many of the poems, however – 'Out of the Bag', 'The Loose Box', 'Known Word', 'The Real Names', the poem in memory of Ted Hughes, the title poem, and several others – it was not a single shape that was thrown, but several. Different sections of the poems represent the different casts made. The pleasure of doing it that way was in following each new impulse, finding and trusting approaches that allowed both oneself and the subject to stretch their wings. The risk was that the poem might then range too freely beyond the reader's ken – but it still seemed a risk worth taking.

'Electric Light' is a case in point. The first and third sections are probably straightforward enough: I don't say that the old woman is my grandmother, but there are clues to show that she is ancient, archetypal and central to the family. The risk is in trusting that the reader will go with the middle section, which is an evocation of my first trips to London, by ferry and train, but is also meant to suggest a journey into poetic vocation. It should signal a connection between the strange and slightly literary word 'ails', spoken by the sibylline grandmother to the distressed child, and the aspiring poet's sense of historical and literary England, seen first from the train window and then deliberately sought out in the Southwark of Chaucer's Tabard Inn and Shakespeare's Globe.

Once 'Electric Light' got written, I had no doubt about it as the title poem. Apart from anything else, the brightness of my grandmother's house is associated in my mind with a beautiful line from the Mass for the Dead, '*Et lux perpetua luceat eis*', 'And let perpetual light shine upon them' – a line which is also echoed in one of the sections of 'The Real Names'. Then, once I settled on the title, I began to see what I hadn't seen before, that there was light all over the place, from the shine on the weir in the very first poem to the 'reprieving light' of my father's smile in the penultimate line of the penultimate poem in the book. And as well as this, there is an almost equally pervasive note of elegy.

'The stilly night' is mentioned and to anyone who knows the Thomas Moore song, the phrase inevitably calls up 'the light / Of other days around me'. At several places in the collection, a brightness of other days falls from the classical air, from the imagined weather of Virgil's *Eclogues* and from the actual skies above sites in the Peloponnese and other legendary parts of Greece. And some of that brightness casts its beams even farther north, to shine on the Bann Valley on the eve of the third millennium, or to turn a rented smallholding in Co. Wicklow at the end of the twentieth century into the equivalent of a farm in the Mantuan countryside, confiscated and resettled on the eve of the first.

The book could even carry a Virgilian epigraph: it is full of *mortalia*, by people and things we must pass away from or that have had to pass away from us. Deaths of poets and of friends, and of friends who were poets. *Sunt lacrimae rerum et mentem mortalia tangunt.*

Electric Light **2001**

John Heath-Stubbs

I have been asked to make a statement. I find this a pretty impossible thing to do; for me, the poems themselves are the only statement I can make.

I suppose there may be a sort of paradox in this, since the concept of poetry, or any art, for that matter, as self-expression, has always repelled me. For me, a poem is a verbal construct, a musical verbal construct. It uses language as a means of exploration and definition. The imperfections of language – its ambiguities (puns), and its sound values (the fact that some words rhyme together, for example) are the stuff of poetry.

A poem is written to be read aloud, or at least to be heard with the inner ear. The statement that a poem is simply something to be contemplated on the printed page, I find ridiculous and puerile.

The Greeks applied the term '*mousike*' to the arts of poetry, music and the dance. For them these things were inseparable. Their language had a pitch-accent – so to recite a poem, you more or less had to sing it. They were a Mediterranean people, and, as Mediterranean people do today, made use of a great deal of body language – gesture and so on – when they sought to communicate. So you had to dance the poem as well. With us these three things have developed independently, but they are still closely related.

The poem then is primarily a piece of music, but in the twentieth century it must be music for our own age. The fact that there is something going on now called 'rhyme revival' simply shows what an amateurish and trivial way poetry is looked upon in this country. In which of the other arts would anyone seriously suggest a return to nineteenth-century procedures? Conventional metres and conventional rhyme schemes, as far as I am concerned, can nowadays only be used for light and occasional verse.

As for my volume of *Selected Poems,* I have had a lot of trouble putting it together. I probably had to discard as many poems which I would gladly have reprinted as are contained in the volume as it stands. A book of selected poems is simply a case of samples. I would refer readers who find my work in any way attractive to my more substantial volume of *Collected Poems.*

Selected Poems 1990

Anthony Hecht

I was born in New York City in 1923, and for many complicated reasons my childhood was a rather bitter and lonely one. Things picked up when I went to college, but not for long. In the middle of my junior year I enlisted in the army in order to be able to finish out that college year, and then was called up. After an infantry basic training, I was sent to a special language training program, presumably to prepare for intelligence work overseas. The program was to last twenty-eight weeks; in my twenty-fourth week the whole thing was abandoned by Congress because it was an election year, and the program seemed to favor college-education men and the sons of immigrant parents who had an edge in languages on the rest of the population. I returned to the infantry, and served in France, Germany, Czechoslovakia, and finally on occupation duty in Japan. In Germany, I was briefly attached to the Counterintelligence Corps. My first encouragement in poetry came from John Crowe Ransom, under whom I studied after the war at Kenyon College, where I also taught for a while. I used to offer Mr. Ransom specimens of my work from time to time. He would harbor them somewhere and never say a word, and I was much too shy to ask his opinion outright. I was hoping of course that he would like something of mine well enough to publish it in the *Kenyon Review*, which he then edited. One day I went to call upon him in his office for some help and advice about a class I was teaching. It had something to do with Shakespeare, as I remember, and we were deeply and hectically into it when I looked past his head to the blackboard where he habitually wrote down the names of the contributors to the next issue of the *Review*, in the order in which they would appear, and with the number of pages they would occupy. And there, to my astonishment, high on the list, and right between Lionel Trilling and Eric Bentley, was my name. At this point Mr. Ransom was being very animated about *Macbeth*, and all for my benefit, but I overcame my good manners and interrupted him to ask whether this meant that I was to appear in the next issue. He turned around to look at the blackboard, smiled, and in his very gentle southern voice said, 'I seem to have made a slight mistake,' whereupon he rose, went to the blackboard and erased the H in front of my name, and put down Br instead. He was apparently going to publish a Brecht story with a commentary by Bentley. He did in fact publish a poem of mine in the next issue, but I have often wondered whether his liking for that poem might not have been tinged with embarrassment.

The Hard Hours 1967

There is a way in which a poet's work is for him always a failure and a disappointment, since he alone once entertained the vision of what it might supremely be. This is no doubt what Paul Valéry and the many poets who like to quote him mean when saying, 'A poem is never finished, only abandoned.' At the same time, and without the cancelling effect of a paradox, there is a sense in which, for the poet alone, and only for a little while after the poem is written, that poem is an achievement of immeasurable worth, won through difficulties that are not necessarily legible in the text, which is itself the chosen solution to virtually countless alternatives and puzzles. To the reader, these fertile, bewildering, and possibly paralyzing options do not present themselves: the poem rolls along its iron rails of necessity like a preordained event. Only the poet knows how near and how often he came to chaos and failure, how unexpectedly he rescued himself when almost all hope was abandoned. After a while, of course, his intimate memory of all those compositional dilemmas fades away and he becomes, as Auden said of Yeats, 'his admirers' – he reads his own poems without any of the anxiety or joy of discovery they afforded him during the writing of them. I dislike most of my early poetry, and in the more recent work 'The things which I have seen I now can see no more.' Accordingly, while the memory of a few details has not quite faded I set them down here, though quite aware they may be of interest to no one but myself.

In the summer of 1977, after a stint of teaching in Salzburg, I came south to Venice with my family for a two-week visit, like some protagonist of a Thomas Mann short story. The city was enchanting to us all, we were very happy while there, and I was filled with a desire to express my sustained delight in a poem of some scope. When we came home, instead of starting right in to write, I read widely and randomly about Venice: guide books, histories, fiction, biographies, plays and poems. I gleaned less from this than I had expected, but this preparatory reading in no way diminished my urgency or watered down to bookishness my zeal to set the city down in an immediate way. So strong was that zeal that finally I began to write the poem in the voice of someone I had not yet identified any further than to know he was deeply troubled, indeed, sick; that his sickness was an analogue of the decay of Venice itself, and when I wrote, in the opening lines, about 'a clean coolness at the temple' I was thinking of the tiles on a bathroom floor, and conceived the speaker to have just recovered consciousness on such a floor. It wasn't until I had gotten well into the poem (my notes contain questions like 'Who's speaking?') that I hit upon who the speaker should be. But even before I found him I knew that he must be American, that his past must be befouled in a way from which he was trying to escape, and that if the decay of the city was an analogue of his sickness, so were its beauties an image of his dreams of redemption. And his concentrated attempt to see things clearly in the famous clarity of Venetian light would be a metaphor for his virtually hopeless attempt to fathom and understand the mystery of his own anguish.

The Venetian Vespers 1980

W. N. Herbert

When my grandmother makes a mistake she says, 'Eh tell a leh.' Maybe it's the Calvin in her makes her confess to lying when she isn't. But I feel the same whenever I use conversational English picked up after fourteen years in Oxford. Or whenever I lapse into a full-throated Dundonian Scots at home and someone announces, 'Ye've no lost yir accent.' Herbert speak with forked tongue.

One strand wiggles back to Blackness Primary and recites, 'Yir heid's daft, yir belly's saft, an yir bum is medd o leathir.' The other coils around Brasenose College and dreams of Marius the Epicurean. But I don't want to choose between them: I want both prongs of the fork. Aren't we continually hopping registers, like socially challenged crickets? My motto is: And not Or. This is what links 'Landfish', which is in Scots, to 'The Cortina Sonata', which is about Scottishness.

For the 'Sonata' I wanted a structure that bound themes together without blurring their distinctness, and found it in the classical sonata, which elaborates on two separate ideas, modulating them from major to minor, and so on. My themes were: my upbringing, and my experience of foreignness. So I talk about my grandfather's love of flowers in one breath, and a Renaissance courtier in Florence in the next. By looking at both the outside and the inside of my Scottishness, I hope to arrive at some melodious conclusions.

'Landfish' could have been a kind of New Demotic verse; boiling the idiolect down to something I'm able to say in a pub. But that would be a poetry that's afraid of getting beaten up.

Most of my Scots, to be blunt, gets the shit kicked out of it. I don't stay 'true' to how 'thi Peopul' speak: I search dictionaries for gorgeous defunct fragments; I make things up. I think that's the poet's task: to invent new ways of saying that are beautiful even after they've had the shit kicked out of them. So 'Landfish' is peculiar, baroque, whatever. It may be a challenge to read, but that's the challenge: come on in, the clytach's lovely.

Then there's 'Ticka Ticka', which is about a certain industrial dispute. I spent my teenage summers 'working' in Dundee's Timex factories. My father worked there for thirty years, as did many of his friends, at managerial and shop-floor levels. Last year's strike was deeply divisive of this community, and the final, inevitable closure left a bitter aftertaste of impotence. 'Ticka Ticka' combines personal memory and voices from Dundee's radical past to try and make some sense of these events. It's not a politically correct piece of polemic, it's an attempt to heal the divisions this dispute opened in me.

The last section is picked from four pamphlets and books, and covers my Scots work from 1983 to 1991. It's called 'Omnegaddrums', which my dictionary defines as 'a miscellaneous collection, a medley, the unincorporated craftsmen of the burgh'.

Forked Tongue 1994

Rita Ann Higgins

I had a strange bicycle. It was a cross between a High Nelly and a chairoplane, but I loved it. On my way home from town, I had to get off the bike and walk up this steep hill, where the male factory workers would loaf during their lunch-breaks. As I passed they would shout things about my bike and say things to me like, 'Would ya?' or, 'Any chance of the ride?' I was always red with rage and exertion passing them and I swore to myself, 'I'll get you bastards.' That's how 'The Apprentices' poem came about.

Some miserable fecker stole my bike and broke my heart. After that I took the Mervue bus. I loved the bus, settling in and daydreaming. One day I was admiring this beautiful woman. After I had made a goddess out of her, she yawned and the goddess flew out of the window. Another disappointment: things are never as they seem and why should we set people up to begin with? I wrote the poem 'Goddess on the Mervue Bus'.

Work was so plentiful in the seventies, we thought the multinationals were the greatest. What did we need unions for when they were giving us hampers with turkeys as big as horses?

Eventually most of the factories closed down. The multinationals left, taking the loot and the turkeys. 'When the Big Boys Pulled Out' was written some time later.

Sunny Side Plucked has other factory poems, like 'Work On', about jiving in the toilet of the shirt factory, and listening to the country girls talk about the boyos they shifted, and the type of cars they drove, and eventually the voice of the bossman telling us we were here to work and could we have our fantasies at the weekend. One time I did a workshop with a group of IRA prisoners; for security reasons I had to be locked in with them. At the back of the room the warder walked up and down behind a glass panel. He yawned a lot. He stretched out between two chairs; he had siestas between stanzas. After that came a poem called 'Reading'.

Shortly after its publication, I received a letter from the prison authorities saying they could not recommend that I do any further work with the prisoners.

Not all the poems in *Sunny Side Plucked* are related to actual events. All the poems about sex go on in my head, except I have met 'The-Did-You-Come-Yets' (how come they never know?). Plato and Petrarch pushed their way in past proletariat and prisoner, making poems about Philistines possible.

The voices are of real and sometimes super-real people throwing wobblers and fighting back. What I want to do is build up the characters beyond a snippet to a believable existence. To get to the poetic truth it is not always necessary to tell the what-actually-happened-truth; these times I lie.

These voices nearly always let rip, but they must have something to say, and they must say it without frilly knickers and hoola-boola. Humour doesn't have to sneak in but it's better if it does.

Revision is endless as it has to be.

Sound is precious, sense can be beat into shape.

Sunny Side Plucked **1996**

Geoffrey Hill

''Tis not my intention to make an Apology for my Poem: Some will think it needs no Excuse, and others will receive none.' Dryden was right, in principle (though perhaps he was not always true to his principles). If explanations are insisted on, I can do no more than point to the book's epigraph, which consists of a few words snatched out of *The Advancement of Learning*: 'From moral virtue let us pass on to matter of power and commandment . . .' If *King Log* has a theme, Bacon's words are relevant to it.

King Log 1968

Mercian Hymns was begun in the summer of 1967; it was finished precisely three years later. From the first I sensed that it would be a sequence, a volume complete in itself. This apparently novel fluency (between my first and second books there had been a gap of nine years), together with the use of what is, for me, a new form, might be seen as evidence of a diversion from earlier beliefs, attitudes, procedures. I would, however, be inclined to stress the likenesses, the continuities, between *For the Unfallen*, *King Log* and *Mercian Hymns*, rather than the manifest differences. In the new volume the occasional comedy is perhaps more extravagant, but (contrary to some opinion) the earlier books were not wholly devoid of humour.

It is now not possible to recall why or how one was drawn into the presence of 'Offa'. It was an enchantment difficult to justify on rational grounds; but, once one had been drawn, the details of the fantasy took on their own rationale. I would not be thought to underestimate the seriousness, the proper commitments, of the craft: diffidence in describing a work should not be misread as indifference.

Mercian Hymns 1971

I accept, though with some reluctance, that my poetry is generally regarded as difficult. At any given time the consensus, or whatever we are to call it, sets thresholds and boundaries of accessibility, and inaccessibility. These are arbitrary and commonly shift with each new generation; but so long as they remain they are immovable.

I have no ambition to be famously – or notoriously – obscure. The difficulties of daily living get in the way and my poems, unavoidably it seems, collide with the densities of common existence.

Speech! Speech! is not a book to be slowly pondered; it is meant to be taken, at least on first reading, at a cracking pace. The scenario is simple: an individual voice battles for its identity amid a turmoil of public speech and media noise, a crowded wilderness of acoustical din.

In his essay on Christopher Marlowe, T. S. Eliot observes that a play such as *The Jew of Malta* is not so much a tragedy as it is a tragic farce. I have pondered that definition since my sixth-form days at Bromsgrove High School. To say that *Speech! Speech!* is an attempt to create the equivalent of that genre would be a fairly accurate suggestion.

I am baffled and saddened when readers, friendly as much as unfriendly, approach my poems as cryptograms to be decoded. I don't have that kind of intelligence. I have a poor grasp of abstract ideas; a seven-year-old child of very average ability can beat me at chess; whenever I played Scrabble I lost.

Milton's description of poetry as being 'more simple, sensuous, and passionate' than other arts and disciplines has always moved me to a fervent assent. In short, I am happy to make my work as generally accessible as I honestly can. But this is less often than many professional and amateur readers consider right and proper. Nonetheless, in the words of Junius (1772), an author new to me, 'I speak to the plain understanding of the people, and appeal to their honest, liberal construction of me.'

Speech! Speech! 2001

I turned seventy in June and have been cheered by a Blake quotation received from a well-wisher, 'In [the Imagination] I am stronger & stronger as this Foolish Body decays.'

At one point in *The Orchards of Syon* (XXIII) I say 'I write / to astonish myself'. This self-astonishment is achieved when, by some process I can't fathom, common words are moved, or move themselves, into clusters of meaning so intense that they seem to stand up from the page, three-dimensional almost.

The main landscapes of the new book are two that I know well: the Bromsgrove area of Worcestershire, where I was born and grew up, and the valley of the River Hodder in north-east Lancashire. There are also a few New England touches here and there.

In strong contrast to the previous collection, *Speech! Speech!*, the new book is concerned with forms and patterns of reconciliation – not the easiest of states to move into, so there are numerous lapses and relapses throughout the sequence. It is about depth of memory and broken memory, but that could be said of all my poetry, most particularly perhaps of *The Triumph of Love* (1998). The cultivation of depths of memory I see as a civic duty as well as a private burden and consolation.

Depths of memory relates to depth of language in some way; and to speak of depth of language raises questions of accessibility.

Some years ago I came across a note by the German philosopher Theodor Hacker (1899–1945). He writes that 'Tyrants always want a language and literature that is easily understood.' I think that legitimate difficulty (difficulty of course can be faked) is essentially democratic.

The Orchards of Syon 2002

Michael Hofmann

My title, *Acrimony*, suggested itself to me quite some time ago, before most of the poems. A cracked code, a concrete significance barely hidden by an abstract noun, a glimpse behind closed doors, a Latin word for Anglo-Saxon exchanges. 'Bitterness of feeling or language.' The meeting broke up 'acrimoniously', 'amid scenes of acrimony', or sometimes (unfortunately) 'without acrimony'. With the word 'riot', it is surely the most swarming, plural and adverbial singular in the language. Accordingly, I have not sought to attach it to any one poem, but have allowed it to colour the whole book, as it sees fit. The publisher's blurb draws attention to the 'honesty' of the book. There is, of course, nothing inherently virtuous about being honest in poetry. The point is to be something – anything – effectively. It is worth remembering a remark of Gottfried Benn's here, that style is superior to truth. I would rather the blurb had said something about style. But although I have become quite good at recognising my style, I would be hard put to say anything authoritative about it. I think it is a question of identifying a certain mass of particulars, contingencies, facts, personalities, whatever (as in prose fiction, in fact), and still being able – or trying, anyway – to energise them, to pass a current through them, a handwriting, a signature: ideas, connections, music, cadence, tone.

Acrimony **1986**

For a long time, I was going to call this new book of mine *Gone*, and maybe I should have done. Three different senses of the word would have covered my three sections, which are to do with the death of my father in 1993; with travelling to, and reporting from, different places; and with quitting one life for another ('gone' here in the sense of 'smitten with' or 'stuck on'). Then it all seemed to me to be getting frantically tidy, so instead I chose a phrase from one of the poems, 'approximately nowhere', to apply, equally, everywhere.

I happen to believe (still) that a poem should have some reason to exist, in the same way that something in the clouds is required to happen to produce a flash of lightning. A lot of poems get written without such a reason: I don't value them as a category, there is something vapid and leisurely about them. However much one might wish it were otherwise, a poet is not the same as a storyteller or a comedian or a rock musician or anything else. Poems are by their nature occasional, unlegislatable, unpredicted. One of the great books of the century, by the presiding deity of this collection and my 'discovery' of the past five or ten years, Eugenio Montale, is called *Le Occasion!* 'Yet why not say what happened?' writes Robert Lowell, at his most Mephistophelean. I have a poem here called 'What Happens'.

This is not the same as 'confessional'. The poem may not get written without its hurt or its drama, but it's not the hurt or the drama that makes it a poem. Those things are, literally and punningly, a 'pre-text'. They are what get you to start thinking in images, and improvising and arranging words. Without them, I wouldn't think it was worth my while crossing the room to look for a piece of paper. I like the formulation of Bernard Spencer: 'a situation, out of which comes a so-far unformulated excitement'. It's not the situation that matters to the reader, or, once he has it, to the writer: it's the excitement. In his *Adagia*, Wallace Stevens makes the crucial point that a poem is not about an event, it *is* an event. A 'confessional poem' is a contradiction in terms: the action is by definition elsewhere. The reader, quite properly, responds to it exactly as he would to a piece of news or gossip: 'Lovely for you!' or 'Oh, you poor thing!' And that's why he's perhaps a little mulish when it's put to him that he might read such a poem – Olds or Sexton or lesser Berryman, to name some names, again. Why should he, he's heard it before . . .

The ideal poem, it seems to me, is one you want to pick up and read right away, and can also endlessly revisit. Montale is like that for me, and Lowell, and the German poet Gottfried Benn. Some of their poems I have probably read hundreds of times and still never tire of reconfiguring in my mind's eye and ear. A successful poem, in my definition, is 'a machine for re-reading'. The sentences on my own things that have most pleased me saw them in just such terms: 'these poems stuck to me like a burr' or 'kept me up half the night'. Funny accolades, you might think, but their undertone of irritation, accusation and surprise authenticates them for me.

And how does it happen, if it happens? What makes some things exhaustible and others practically not? If I really knew the answer, I'd bottle it, but part of the answer must lie in shifting as much as you can into the language: thick textures, odd combinations, words and turns that are both concrete and collusive. A line like a mosaic of magnets, charges and repulsions in every word. Otherwise, there is a process called annealment, the heating to a high temperature and slow cooling of glass or metal, to toughen them. Making a poem feels like that: writing as yourself, and reading it back as someone else. Distance, perspective, irony, derision, all come into the picture. The poem acquires independence; the poet, in Montale's comparison, is like the props man who's stumbled upon it, 'unaware that he's / the author'.

Approximately Nowhere 1999

Ted Hughes

What do I write about? After thinking the poems over, I have decided to say this: What excites my imagination is the war between vitality and death and my poems may be said to celebrate the exploits of the warriors of either side. Also they are attempts to prove the realness of the world, and of myself in this world, by establishing the realness of my relation to it. Another way of saying this might be: The poems celebrate the pure solidity of my illusion of the world. Again – and probably this is the first near-truth I have put down yet – they are the only way I can unburden myself of that excess which, for their part, bulls in June bellow away.

In each poem, besides the principal subject – and in my poems this is usually pretty easy to see, as, for instance, the jaguar in the poem called 'The Jaguar' – there is what is not so easy to talk about, even generally, but which is the living and individual element in every poet's work. What I mean is the way he brings to peace all the feelings and energies which, from all over the body, heart, and brain, send up their champions onto the battleground of that first subject. The way I do this, as I believe, is by using something like the method of a musical composer. I might say that I turn every combatant into a bit of music, then resolve the whole uproar into as formal and balanced a figure of melody and rhythm as I can. When all the words are hearing each other clearly, and every stress is feeling every other stress, and all are contented – the poem is finished.

I have gone to some lengths, I see, to give what is perhaps a generalisation about the composition of poetry, as well as a description of my own particular experience. I hope, though, to have defined the making of a very special kind of verse. There is a great mass of English poetry in which the musical element – the inner figure of stresses – is not so important as other elements. To me – no matter what metaphysical persuasion or definable philosophy a poem may seem to subscribe to – what is unique and precious in it is its heart, that inner figure of stresses. And in composing these poems I have been concerned to give to them – as well as good faces, clear brains and strong hands – sound hearts.

The Hawk in the Rain 1957

Wolfwatching is a gathering of occasional poems, none of them written to any conscious larger plan. I began to think of it as a group only as I realised how sharply the nucleus of it was rejecting certain pieces.

I say none was written to a larger plan, but in fact some were written partly as a correction of the over-determined plan of an earlier book. At one time I composed a text to accompany a sequence of Fay Godwin's powerful photographs of the upper Calder Valley, in West Yorks. In that book, knowing how photographs tend to contradict and displace any associated verbal imagery, I decided to stick to something simple and atmospheric. Also, I wanted to avoid hijacking Fay's inclusive vision with the exclusive autobiography (which I saw as a danger . . . after I'd made a beginning with three or four pieces in that vein). My guiding metaphor was film music: non-visual, non-specific, self-effacing. Since then, I have felt that what the book needed was exactly what I took pains to avoid: a gallery of detailed, quite subjective portraits of some of the people whose lives gave those dramatic backdrops their meaning. I became aware of the lack as a vacuum to be filled. And here and there, without my approaching them as a project, the odd piece about members of my family began to emerge, as reminiscence or tribute.

Some of the other titles answered a more definite prompting. A direct request, to help raise funds for the Rhino Rescue scheme in Kenya, produced 'The Black Rhino'. Thanks mainly to the *Daily Telegraph* it has raised quite a bit. When Greg Gatenby (Literary Director of Toronto Harbourfront) asked me for a whale-poem for his whale-size *Whale Anthology*, I deferred my response till it was too late, so I dedicated 'Little Whale Song' to another seagoing singer. 'On the Reservations' is a salute to the South Yorks poet Jack Brown, and my old schoolfriends in the South Yorks coal belt.

Accident seems to account for much of what we write. But sooner or later, if it has any life, we begin to see that it belongs to a pattern more like necessity. Certain books of poems are a kind of totem-pole: I suppose there is that aspect to this collection. The only question is (in so far as there is a question at all), why consult just these familiars at just this time?

Wolfwatching **1989**

Kathleen Jamie

My Scottish Book. I was writing, for once, with Scotland in mind, and discovered a rich seam. I wrote it quite quickly, though it wasn't a premeditated book. It just so happened that the poems I was writing seemed to hold either Scots words, or landscapes, or memories of growing up here, being a girl here.

I suppose I feel for Scotland what everyone thinks of their country. Irritation, exasperation and love. I'd been away for a couple of years, and coming home meant seeing afresh. (And hearing, of course, I fell in love with the Scots language – its words and cadences are there throughout the book.) We were having one of our occasional convulsions of proud despair, and I was able to wonder what kind of Scotland we could/would have, were we brave enough.

Some of the poems, like the title poem, are much more public than my earlier work. Some are political ('Crystal Set', 'Mr and Mrs Scotland are Dead'). The first line of 'In Praise of Aphrodite' is 'These are wicked days'. It's Tsvetayeva's and I saw no reason to change it.

'Den of the Old Men' and 'Jockey in the Wilderness' contain everything from folklore to Celtic shamanism, to redundancy. There is a grudging fondness there, but Scotsmen are being asked to make changes, and they're not doing it too successfully, as yet.

I take my solace in the natural world. I live by the Tay, a wide clean river; hills and birds seem to be entering the poems; my local landscape, the energy of the land. To my mind, these poems are more interesting than 'political' and 'gender' poems.

Maybe we are always discovering what kind of poets we are; using poetry to explore our own condition as poets.

Those avenues (Scottishness, woman-ness) were interesting enough, and I've discovered things, and rid myself of bogles. As if, by examining and throwing off (laughing off) the constraints imposed on me by being a Scottish girl, I was giving myself permission to go a wee bit farther. Empowering – that's the buzz-word. 'Duty' is too strong but I felt under some obligation to explore these areas, and now I have. So, for the time being, I can move away from them. Much in this culture wants reworking. Perhaps we can do it one at a time, each for ourselves. This is what the poem 'The Queen of Sheba' did for me. The Queen of Sheba was a figure of my girlhood. If ever you threw a tantrum or wanted, or didn't want, or flounced, or displayed some degree of emotion embarrassing to our Presbyterian sensibilities, you were asked, 'Who do you think you are? The Queen of Sheba?' I mean, permissions were Not Given. Neither to boys nor girls. I enjoyed bringing the Queen of Sheba – clever, huge, sexy, audacious powerful woman – riding into our mean streets. I think all art is about liberation. (Not selfish individualism.) Now I want to go back to the places of the imagination. A-travelling, mapping some new places. To something a little more . . . metaphysical. Don't ask me what I mean.

The Queen of Sheba 1994

When I read that Louise Glück recognises the end of every book as a 'conscious diagnostic act, a swearing off' I was grateful to her. She had articulated something which I'd been grappling with. To become conscious of a book's themes is to come out of the place where the poetry happens. It was very much the case with *Jizzen*. Once I knew what the book was 'about' it was done. The last word I wrote was 'proven': the last word of 'A Green Woman'. When that line was in place, it was like finishing an exam. It was time to put down the pen and walk, empty-headed, out into the sunshine. 'Proven' was my last word and I was out of there.

There were a couple of titles I could have used but *Jizzen* was the one which wouldn't go away. It's an old Scots word which doesn't translate very well. It means 'in labour', 'in the act of giving birth'. *The Concise Scots Dictionary* gives it as 'childbed'. I have never heard it spoken. There is the tender poem by Douglas Young, 'For a Wife in Jizzen', which begins

Lassie, can ye say
whaur ye ha been,
whaur ye ha come frae
whatna ferlies seen?

'Jizzen' is a strong, strange word. It names a strong strange experience, in a language which itself needs to be reclaimed and used. Though I'm loath to use words which I don't hear spoken, I thought, what the hell, it's a poet's prerogative to bring words back into usage, to shift their meaning, to dust them down and refresh them.

The poems in this book were written between 1995 and 1999. My two children were born in '96 and '98. The Conservative government, which came to power when I was a lassie of seventeen, eventually fell. The referendum on the issue of the Scottish Parliament was held in '97, and this year we took the two infants to Edinburgh on the day of its opening. Births of children and of nations. Acts of Union and of Separation. New life. Stuff like that.

There was an issue, too, of working with experiences which are wholly female – in an art form which still, at times, likes to imagine that real, proper poetry cannot have women's experience at its centre. Being in the thick of it rather prevents one from wandering lonely as a cloud. I'm still puzzling about these things – What is authority? What is tradition? What does lie at the heart of women's experience? I'm surprised at myself, but I think it is an act of choice. As women we still find ourselves in a tangle of briars. We are told what to write, and then told that real art can't be made from those experiences anyway. We have to spend energy clearing space. Having cleared the space to do otherwise, I seem to have chosen, for the time being, to write from women's experience.

So, in short, *Jizzen* is a book about coming to maturity, about birth and politics. Enjoy.

Jizzen **1999**

Alan Jenkins

When *Harm*, my last book, came out I told myself that if I ever published another collection it would not be like that one, a very short book of intensely personal poems. Things looked good for a while – the first two poems I wrote after *Harm* both employed a fictional or 'dramatic' voice: one was spoken by a (dead?) English adventurer who has 'gone native' in the Amazon and the other by a Leesonesque City wide-boy in free fall, his mind confusing images of a recent earthquake with shots of the atomic bomb on Hiroshima and the Great Storm of 1987. All of this, though drawing on experiences or dreams – or dream-like experiences – of my own, seemed far enough from my personal life or most pressing concerns to encourage me in the belief that I was on the right track, one that led pleasingly away from the 'confessional' poetry I'd been writing two or three years before. These poems had come quickly, which allowed me to hope that I would go on in this vein and produce a big, generous outward-looking book, soonish, perhaps even in a year or two. Now, six years later, here is *The Drift*: a very short book of intensely personal poems.

What happened was that *Harm* won a prize, which though very gratifying also pretty effectively shut me up, closed me down, whatever. (I've since discovered that this is a fairly common reaction to any sort of recognition, another mental mechanism we don't seem to have much control over, but one with awkward, paradoxical consequences if you're trying to practise any kind of art.) When I got started again, it was in response to the news of an old friend's terminal illness. We'd met on our first day at university and had been inseparable all the way through it. As well as all the fun we'd had, I couldn't really imagine being who I was if it hadn't been for him. He had married immediately after graduating, and our lives had gone in different directions. We had even had a kind of falling-out that had never been put right – in the way of these things, I thought there was all the time in the world and so, probably, did he.

Now he only had a few months to live, and I never saw him again. But I began writing 'The Short Straw' – 'So I've drawn the short straw' was what he'd said when he heard he was incurable – as a tribute to him, and over the year or so it took me to write, it became an elegy. (To him, or to the life I'd shared with him? It didn't seem a distinction worth making.) I also began working on a prose introduction to the brief life and brilliant art of Bruno Fonesca, a painter of my acquaintance who had died of AIDS. And during that period two other friends died too, both poets, utterly different in their natures and approaches but both much loved by me, and by many others: Joseph Brodsky and Gavin Ewart. Feeling very much in the midst of death (and though the death of one's elders and betters is bad enough, having an exact contemporary die placed me squarely in the death zone myself), I recalled one of those elders and betters once telling me, 'Your subject is loss. Stay with that.' I attempted an elegy for Joseph, began one for Gavin, and though neither poem really worked, the elegiac tone of the book had arrived, and it wasn't going to go away. My only choice was to go with it or give up.

For it's true that we don't choose our subject, it chooses us. Next was my mother. And though this was 'only' what my gay male friends had been going through, on a daily basis, for the past ten years – the loss of, in some cases, practically everyone close to them, with terrible rapidity and inevitability – it began to seem inescapable. From my drift towards middle age – the 'somehow-getting-to-be-forty', as Ian Hamilton wrote, unforgettably – I was sending distress signals about the losses it had entailed. Chief among them was the loss of a kind of innocence – not sexual innocence but the child's (and if you're lucky, as lucky as I had been, the young adult's) innocence of death itself. From this point of view childhood was the lost paradise before people started leaving me, that is, dying. There had been other kinds of leave-taking in the intervening years, and they began to find their way into the poems. I was writing with an equal commitment to order – a more careful organisation of stanzas and line-beats than I'd ever wanted before – and to a certain raggedness. I had rediscovered for myself the ancient truth that poetry consoles while offering no consolation (something I only needed to go back to Larkin, as I did all the time, to have confirmed); I was consoled by shapeliness, but I wanted to stay true to the dishevelment I felt as well. The poems would have nothing in them that needed to be explained or apologised for. Then one day I started cutting back and weeding out. *The Drift* has twenty-seven poems, like my last book and the one before that. 'There is no safety in numbers, or in anything else': James Thurber. But on the other hand, Samuel Beckett: 'Not count! One of the few satisfactions in life!'

The Drift **2000**

Elizabeth Jennings

I do not like writing about my poetry. Poems, if they succeed at all, are autonomous, they stand alone; no contemporary poem should need footnotes. However, there are perhaps things which one can usefully say about one's attitude in general towards one's poetry. Whether a poet writes his poems in bed, while smoking, eating or drinking, whether he writes them slowly or quickly, works through many drafts or few – these things are not, in my opinion, in the least interesting to other people; they are the poet's own affair and should be as private as making love.

But, as for my attitude towards my own work – writing poems is for me always a discovery; it is also the gradual building of a world. The making of a poem starts as a personal matter (though never as a mere device for introspection) and, if the poem is successful, ends as something quite objective. There is a kind of passionate detachment about the whole process. It is, however, a mistake to think that a poem always begins in the same way in the imagination of the poet. In my own experience, a poem sometimes declares itself as a vague but violent physical reaction; at other times, what started as a technical experiment may end in the resolution of a mental or emotional conflict. That is all I shall say about the genesis of poems.

I would like to say something now about the poet's audience. I don't suppose a poet ever thinks about his possible readers while he is actually writing a poem, but I am sure that most poets afterwards want their work to be read, understood and enjoyed as widely as possible. Robert Graves must surely be in a minority in thinking that a poet only wants the appreciation of his fellow poets or of a few select friends. For myself, I find few things more gratifying than the approval of someone, perhaps not a poet himself, who doesn't know me. One has plainly made contact and that is a delightful thing.

Influences are perhaps interesting and I should like to think that I have been influenced by the modern poets whom I most admire – Yeats, Edwin Muir and the American Wallace Stevens. I do not think I have been strongly influenced by any of these poets in the matter of technique. Rather they have acted as liberators, have shown me the most direct way into my own world.

Prose has always seemed to me an attempt to find words for something which I already know, whereas my best poems manage to say in a strict inevitable form something that I did not know before. Consequently, I feel uneasy writing this kind of apologia: all that I have tried to say about my own poems seems somehow not quite to be the truth. It is an approximation merely and perhaps rather a pompous one. I hope to be judged by my practice, not by my theory.

A Way of Looking 1955

Song for a Birth or a Death is my fourth book of poems but I feel scarcely more capable of discussing my work now than I did when my first book appeared. I find that the more poems one writes, the more mysterious the whole creative process becomes. Writing poems has been my most vital occupation since I was thirteen years old and now, having given up in turn advertising copywriting, working in two public libraries and reading for a publisher, I am devoting all my time to writing. This means, of course, that I am producing a good deal of prose as well as poems. Unlike some poets, I do not feel that prose diverts me from poetry; on the contrary, it often both stirs up the sources of poetry and also acts as a restful interlude during those frustrating periods when poems simply will not come. Briefly, I can write prose at almost any time, whereas poems have to be waited for patiently and, odd as it may sound, disinterestedly. Though I can never explain satisfactorily why I write poems, I can, I think, say one or two things about *Song for a Birth or a Death* which may prove illuminating to the reader. The poems in this book are more directly personal than most of my earlier ones; many of them are concerned with my childhood, my religion, and my relationships with people I love. I have written of these subjects as honestly and as simply as I can because I am well aware that though, in one sense, all poetry is and must be personal, in another, it is something quite separate from the poet himself. His own experiences may be part of his poetic material but those experiences have to be shaped, ordered and understood before they can ever crystallise into satisfactory poems. Many readers fail to understand this shaping and distancing process and are, as a result, inclined to ask a poet why he is not embarrassed when people read poems of his which are based on intimate personal experience. If the poems in question are at all successful, the poet is never embarrassed simply because these poems are no longer part of him but have taken on an autonomous life of their own.

When I look back on my earlier books of poems, I can see now certain obsessions, preoccupations, experiments and styles. My poetry has changed, I think, but the change has been almost wholly unconscious. I never know what my next poem will be like, though I may have a very clear idea of what I don't want it to be like. To say this may seem to be giving a very minor role to the intellect in the making of poems. In fact, I believe that intellect is just as important as imagination, emotion and technical skill. When one is actually writing, however, one is never aware of these things as separate faculties or functions. One writes as a whole person, both with all that is conscious in one and all that is unconscious, or, as Yeats put it, with 'intellect, blood and imagination all running together'. And when one is writing poems, one is at a pitch of nervous and mental intensity that is quite unlike any other experience I know.

The qualities I admire most in poetry are clarity, concentration, and a tremendous pressure of feeling controlled by a flawless sense of form and rhythm. I find these qualities, in different degrees, in Vaughan, Herbert, Hopkins, Yeats, Robert Graves, Edwin Muir and Wallace Stevens. I have, at various times, been influenced by all these poets, although I hope that these influences are becoming less obvious in my own work. The best influences are always springboards towards a style and a voice of one's own. I write poems in order to know, to discover, to get things clear. My writing is also a search for order. I wish to communicate too, of course, though this is never a primary consideration when I am in the act of writing a poem. Poems must be truthful but they must also be well made. In prose one may be able to dissimulate, in poetry the truth always emerges and, if one is not being really honest, it can destroy a poem utterly. The standards of genuine poetry are high and nothing less than formal perfection and complete truthfulness will do.

It is an honour and a responsibility to be a poet; it is also painful, precarious and deeply disturbing. The perilous process of making a poem is so mysterious, exquisite and absorbing, however, that it more than compensates for the long dark periods when poetry seems to have dried up in one for ever. I cannot say what my next poems will be like; writing a poem is, like mystical experience, a gratuitous gift. One can prepare oneself for it but one has no right to demand it.

I am never satisfied with any of my poems for long. It is the one which seems just ahead but tantalisingly hidden that really interests me. The pursuit will be fascinating, full of snares and, perhaps, finally fruitless. I only know that this strange occupation seems to me intensely exciting and worth devoting one's life to.

Song for a Birth or a Death 1961

P. J. Kavanagh

I began to write rhymes as soon as I could read nursery ones; when I started to read poetry, I sedulously and helplessly wrote other people's poems, and continued to do so until I fell in love. This permanently disturbing experience coincided with a long period of separation from my love and then it was that I found myself scribbling in a Barcelona restaurant, on the back of an envelope, words that seemed to be in my own voice. These words are now, some years later, the first in my first book. I was so excited I couldn't stop, and although I've scrapped nearly everything I wrote at this time, I knew then as I know now, there is no turning back.

I find it difficult to write about my 'poetic aims'. My primary aim is to be truthful to the initial impulse wherever it may take me. There are those who might call this an anti-poetic aim – 'The truest poetry is the most feigning' – and I sometimes think they may be right. To tell the truth, I don't know. But these pieces of myself, pared suddenly onto scraps of paper, or scraped, slowly and laboriously in locked rooms, in different moods, in different parts of the world, I can't imagine what they mean to anyone else. But it is fine they mean something, because that, mysteriously, is what one intends.

I showed the typescript of this book to a great friend of mine who does not normally read poetry. He returned it somewhat abashed. 'Extraordinary,' he muttered, 'you poets, you must feel absolutely stripped naked at the thought of people reading such intimate stuff.' He couldn't have said anything less gratifying. The poem worn like a heart on the sleeve is nearly always sorry stuff. Startled, I re-read the book from beginning to end, and I still can't see what he meant. I think a poet goes so deeply inside himself to write a poem that he ceases to be himself at all. Of course he can only find what is already there, but it is what seems to him non-private, universally applicable, that finds its way into the poem. That is when he does make a poem and not something that he only hopes is one; and alas, it is into this latter category that the greater part of the work of all poets must fall. (The tiny preface to Auden's *Collected Shorter Poems* seems to me the last word on this point.)

A great poet at the moment of creation becomes himself so entirely that he becomes all men. Perhaps this is Eliot's 'denial of personality', even Keats's 'negative capability'. It is near to what is called 'a state of grace' and indeed has something of virtue in it. Everyone knows how brief, how elusive, and how exciting the glimpses of such moments are, and should therefore not be surprised at the scarcity of good poetry, or at the quantity of boss-shots, but should be grateful rather, and reassured, that there is any at all.

One and One 1959

When a man looks at a pile of his poems it astonishes him how many of the great events of his life, of his time, are not recorded there – not directly. There he is, churned up with loves and aches and horrors, private and public, a man of his time like everybody else, and he finds he has written (say) of a path through woods, and remembers that seemed to say it all, or nearly all. Philip Larkin remarked years ago, 'The poems a poet thinks he ought to write are not necessarily the ones that get written.' This can dismay him, and shake his nerve.

It can disappoint the public, too, who look for newspaper importances whereas he talks of moss, or moons. So he has been shuffled from the centre of things, where he was once, to the fringes, a tolerated irrelevance. There are exceptions, and they are rewarded. Wilfred Owen talked directly of the Great War and was heard. Edward Thomas barely mentions it and has had to wait sixty years. But the evident importance of its subject bears only a slight relation to the importance of a poem.

Coleridge planned great poems on politics and God but found himself writing (and found himself when he wrote) letter-poems to his friends. It seems that a poet can't go fishing for poems, he has to become the fish and be hooked. Should he feel the strange twitch in his imagination, the inexplicable pull of excitement, when his eye falls on some particular piece of moss (or particular bus-stop – anything, so long as it surprises him), then so be it, he must allow himself to be pulled. If luck attends his journey he will express enough of his own humanity to reassure others of the importance of their own. Which is why dictators, those most effective of literary critics, do not like poets. A good poem is a political act, unbiddable, and they know this.

Which is why poets, sometimes apparently arrogant, but always humble before their task, should not lose heart. Sometimes we think we footle, and sometimes we do. At times, too, we could wish the Muse used bigger bait, more brightly coloured; the water is murky. But it always has been, and the same water for all.

Selected Poems 1982

Patrick Kavanagh

My beginnings were so peculiarly humble and illiterate that I have never dared to write about them. I dislike talking about myself in a direct way. The self is only interesting as an illustration. I can begin only when things are moving into the comedy of humility. I used at about the age of twelve to make up ballads in my head and these I sang to the neighbours. They were useful ballads telling about football matches, dances, etc. More than thirty years later I heard one of those ballads being sung. It was about a wedding dance which a number of men tried to crash.

Farrelly climbed in by the window
But Dooly fell back with a souse
And the singing and shouting was terrible
Around the half barrel of stout.

My misfortune as a writer was that atrocious formula which was invented by Synge and his followers to produce an Irish literature. The important thing about this idea of literature was how Irish was it. No matter what sort of trash it was, if it had the Irish quality. And that Irish quality simply consisted in giving the English a certain picture of Ireland. The English love 'Irishmen' and are always on the look-out for them.

So it was that, in the sign of this horrible constellation, I wrote a dreadful sort of stage Irish autobiography called *The Green Fool* (1938). I have never been able to live it down. My second greatest misfortune was that I came to live in Dublin. That was at the start of the Hitler war. My lot was cast in the midst of a crowd of the usual kind of lying journalists. Never in touch with anyone who would give me a line on the situation. One quality the school demanded of me was that I express peasant life. I was the authentic peasant. Several other Dublin bards were contending for the peasant title but I don't think any of these ever deposed me. Through hopping and trotting in the end I woke up.

I wrote a novel, *Tarry Flynn*, which I am willing to say is the only authentic novel of life as it was, and is, lived in rural Ireland. One must not hesitate to tell the truth, even when it is in favour of oneself. The Pilot Press, which published *Tarry Flynn* in 1948, went broke immediately and the novel was remaindered at a shilling. It is now hard to get. Then it dawned on me that the whole school of Irish writers and poets had nothing but 'Ireland' to offer. So I started a campaign to destroy the school. That campaign succeeded and the 'Irish' thing has fled either to America or the BBC.

But my real awakening came later, in 1955 and 1956, and most of the poems in *Come Dance with Kitty Stobling* were written in that period. I wrote all these new ones in an orgy of energy in about a week. It takes colossal energy to write a good poem and I have only the one lung; the other one had the misfortune to contract cancer and had to be removed in 1955. That's about the size of it for the present.

Come Dance with Kitty Stobling 1960

X. J. Kennedy

A remark of Eliot's has stuck with me: his comparison of the meaning of a poem – the prose sense of it – to the burglar's bit of meat. There in the darkened house sits the mind of the reader, a house-dog given a kidney to keep him quiet, while the rest of the poem stalks about its business: making off with the first editions and the silver gravy-boat. Eliot's metaphor is the source of my title, *Breaking and Entering*. As a reader of poetry, I have often felt dog-like, especially when confronted by poems that seem just wild and whirling words. Such poems cause the hackles to rise until one wants to bite the poet in the leg. And yet, while trying to write poetry myself, sometimes I neither know nor care what I mean by the words that start coming in stealthily. Usually, it is a happy surprise when a wild mess of verbiage makes sense to me. I believe that, as a friend, W. D. Snodgrass, puts it, writing a poem is often a matter of groping down through many top-of-the-head ideas and many self-deceptions. If the poem is lucky, it arrives at some facts that its writer had not known he knew.

Lately, I have been writing more song lyrics. When toiling in vain over a would-be poem that obstinately remains just a word-hash, I remember the advice of that old Boston Irishman heckling a political speaker in a public park, 'Aaaaghh, won't ye shut up or else give us a tune, ye blatherer!'

Breaking and Entering **1971**

Philip Larkin

It would, perhaps, be fitting for me to return the heartening compliment paid by the Selectors to *The Whitsun Weddings* with a detailed annotation of its contents. Unfortunately, however, once I have said that the poems were written in or near Hull, Yorkshire, with a succession of Royal Sovereign 2B pencils during the years 1955 to 1963, there seems little to add. I think in every instance the effect I was trying to get is clear enough. If sometimes I have failed, no marginal annotation will help now. Henceforth the poems belong to their readers, who will in due course pass judgement by either forgetting or remembering them.

If something must be said, it should be about the poems one writes not necessarily being the poems one wants to write. Some years ago I came to the conclusion that to write a poem was to construct a verbal device that would preserve an experience indefinitely by reproducing it in whoever read the poem. As a working definition, this satisfied me sufficiently to enable individual poems to be written. In so far as it suggested that all one had to do was pick an experience and preserve it, however, it was much over-simplified. Nowadays nobody believes in 'poetic' subjects, any more than they believe in poetic diction. The longer one goes on, though, the more one feels that some subjects are more poetic than others, if only that poems about them get written whereas poems about other subjects don't. At first one tries to write poems about everything. Later on, one learns to distinguish somewhat, though one can still make enormously time-wasting mistakes. The fact is that my working definition defines very little: it makes no reference to this necessary element of distinction, and it leaves the precise nature of the verbal pickling unexplained.

This means that most of the time one is engaged in doing, or trying to do, something of which the value is doubtful and the mode of operation unclear. Can one feel entirely happy about this? The days when one could claim to be the priest of a mystery are gone: today mystery means either ignorance or hokum, neither fashionable qualities. Yet writing a poem is still not an act of the will. The distinction between subjects is not an act of the will. Whatever makes a poem successful is not an act of the will. In consequence, the poems that actually get written may seem trivial or unedifying, compared with those that don't. But the poems that get written, even if they do not please the will, evidently please that mysterious something that has to be pleased. This is not to say that one is forever writing poems of which the will disapproves. What it does mean, however, is that there must be among the ingredients that go towards the writing of a poem a streak of curious self-gratification, almost impossible to describe except in some such terms, the presence of which tends to nullify any satisfaction the will might be feeling at a finished job. Without this element of self-interest, the theme, however worthy, can drift away and be forgotten. The situation is full of ambiguities. To write a poem is a pleasure: sometimes I deliberately let it compete in the open market, so to speak, with other spare-time activities, ostensibly on the grounds that if a poem isn't more entertaining to write than listening to records or going out it won't be entertaining to read. Yet doesn't this perhaps conceal a subconscious objection to writing? After all, how many of our pleasures really bear thinking about? Or is it just concealed laziness?

Whether one worries about this depends, really, on whether one is more interested in writing or in finding how poems are written. If the former, then such considerations become just another technical difficulty, like noisy neighbours or one's own character, parallel to a clergyman's doubts: one has to go on in spite of them. I suppose in raising them one is seeking some justification in the finished product for the sacrifices made on its behalf. Since it is the will that is the seeker, satisfaction is unlikely to be forthcoming. The only consolation in the whole business, as in just about every other, is that in all probability there was really no choice.

The Whitsun Weddings 1964

James Lasdun

Unlike anything else I've written, these poems came swiftly and – dare I say it – easily. I wrote them over two summers, working on the porch of an old barn in the Catskill Mountains near Woodstock, New York, where I moved with my family a few years ago.

Having led a mainly urban, more or less peripatetic existence for most of my adult life, I found myself for the first time living in a place where I felt suddenly, strangely and euphorically at home. Why this should be so was something of a mystery, and the poems come largely out of this: this unexpected feeling of belonging somewhere, and the attendant question of what had all along been giving rise to its opposite: a kind of perpetual, low-grade feeling of estrangement.

It isn't the prettiest of landscapes here, or the most hospitable. Most of the enterprises launched from it – farming, quarrying, tourism – have failed, and after a couple of long, hard winters you see the point of Auden's remark that America wasn't really supposed to be inhabited by people at all. Anything you succeed in growing on the rocky soil, for instance, is fair game for the deer. If you manage to fence them out, the woodchucks and chipmunks will burrow in, and even when you've learned to sink a fine-gauge wire mesh in the ground to keep them out, the wild turkeys will come along sooner or later, flap in over the fence like a squadron of pterodactyls, and make quick work of anything left. You might think your house itself is inviolable, until you come face to face, as we did, with the rattlesnake peering through the broken plaster of your laundry room where it has decided to spend the winter, or find yourself woken in the night by the Black Bear slashing the window screen to get at the kitchen scraps. And then there are the trees, your vertical brethren and most patient rivals, encroaching a little further into your clearing every year, waiting for your venture to subside into ruins like all the others they've grown back over since the Dutch first settled here, until you begin to understand that as far as making a viable life in this spot, it's either you or them. At which point, being human, and of the technological era, you realise you are going to have to get your hands on – among other things – a chainsaw.

And if, like me, you think of yourself as a person of staunch nature-loving, even tree-hugging, principles, you find yourself suddenly in an interesting situation: face to face with the unpalatable terms of your own continued existence, which are after all the terms of anyone's existence, just laid a little more bare than usual. And perhaps it's just this that makes living here so oddly compelling.

Landscape with Chainsaw **2001**

Peter Levi

The slow mechanics of publishing make it hard to be exact about one's poems, by the time they appear in a book. By now one's mind is full of something else. The special excitement of poems attends their birth and their rebirth in the mind and on the tongue, but not their publication. This excitement is impossible to counterfeit, not because of its intensity or its resonance but because of its strange and individual quality.

I can promise nothing about the future and express nothing about the past; no poet has anything better to say about literature than his poems. Sometimes I think of writing in prose, but I doubt if I shall ever get the comprehensive clarity one would need, supposing one were to say what matters. This feeling that one must only say what matters, and at the same time the stress and confusion of what does matter to one, and the inability to cope with it, are an important source of romantic poetry.

But romantic art seems to me terrible and worthless, except for the value which human beings share with their own self-portraits. One can learn a form in art and this form might be unromantic. A society which was functional and scientific could perhaps (if it were at the same time free) produce its own forms. These would not be romantic (the ballad of the bankrupt prince, the rootless intellectual) or epic (epic poetry depends on a far different society from ours and had in that society a far different meaning); if it were possible to work towards these forms, I should like to do it, but I doubt if I have been doing so.

When one looks at the great poets of the last generation, one despairs both at their inimitable power and at their ineluctable impotence. In a sense I believe that both the impotence and the power came from the divided consciousness of the same situation. My situation is different. I have and want neither. The power that I want is Henryson's, Chaucer's, John Clare's, Skelton's and Smart's, and the impotence I am prepared to accept is that of Robert Southwell and George Herbert. This is not a new formula (it is not a formula at all) or the ritual chanting of a new ars poetica, but only one way of being honest. Honesty is itself an art, and difficult to attain. The degree of its attainment differs, and the level differs.

How to alter what poetic honesty cannot but reveal is another question which can never be solved in poems themselves. The intensity and the confusion are too great there. And we can judge the poems themselves on the same criteria as the poet judges his own past work; but never on the rigorous and far-reaching criteria by which his future work was likely to have been determined. Once the decision has been made, nothing can exist but the poem. Decisions of this sort are incommunicable and often subconscious. If one tries to discuss them, all one's words turn out to have private meanings. But the poem can be as clear as 'the orchis . . . rotting in a grave of dew'.

The Gravel Ponds 1960

Christopher Logue

Poetry is gratuitous, it is the art in which we excel. That is, the Dutch are painters; the English, poets.

Poets are not paid, they are housed or fed, well or badly, according to their period and their behaviour. Though a poet claims to serve or to ignore his community's interest in his work, no price can be set against his endeavour or his ignorance.

The chief preoccupation of a serious poet today is politics. How and what he writes about is his own affair. Apart from Milton, and, to a lesser extent, Pope, there are no English precedents for this preoccupation. This is one of the reasons for the present degradation of English poetry. Talent is thin on the ground, ability to face outwards, using personal predicament as a spur and not an end in itself, is almost totally lacking. The indifference of the educated public to poetry is justified. Organisations such as the Poetry Society and the Poetry Book Society emphasise this indifference but do almost nothing to change it. Many poets and their few readers think of themselves as the guardians of culture, an educated elite. This sentimental ideal could not be further from the truth.

The solution to this problem lies in the development of narrative and dramatic poetry, the complete abandonment of the passionate or academic lyric, the introduction of argument and situation, the avoidance of literary imagery and psychological obsession with self.

The workers are not interested. They have other fish to fry. Nevertheless, the future of English poetry is bound tight to the future of the working class. Laments over the decay of religion, the loss of this or that sex partner, the glories of Italian summer holidays &c., are meaningless and destructive.

I hope you buy my book.

Songs 1959

Michael Longley

For a long time I have been preoccupied with form – pushing a shape as far as it will go, exploring its capacities to control and its tendencies to disintegrate. Ideally this should be an inner adventure; plan and passion, improvisation and calculation should coincide.

After I've flown my rickety biplane under the Arc de Triomphe and before I perform a double back-somersault without the safety net and – if there's time – walk the high wire between two waterfalls, I shall draw a perfect circle free-hand and risk my life in a final gesture. As an Ulsterman I realise that this may sound like fiddling while Rome burns. So I would insist that poetry is a normal human activity, its proper concern all of the things that happen to people. Though the poet's first duty must be to his imagination, he has other obligations and not just as a citizen. He would be inhuman if he did not respond to tragic events in his own community, and a poor artist if he did not seek to endorse that response imaginatively. But if his imagination fails him, the result will be a dangerous impertinence. In the context of political violence the deployment of words at their most precise and most suggestive remains one of the few antidotes to death-dealing dishonesty. I like Pound's equating of an artist's technique with his sincerity.

In Elizabeth Bowen's novel *The Heat of the Day*, there's a marvellous definition of love which underwrites my intuitions about poetry, especially if I allow myself the unfashionable concept of the Muse: 'To have turned away from everything to one face is to find oneself face to face with everything.' I believe that in a sense most poems are love poems; that because a poet is someone for whom no experience is complete until he has written about it, most poems are elegies as well –

That poetry, a tongue at play
With lip and tooth, is here to stay,
To exercise in metaphor
Our knockings at the basement door,
A ramrod mounted to invade
The vulva, Hades' palisade
The Gates of Horn and Ivory
Or the Walls of Londonderry.

The Echo Gate 1979

A visit to Japan in 1991 modified the way I look at the world. It also made me surer of my own artistic practice. In Ireland my poems about landscape, flowers and animals are sometimes dismissed as escapist ('your wee poems about swans and primroses', to quote a younger contemporary). I sensed that I was soon on the same wavelength as Japanese audiences when I read them my nature poems. I was captivated by the Japanese appreciation of everyday objects and their sacerdotal potential: the pretty boxes and paper wrappings; the napkins that contain poems as well as chopsticks; the bowls that make hands look beautiful; the tea ceremony that elevates modesty and epitomises the virtues of this least slipshod of cultures. Then there were the shrines, often in unexpected places, some very humble, one dedicated to the spirit of the silk worm: alcoves in the quotidian, 'places where a thought might grow'. I celebrate all this in *The Ghost Orchid* – not only in the Japanese pieces and in the interrupted sequence of reconstructed Chinese poems, but also, I hope, throughout the collection. I aspire to a lightness of touch, and value art in which not a single word or brushstroke is superfluous; in which deep matters are essayed without fuss. The Japanese have a single word for this aesthetic: *karumi*, private. This was an exception: I am still warmed by the response of several readers, some of them damaged or bereaved in the Troubles. I had long wanted to make a self-contained lyric out of the scene in Book XXII of the *Odyssey* where Phemios the bard and Medon the herald beg for mercy from Telemachos and Odysseus, who have just finished slaughtering Penelope's suitors. By serendipity or subconscious design, I was leafing through an Ulster Scots dictionary, and found that dialect from my region was making available to me the terror and comedy of this scene out of Greek epic. Words such as *banny*, *barn*, *gabble-blooter*, *keeking* made fresh sounds and suggestions. Ulster Scots words are still part of everyday speech here and crop up elsewhere in *The Ghost Orchid*. Although I believe that they should be decipherable and work on their own without a glossary, it pleases me to imagine a reader somewhere far from Ulster discovering what these words mean by going back to Homer. The long way home.

My main preoccupations continue to be Eros and Thanatos and their reflections in summer and winter, day and night, the evanescence of plant and animal, 'the merry go / Round around the sun and the roundabout of death'. I write for everyone and for no one in particular. The first person I try to please is myself. I live for those moments when language itself takes over the enterprise, and insight races ahead of knowledge. Occasionally I have things to say, or there is something I want to describe. But these are not my main reasons for writing.

The Ghost Orchid 1995

The first poem in this selection, 'Epithalamion', is the first poem of mine to survive. I wrote it in the summer of 1963 when I should have been studying for my finals. Two long sentences are woven through an intricately rhymed stanza of my own invention. From early on I was preoccupied with formal challenges. At the same time 'Epithalamion' is a love poem with a religious undertow. Horace calls the poet *musarum sacerdos*, priest of the Muses. The Scottish word *makar* is a straight translation of the Greek *poetes*. The poet oscillates between notions of craft and vision. If he settles too long for one or the other, he becomes boring. Ideally, plan and passion, improvisation and calculation coincide.

A poet makes the most complex and concentrated response that can be made with words to the total experience of living. The experiences out of which I write include falling in love and marriage; fatherhood; being the son of a brave soldier who survived the First World War; friendship with botanists and ornithologists as well as with poets and painters; rediscovering in my forties the classics, especially Homer; listening to music every day; exploring over a period of thirty years a remote corner of County Mayo; discovering more recently the mysterious landscape of the Burren in County Clare, and a small village on a mountain top in Tuscany; meeting people of like mind in Japan; living in a society disfigured by fratricidal violence; and believing throughout the Troubles that the arts are central to life.

I wrote the latest poem included here in August 1994, when there were rumours of an IRA ceasefire. I was reading book XXIV of the *Iliad* and managed to fit into a sonnet the episode in which the old King Priam bravely visits Achilles' tent to beg for the corpse of his son Hector and enough time for a proper funeral. The IRA did indeed call a ceasefire and my poem 'Ceasefire' appeared in the *Irish Times* two days later. The sort of poetry I write usually makes its occasion in private, but this poem enjoyed a modest public role which I still find a replenishment. Though I hope that the time has come for 'Ceasefire' and a number of related poems to elude their topicality, I keep as talismans at the back of my folder of new work letters from people who in their bereavement have found my lines of some use. Living in Ireland has taught me that poetry is not just an individual but also a communal process.

Selected Poems 1998

George MacBeth

Publishing this volume at about the age (not far from sixty) when Thomas Hardy was assembling the verse for his first book, one feels an eerie sense of hope. Is there, after all, to be life beyond a *Collected Poems*? The answer might well be yes, and the ageing writer approaches his not quite terminal reviews in the spirit of caution. As I hint in the foreword to my book, the question of quality, inviting a resting on a laurel, seems less important than the question of clarity, from which some tips on improvements might be drawn.

Several poets I know admire the resonance of obscurity, and think one should do a little better than say what one means. I don't agree. When one is wrestling with a strict or novel form, as one could be in writing a poem, invention comes far easier than accuracy. Approximations can stand in for inspiration where plain talk would sound banal. Nevertheless, there is a place for happy accidents, and for changes of direction, and for speaking with one's tongue in one's cheek. That said, the point is to have some kind of plan, and to stick to it, even in the rain, with page four missing, and the troops mutinying.

My own plan has been rarely understood, and insufficiently followed. I'm not even sure, now, that I know what it was, but it may have been something to do with a sense of aristocracy. If it were useful to define an aristocrat as someone who sees his parents as better than himself, and yesterday as generally better than today, then I could accept the responsibility of writing as an aristocrat. The opening poems in my book are about my father and mother, and how I see them as heroes, and ikons.

This theme gets quickly lost – and a muddled sense of chaos and violence may seem to supervene – but I try to regrasp the theme as the book goes on, albeit in snatches and through keyholes. What may distract from this accent on conserving – something not uncommon perhaps among poets, and conspicuous in Yeats and Byron – is a much-cultivated pleasure in experiments with structure, or playing games, as more denigratory critics have called it. I plead guilty to this fault, if such it be, but excuse it as the muscle-flexing of a poet who would like to have been an architect. This is hardly a surprising ambition. My father was a draughtsman.

So that you see the author – on the cover of this book you may like to buy, or borrow – stepping down rather gingerly from the roof of a house he hasn't built, and hoping for the indulgence of a careful reading, but willing, being weak, to accept what mead of praise he can get.

Collected Poems 1989

Norman MacCaig

It's hard to know what to say about this new book – or any other, for that matter. Are there changes? Do any of the poems in it give off a whiff of that dubious concept *progress*? If they do, or if they don't, it's not by premeditation and intention. I sit by the fire, a blank mind over a blank page, and do my best, hoping the result will be a poem and will be a poem that might interest other people. This means that if I have changed a little, why then, the poems will have changed a little, too.

Of course one gets notions that modify these results – like, in my case, wanting to write a poem or two longer than my usual ones; and it seems I've done this: not that I think there is any intrinsic value in mere length. Whether one wants any very marked change in one's work (length, form, subject matter and all the interesting rest of it) depends on whether one is the sort of man who believes that the devil you know is better than the one you don't know or the sort who believes that a change o' deils is lichtsome. Lichtsome. I don't agree at all with those who think that in these terrible times one must write only 'terrible' poems, that it is a sort of treason to the million suffering people in the world to write about the pleasures and graces that happen to one's own self. I should suppose, in fact, that while it is a very solipsistic creature indeed who can shut his mind to that suffering, it is all the more important in this sad world to notice, record and praise the good things that are still there. And my own self is the only one I've got. It's a lucky self to which many pleasant things happen, and, if I do write gloomy poems, I write also in praise of these things. If I ignored them I wouldn't go off my head, but I wouldn't lie telling my truth either.

The White Bird 1973

MEDBH MCGUCKIAN

I had been afraid my breaks and changes could never look like bridges, they have made me as coherent as I would like to be, and it is no small sense of privilege to have Seamus Heaney's encouragement on the back cover of the book. He was speaking at the new Waterfront Hall in Belfast, briefly, on the way art is stretched to bind us now where religious rituals seem to fail. It was the aftermath of funerals for once more devastating than even we are used to here. (I am reading Paul Muldoon's exquisitely pessimistic 'Aftermath' in the *Sunday Times.*) For millions, it was 'A yesterday I find / almost impossible to lift.' Princess Diana's half-lived dates, so catastrophically complete inside and beyond my book's dates, somehow connected to all the gathered violent deaths from the Hunger Strikes to the Ceasefires, which pitch themselves at people who love through love. At Casement Station in Tralee I had a lament for her in one pocket, a commemoration of Michael Collins's seventy-fifth anniversary in the other. Both belonging to both and neither world. How can I possibly as a poet be as stirred by the long-ago assassination of the Corkman responsible for both whatever freedom Ireland achieved in this century and its unsuccessful partitioned state, as by the careless hounding down of a once-future queen? Because of my own sense of tragic non-identity, I identify positively with them both, and many people where I live feel the same dilemma, the anguish of being neither one thing nor the other, the highs and lows of dual citizenship.

One does not express such a complicated search for and escape from selfhood easily. My methods have often been described as obfuscating, but reading Eavan Boland's 'Object Lessons' I thought of Mallarmé in 1885 describing the new school of Symbolism:

> The contemplation of objects, the image that rises out of the reverie the objects provoke – those are the song. But the Parnassians take the thing in its entirety and point at it: thereby they lack mystery. They deprive the reader of the delightful illusion that he is a creator. To name an object is to destroy three-quarters of our pleasure in a poem – the joy of guessing, step by step. The ideal is to suggest the object. We derive the most from the mystery that constitutes the symbol when we evoke the object step by step in order to portray a state of mind. Or, the other way round, when we choose an object and derive a state of mind from it by a sequence of decipherings.

I would simply disagree with Mallarmé's condescension towards what he calls 'the reader' – often I have the certainty that it is the students who really create, I being more a mere reader of non-poetry than they, and lost without them.

The latest book I'm reading is by Vivienne de Watteville, Maria Edgeworth's great-niece, who went big-game hunting in 1928 to understand silence – 'Peace can only be won in exchange for the total surrender of personality' – no more likely than going to church not to have to think our own thoughts.

Selected Poems 1997

Jamie McKendrick

Way back, in a flunked local radio interview, I was asked whether I ever wrote about Oxford (where I've been living for some years). It wasn't so much the ruffled tone of the question that made my mind go blank as the whole idea of what poems are about. Many poets must experience a similar embarrassment when asked, politely or sceptically, what their work is about – that of not knowing the simple answer they of all people should know. My first impulse is to reach for some momentous theme like the behaviour of pigeons. It's not that poems *aren't* about things – this, that or whatever – and I don't for a moment, or much longer than a moment, mean to belittle the importance of subject matter. But saying, for example, this poem is about a compost heap, hardly helps anyone. Saying instead that the poem is a subtle quarrel between the pentameter and the hendecasyllable only shifts the burden from one shoulder to the other (probably the stronger to the weaker). It's the *way* that a poem is about what it's about that matters, but on this topic it's probably underhand for an author to intervene.

As for poems about Oxford, precious few. One set in the Botanical Garden there finds its way soon enough to nineteenth-century Seville. Though with this book I had hoped to move a bit closer to where I live at present and, for that matter, a bit closer to the present moment. It began promisingly. The first poem, 'Ancient History', is set in an ancient Rome roughly half lifted from Livy, half forged by myself. 'Paestum' follows soon after, further south, further back in time, with its Greek temples on Latin soil. Other times and places permeate these poems but then they also permeate our lives. 'Span', for example, which begins and ends with the dismal squalor of the room I was renting (no fault but my own), by way of a chance encounter with the dictionary on the floor, traces the root of the word 'crimson' back to the Arabic *qirmizi.* Omitted are the vowel shifts on the consonantal shelf – *cremisi* (It), *cramoisi* (Fr) or the Scots *crammasy*, as in MacDiarmid's great short poem which begins 'Mars is braw in crammasy'. Qirmizi is an Arab word for a small insect that breeds on the kermes oak, and from which the dye is made: an insect which in its own way has stained a host of different tongues. It's one small insect among many others in the book, including the monumentally lightweight 'Marble Fly' of the title.

The Marble Fly **1997**

Louis MacNeice

The poems in *Solstices* were mainly written in 1959 and 1960; in particular, in the spring and early summer of 1960. I underwent one of those rare bursts of creativity when the poet is first astonished and then rather alarmed by the way the mill goes on grinding. Now that I look at the whole collection in cold blood I find that, while it has much in common with my last volume, *Imaginings* (1957), fewer of these later poems strike me as forced (in revising I eliminated one or two compulsive bits of trickery) and more of them seem to be 'given'. And the chronic problem of order did not seem so difficult as usual. These forty-odd poems include personal lyrics (felt and caught in a flow), personal reminiscences of the war years, a little direct or indirect satire, a few 'travel poems', several sequences and a large number of overt or covert parables; yet, while some deliberately lilt and some deliberately drag, I find that they seem mostly to be scored for the same set of instruments.

Poets are always being required – by the critics and by themselves – to 'develop'. Most critics, however, to perceive such development, need something deeper than a well and wider than a church-door. In certain poets of our time the changes are conspicuous enough; in others, such as Robert Graves, a careless reader might complain that the menu is never altered. To assess one's own development is difficult. I would say of myself that I have become progressively more humble in the face of my material and therefore less ready to slap poster paint all over it. I have also perhaps, though I venture this tentatively, found it easier than I did to write poems of acceptance (even of joy) though this does not – perish the thought – preclude the throwing of mud or of knives when these seem called for. Several poems in *Solstices*, e.g. 'Country Weekend', were deliberate exercises in simplicity or at least in a penny-plain technique where fancy rhythms and rhymes would not obtrude too much.

Then of course there is the question of 'commitment'. Some people complained that my long rambling *Autumn Sequel* (1954) was much less committed than its long rambling predecessor *Autumn Journal* (1939); their reasoning seemed to be that the proportion of myth to topicality was much higher in the later work. I do not follow this reasoning. In *Solstices* there is a sequence of four poems suggested by the literature of the Dark Ages; these seem to me just as 'topical' as the poem called 'Jungle Clearance Ceylon' or two that are about the last war. Similarly, when my central image is a wind-screen wiper, I feel myself just as mythopoeic as if I were writing about the Grael (though I notice, to my own surprise, that *Solstices* contains practically no allusions to either Graeco-Roman or Christian legend). My own position has been aptly expressed by the dying Mrs Gradgrind in Dickens's *Hard Times*: 'I think there's a pain somewhere in the room but I couldn't positively say that I have got it.' So, whether these recent poems should be labelled 'personal' or 'impersonal', I feel that somewhere in the room there is a pain – and also, I trust, an alleviation.

Solstices 1961

When I assembled the poems in *The Burning Perch* (I am not happy about the title but could not think of anything better), I was taken aback by the high proportion of sombre pieces, ranging from bleak observations to thumbnail nightmares. The proportion is far higher than in my last book, *Solstices*, but I am not sure why this should be so. Fear and resentment seem here to be serving me in the same way as Yeats in his old age claimed to be served by 'lust and rage', and yet I had been equally fearful and resentful of the world we live in when I was writing *Solstices.* All I can say is that I did not set out to write this kind of poem: they happened. I am reminded of Mr Eliot's remark that the poet is concerned not only with beauty but with 'the boredom and the horror and the glory'. In some of the poems in *The Burning Perch* the boredom and the horror were impinging very strongly, e.g. the former in 'Another Cold May' or 'October in Bloomsbury' and the latter in 'Flower Show', 'After the Crash', 'Charon' or 'Budgie'. I find, however, that in most of these poems the grim elements are mixed with others, just as there are hardly any examples of pure satire in this collection; 'This is the Life', I suppose, comes nearest to it but still seems to me no more purely satirical than, for example, a medieval gargoyle. When I say that these poems 'happened', I mean among other things that they found their own form. By this I do not, of course, mean that the form was uncontrolled: some poems chose fairly rigid patterns and some poems loose ones but, once a poem had chosen its form, I naturally worked to mould it to it. Thus, while I shall always be fond of rhyme and am sorry for those simple-minded people who proclaim that it is now outmoded (after all, it remains unbeatable for purposes of epigram), a good third of the poems in this book are completely without it. Similarly with rhythm: I notice that many of the poems here have been trying to get out of the 'iambic' groove which we were all born into. In 'Memoranda to Horace' there is a conscious attempt to suggest Horatian rhythms (in English, of course, one cannot do more than suggest them), combined with the merest reminiscence of Horatian syntax. This technical Horatian-ising appears in some other poems too, where, I suppose, it goes with something of a Horatian resignation. But my resignation, as I was not brought up a pagan, is more of a fraud than Horace's: 'Memoranda to Horace' itself, I hope, shows this. So here again, as in poems I was writing thirty years ago (I myself can see both the continuity and the difference), there are dialectic, oxymoron, irony. I would venture the generalisation that most of these poems are two-way affairs or at least spiral ones: even in the most evil picture the good things, like the sea in one of these poems, are still there round the corner.*

The Burning Perch 1963

* This was written shortly before MacNeice died, on 3 September 1963. He sent it with a letter dated 26 August, apologising for the delay and saying, 'My doctor won't let me go to London yet, so everything is awkward.'

Barry MacSweeney

The Book of Demons (which includes the sequence of poems 'Pearl') is a book of experience and innocence. 'Pearl' was written first, inspired by the first loves of my life, natural and human and both wild. The physical setting of this entire lyrical sequence is the high lead-mining country of a remote part of the Northumbrian border country near Cumberland and Durham. It is on the East Allen River by Allenheads, Alston and Nenthead. It is spellbindingly beautiful. Pearl was a mute girl who lived at the top of the lonnen (or loaning) who was also spellbindingly beautiful and the first girl I saw naked, swimming in the East Allen. She could not speak and was treated locally like an idiot. We lived fifty yards apart. Being the same age, we got on. I spoke, she didn't. I took – one day in the rain – a slate from the byre where we used to make sure the heifers were in from the marigold beds. And I taught her to read and write, high on the law. She was fierce and majestic like the landscape – the skies are like Wyoming – and her eyes blazed with frustration at lack of speech and positional attitudes of others more ignorant. It is a celebration of her. Totally.

The Book of Demons is a hard experience. From the years of harmlessness with Pearl, I am now an alcoholic – recovered. And recovering. I spent the last three years in various hospitals and in a clinic (for two months), once on a life-support machine at the edge of death and with great help from family and friends. I have sat at the bedside of those who did not recover and are now dead, including royalty and others. *The Book of Demons* is a record of my addiction and sickness – it is sometimes harsh and brutal, but I have tried my lyrical best to make all of the sorry experiences sing out loud. And also the love that grew from recovery and from those who gathered around to help.

The Book of Demons 1997

Sarah Maguire

It was only when I was going through the last, agonising stages of assembling the manuscript of *Spilt Milk* that I began to realise how it was beginning to form a whole, an argument of sorts: the different poems extending into each other through the repetition of images and motifs. 'Trope' is the correct term, I suppose, from the Greek word meaning 'turn' – that is, to turn language, to make a figure of speech (I like the sense of movement in the term trope: metaphor seems more frozen, metaphorically, that is). Now, this is inevitable: all writers have their own unconscious triggers and obsessions to work out, things which affect us and move us into writing; so, to a large extent (the unconscious part), I'm not in full control of these tropes: they turn me.

So what crops up? The first obvious theme is indicated by the title of the book: spilt milk. What does that suggest? Initially the cliché 'there's no use crying over . . .' Yet in so naming the book I'm explicitly suggesting that there's a lot of use crying over mistakes and losses. There's a good deal of spilling and slipping in the poems, intimating that boundaries are being overcome, that nothing is quite as stable as we might like to think. So the idea of transgression is crucial.

Next 'Milk'. There's no getting over the fact that this is a very oral book: milk, fruit, sperm, aubergines, whisky, shark – I'd like you to feel well fed by the end of it. Why so much food? Is there anything more simply pleasurable (well, maybe – but that's never simple) and more culturally significant than eating? Nothing seems more innocently personal and intimate; nothing carries such a freight of culture, class and caste. Again, it's the issue of boundaries: food is something we take into ourselves which changes us very effectively (and affectively).

Now milk of course is perhaps the most emotive food of all, which leads us on to femininity, the theme I think is most important to my work. In a number of poems I've tried to ask, what does it mean to be 'feminine', to be a woman? How then to make sense of the connections between what is most subjective and wider, more 'political' issues. You'll notice lots of gardens, as well. This stems partly from my training as a gardener when I left school, and partly from my fascination with the concept of gardens: the way they act as boundaries between notions of the civil and the wild, being a highly constructed space which signifies spontaneous nature.

Above all, what I've tried to do in these poems is to push out of the lyric tradition, with its connotations of hermetic intimacy, into the broader contexts of the historical and the social, without employing the exhortations of polemic, without losing sensuality or richness of language. A small attempt at transgressing yet another boundary.

Spilt Milk 1991

Derek Mahon

I am not sure that I can write very meaningfully about my own work. The poems in *Night Crossing* are already at a distance from me (the latest is a year old), and have begun to seem like the work, not of myself but of an old friend, perhaps, who emigrated and from whom I receive only the occasional postcard at longer and longer intervals. My preoccupations have changed and go on changing, and my sense of desirable form changes with them. Poetry, for me (as for most poets, I suppose), is basically a struggle with the exigencies of form, and may, if one is very lucky, reveal certain declivities of the language that have not been revealed in quite the same posture before. It is in these declivities, I am convinced, that the unparaphrasable displacements of human thought and feeling lie – things that language cannot, in the normal course of things, encompass. Wittgenstein saw 'poetry' as the enemy of language, but I prefer Wallace Stevens –

The whole race is a poet that writes down
The eccentric propositions of its fate.

I wonder what eccentric propositions my own poems embody. A Dublin editor, writing recently about the young Irish poets, remarked that much of my own work was concerned with the 'dispossessed'. I had never really thought about it in these terms, but I see what he meant. Owing, perhaps, to the peculiar circumstances of life in Northern Ireland, where I was born, brought up, and now live, I have always felt something that might be described as 'dispossession' – a cultural dislocation, a nostalgic (and slightly guilty) independence of community, and a resulting self-consciousness. This experience is both tragic and potentially comic.

Night Crossing 1968

I must have been sixteen or so when, in whatever anthology of French verse we were studying at my Belfast grammar school, I came upon Vigny's line, '*Dieu, que le son du cor est triste au fond des bois!*' and it has remained with me ever since, like the refrain of Yeats's 'The Stolen Child', its echo reverberating down the years. The closest visual analogue I've met with is the Uccello in the Ashmolean from which this collection takes its title: tense figures, stylised yet realistic, in pursuit of what unseen prey? There's a sententious platitude here somewhere, which would explain the self-guying (surely) formalism of the title poem itself. The poem is hardly more than decorative, but it serves to introduce a theme picked up later in what I sincerely hope is a more considerable piece of work, 'The Globe in North Carolina'. I won't try to describe the sequence of events for which the title also serves as a euphemism; had I done so in verse, I might have produced a more interesting volume. More probably I'd have been criticised for spending too much time among life studies and dream songs. In any case, there's a helplessness involved: one does what presents itself to be done.

'Courtyards in Delft' and 'Girls on the Bridge' are about pictures too, but also about 'real life'. 'A Lighthouse in Maine', 'A Postcard from Berlin' and 'The Terminal Bar' fall into the same category, each having been set off by a picture postcard – a reproduction of Hopper's *Highland Light*, a Berlin street scene, a rocky-horror glimpse of New York night life. The same is true of 'A Garage in Co. Cork'. I didn't see the garage and start writing the poem. The trigger was a postcard photograph by one Fritz Curzon entitled *McGrotty's Garage, Eire* (*sic*). The photo shows an abandoned filling station with the remains of two ancient pumps in front of it, and over the door the legend: 'McGrotty's Garage'. Ho-ho. Irish joke. 'Grotty' isn't a word you would hear in Ireland. It's a London yob-word, and I suppose it was some patriotic reflex that got the poem going. I set it in Co. Cork because Cork is one of my favourite counties. The ruined garage is probable somewhere else altogether – Wicklow or Donegal. I can see I'm not being very helpful. I find it hard to comment on my own work in a general way.

A note on the dedication, though. A friend described to me how she had watched the late J. G. Farrell, author of *The Singapore Grip*, sit entranced before *The Night Hunt* in the Ashmolean shortly before moving to Ireland, there to be washed from a rock while fishing in Bantry Bay. We were friends, and I'm one of the many who remember him with an acute sense of loss.

Now, Lycidas, the shepherds weep no more.
Henceforth thou art the genius of the shore
In thy large recompense, and shalt be good
To all that wander in that perilous flood.

The Hunt by Night **1982**

Glyn Maxwell

These things begin and end on an empty playing field, though in between we do roam the eleven parts of the town. What town? This: the pioneering work of decent men, still green and floral at its centre after seventy years, yet sits among the derided, for its clumsy name and novelty, and slowly, with them all, capitulates to the self-interest and legerdemain of the disgracing powers.

Welwyn, it's neither a Garden nor a City, but England is playing itself out here, as much as in Whitehall or Wapping, around Stonehenge or Toxteth, to the tune of 'Fences, everybody needs good fences' and 'Rule Britannia', 'Chariots of Fire' and both versions of 'God Save the Queen'. Our MP feels the government has done too much for the homeless. McDonald's must open and the hospice must close. My beloved wood won't need another hurricane to bring it down. The lord who owns the parkland owns forty Ferraris. A lady brought round a petition against the war memorial. Churchgoers call for hanging. Nobody goes to town at night, where when I was a child our famous fountain would change colour, red, white, green. The bridge under the A1/M reads 'Rudolf Hess' and 'St Albans killed Welwyn'. We will send Hoodhead to St Albans, but you cannot satirise this age.

The mayor's son, though, is at least liked, I have it on good authority; and gloved hands are held, virginities kept and lost, fair games still played and some children mind their language. Well, I mind mine, standing at the top of the stairs waiting to ask the impossible questions worth asking, and keep asking. Welcome to this book of first poems.

The best poem is birdsong, Hopkins's halcyon: 'Crying *What I do is me; for that I came.*' So she can't say much about influences, techniques, she doesn't know what's going on – one doesn't love words, one is inhabited by them. One starts here. Does one love life? Or home? Most things I try to say go quite happy unsaid. Between the black option and the English words 'I love', though, come the incorrigible imperfect games – Rhyme, Don't Rhyme, Laugh or Differ, Explain or Shrug – with inevitable heroes, of encompassing, independence, tolerance, respect.

Like most of this fancied and unwary generation, I'd just as soon have been a rock singer or sports star, and, though it's grown too late for either, as I embark on my all and am now braced for filing-under if not filing-away, I can say that this little stream ran nearer to the man who sang 'My love she speaks like silence' and 'Money doesn't talk it swears' and 'You're gonna make me lonesome when you go' than to any book, that echoes that appear may be happy to appear, and that, if a reader opts to tax me with derivativeness, and has a certain wrinkled old New York exile in mind, I would trust my smoother features to assume the same expression as John Barnes's might, were he to be accused of playing too like Pelé. As I say, these things begin and end on an empty playing field, and the truly imaginative child doesn't care if no one is watching for it is, however you look at it, his turn.

Tale of the Mayor's Son 1990

W. S. Merwin

I have been asked to say something about myself, about my writing, and about poetry; and in the circumstances I hope it won't seem ungracious if what I say seems a little like blood wrung from a stone. I don't think I talk about any of those subjects easily, and I know I talk about the latter two very unwillingly.

That is to say, I don't usually like literary conversations, though I deeply enjoy talking with writers other than poets about the practical side of getting things written. I like talking with some people about particular poems; though I think that in such conversations all I usually do is to try to describe a quality that excites my enthusiasm in a poem. I do not like writing about poetry. This is both an intellectual distaste and something which amounts to a physical aversion. Above all, I do not like trying to generalize about poetry, on the one hand, or to say something about my own poems, on the other.

It even occurs to me (conveniently enough) that if I were to describe some of the reasons for this dislike, they might be as pertinent as anything I could say about poetry, or my own efforts. At least I shall try to do that first, by way of a disclaimer, if nothing else. Part of my dislike, though a very unimportant part, is a reaction against the vast influence of criticism in modern poetry. I think that one of the dangers of modern poetry has been a tendency to become inbred. Its small audience enhances the danger. It even seems possible for some poets to write as though critics, even particular schools of critics, were a fit and sufficient audience for poetry. I used to read all the articles in which critics kept working out reasons to prove how necessary and useful they are; but I don't read those articles, or indeed critics, any more, and I can't remember what the reasons were, even if I try very hard.

The other, main roots of my dislike, I suppose, are a distrust of generalization and abstraction; and a superstitious unwillingness to dissect the goose whose eggs, whatever their metal, are vitally important to me.

Which leads me around to one of the few general statements I feel safe in making about poetry. It is a mystery. It is a metaphor of the other mysteries which comprise human experience. But, like some other mysteries, it gives us a feeling of illumination – one mystery giving us a name by which to know another. I confess I think of poetry in a religious way. But I don't mean by that I regard it with any hushed and special reverence. I mean simply that I think of it as a way of using what we know, to glimpse what we do not know.

I remember, quite young, reading for the first time:

Thus have I had thee as a dream might flatter,
In sleep a king, but waking no such matter

and becoming aware that there was a power in the words which the words themselves could not seem to account for, and which I felt strongly but could not understand. I realized that this power must be the poetry of the lines. And I was awed to think that men must have been aware of this power for a very long time. They must, in fact, have recognized it and been able to invoke it sometimes, without ever completely understanding it, since they first began to have names for their own experience of Creation.

Having said that, I want to say at once that I think poetry should be intended to give pleasure, in the most ordinary and old-fashioned sense. I don't suppose that pleasure is the end of poetry, but I do believe that it is an indispensable means to that end. No amount of 'understanding' of a poem is of any use, I am sure, if the reader does not in the end enjoy the poem more than before. I do not believe that obscurity is a virtue, though I would be the last to claim that it can always be avoided.

I am far from sure that what I have been saying is of much import, or is even very coherent. I am even less sure that I can say much about my own work. Anything I could say about the poems – except for actual descriptions of writing them, which would be irrelevant even if I could remember entirely and describe exactly – would be things I have discovered about them since I wrote them.

As for what I want to do, I don't think I'm very different from most other poets. I hope to have a chance to make my work contain a wider range and depth of experience, and contain it more fully, and exactly, and perfectly. I feel lucky when I have an illusion that I know where I'm going, though with part of my mind I'm quite aware that it's an illusion. I very much want to write plays. I seem to be learning to do it very slowly, if indeed I am learning at all. I certainly do not think that poetry is confined to verse, especially in the modern theatre. But I don't think I can say much more than that. When I was being given my discharge from what was then the U.S. Navy Air Corps an officer asked me what I wanted to do. 'Write poetry,' I said. I realised that he'd meant what was I going to do with my life and so forth, and I realised that I had answered most of what he was asking, but that it didn't seem like that to him. Probably just to parry so strange an answer, and show that it hadn't thrown him, he asked, 'What kind?' And he won. I was stumped. I didn't know how to answer that one then, and after several years at it I still don't know the answer. Only now I realize that I'm glad I don't.

Green with Beasts **1956**

Christopher Middleton

The best I can offer, by way of self-questioning rather than statement, is the following group of texts to be thought about:

Harold Rosenberg: The poet feels a tremendous need to turn off the belt-line of rhetoric that keeps automatically pounding away in his brain twenty-four hours a day. Before any poetic event can happen the cultural clatter must be stopped.

Arthur Schopenhauer: Art consists in the fact that with the smallest possible expenditure of outward life, the inward is brought into the strongest relief, for the inward is properly the object of interest.

Franz Kafka: There exist in the same human being varying perceptions of one and the same object which differ so completely from each other that one can only deduce the existence of different subjects in the same human being.

The Polish Count in Norman Douglas's *Fountains in the Sand*: What in the name of heaven do I care for art and politics, with the knife at my throat? I only utilise these things; yes, I utilise them for conversational purposes, in order to deceive others as to my true, incessant and miserable preoccupations. Laughable, is it not? Why don't you smile, Monsieur – you, who have never known the bitterness?

Alfred North Whitehead: Life can only be understood as an aim at that perfection which the conditions of its environment allow. But the aim is always beyond the attained fact . . . In nature, the soil rests while the root of the plant pursues the sources of its refreshment. In the Western Empire there was no pursuit. Its remnants of irritability were devoid of transcendent aim.

Dairine O'Kelly: I sing to myself in bed, I play jigs on my pennywhistle too, but whoever can they be, the people who read poetry?

Nonsequences 1965

John Montague

A book of poems is, for me, a temporary exhaustion of an obsession. So *Tides* ends where it began, with the sound of water, rising/falling. In 1966 W. S. Hayter asked me to provide poems to go with a series of his engravings on the sea. I protested: the only water I knew was inland (already a discovery). But soon I cast off, and found myself in deep water, dealing with subjects I might previously have protected myself against through irony, implication. (I don't mean that I scorn these weapons but I only reach for them when the monster can't be caught by more direct means. Crossing the Irish Sea, I was re-reading the third chapter of *Moby Dick* when in walked my cabin mate. He was as highly coloured as the harpooner Queequeg.)

So the real subject of the 'Sea Changes' sequence, and of the rest of the book, is the interior, the human sea, with its rhythms of life and death. In the first section they are inextricable: an emergency operation, lovers quarrelling bitterly, the attempted rape of an old woman. Another meaningful coincidence: I was translating from the old Irish and for the first time found myself able to face up to that concentrated masterpiece, 'The Hag of Beare', in which the old woman compares her life to the ebbing sea.

In the second section we meet the Muse as death, death naked. I would prefer not to discuss these poems casually, except to say that I am glad I was able to write them, for the experience behind them had been festering a long time. They may seem morbid, but I think they are true, and, having mirrored the Medusa, the artist may return. Some of the best modern poetry inhabits this area, but there is also the great opposite, life-giving rhythm.

So the third section is ruled by a different kind of nakedness: the Muse as energy, love, the full moon. Here, and elsewhere, I was delighted to find the shape of the poem growing more open: much Irish poetry, at least, is conventionalised by the iambic line, and lacks the energy of the spoken, as opposed to the 'written' word.

The moon, mistress of the tides, appears in another phase, in the second-last section of the book, which deals with death as process, a wearing down, a waning. As in 'Omagh Hospital' if we have drifted far enough out, we are ready to submerge again . . .

Tides 1970

Dom Moraes

People constantly ask me whether I, an Indian, don't feel rather peculiar writing English verse. It isn't only English people, but Indians as well, who ask me this. My answers therefore tend to vary: but when I think about it honestly, I must admit that I don't feel in a peculiar situation at all. An accident of birth landed me in the bosom of an Indian family which spoke no Indian language. So my native tongue is English; and Indian languages are like French or German to me. This is probably rather sad, in so far as I am entirely rootless, linked by an accident of language to one country and by an accident of birth to another. But perhaps one's home, under such circumstances, is wherever one lives. I have chosen to live in England.

I have been lucky, I think, not to feel confused by this situation, but I owe a great deal of this luck to my friends, and to the fact that most of them do more or less the same work as I do; so that perhaps I belong to a race after all. I owe most to David Archer, the most eccentric genius in the history of publishing, who under the imprint of the Parton Press put out the first books of George Barker, Dylan Thomas, David Gascoyne, and W. S. Graham in the thirties, and in 1956 flattered me by publishing my first book of verse.

I have been asked to say how I write. Reading over my poems and trying to feel like somebody else about them, it seems to me that they mostly try to express a personal situation or a personal perplexity (sometimes staged in a mythological landscape) as directly and with as much simplicity of language as possible. Of past poetry I prefer Clare, Wordsworth and Blake to the Romantics: Vaughan and Herbert to Donne. The recent poets I most admire are all people who do totally different things from me: of those who have written since the war, Patrick Kavanagh, David Wright, Peter Levi and Brian Higgins. Nobody is qualified to criticise his own verse: I shan't attempt to do so with my own.

As to my methods of writing, I take notes always, except in pubs late at night, and make poems in sporadic bursts throughout the year. While writing I chainsmoke and stand a bottle of whisky in front of me, not to be consumed but so that it can admire me at my labours. As to why I write, I think that is a ridiculous question to ask any poet. If two poets come across each other in the street, they may (if they are on speaking terms, that is) discuss a variety of topics: their wives, their publishers, their Derby losses, or the prospect of landing a man on the moon. There is only one thing which neither is likely to ask the other, and that is why he writes verses. This is not because each knows the other knows; it is precisely because if a poet knew why he wrote poetry he would cease to write it. All that a poet needs to know about his work is that it requires labour and paper, and a great deal of luck.

Poems 1960

Blake Morrison

A group of Jesuits travelling among Algonquin Indians in 1653 were told of a land so cold in winter that everything spoken freezes to ice – each spring the frozen words melt and all that has been said during the winter can be heard as if in a single moment. The story could be interpreted in various ways: as a myth of an enchanted kingdom or even as a metaphor for what poetry should do – retain and transmute living speech then release it in one passionate outburst. Chiefly, though, it is an image of secrecy and confession – of holding back, then letting go.

Dark Glasses is much concerned with secrets, and with people who do or don't keep them. The language of secrecy is often pejorative – we talk of dirty secrets and coming clean – and many of us dream of a more open society than that in which we live. But is candour always a good thing? Do we need reserves of privacy? And if so how far can anyone be understood?

Questions like these lie behind the title poem, whose four stanzas seemed to me straightforward when I wrote them, though readers have called their argument difficult: 1) some people are highly secretive, 2) others appear to be frank but in practice give little away, 3) discovering the truth about someone or something is therefore very difficult, 4) there are, nonetheless, brief and enriching moments of illumination.

If trust and secrecy are a shaping obsession in *Dark Glasses*, a more obvious shape comes from the division of the book into two halves. Part One contains a selection of poems written over a longish period (I reckon to write only four or five poems a year). Several speakers – see 'The Renunciation', 'Grange Boy' and 'Long Days', for example – are young men from a decaying, guilt-ridden bourgeoisie, unwilling or unable to uphold its values. They have the sort of death-wish also explored in 'Flood'.

But not all the poems, I hope, are bleak and pessimistic. There are domestic celebrations, general comedies, a piece of manic science fiction. Even 'The Renunciation' ends on an up-curve, with images of children and renewal.

'The Inquisitor', which takes up Part Two of the book, arose from a dissatisfaction with the clench and clinch of short poems. I wanted a form (nine-line stanzas, as it turned out) loose enough to accommodate diverse material – adventures, journalistic sources, parody, allusions to other poets, jokes, scraps of autobiography. The story concerns a man who enters the Intelligence Service as if by accident (a traditionally youthful sort of accident), drifts along, is assigned a particular though undefined case, falls in love, struggles, fails, is betrayed and waits his end. The atmosphere probably owes something to Le Carré – but then again references to spying have appeared in English poetry ever since Ben Jonson ('Spies you are lights in state but of base stuff'). To me the thriller at its best is close in spirit to poetry, which, however it expresses itself (and my own preference is for the sighing undertone not the yawping declamation), must always be a contemplation or unravelling of mystery.

Dark Glasses 1984

Andrew Motion

Whenever I read my poems in public, I'm struck by how little I have to say about them, except at the level of narrative and structure. Why? I can think of three possible reasons. My wish to write a poem is inseparable from my wish to explain something to myself, and once the thing is finished, any further comment seems superfluous. I believe poems should be self-sufficient – accessible to readers, of course, but not dependent on the after-care of their author. I think my poems (like many other people's, I dare say) are only partly the product of conscious workings; they also rely deeply on primal, swampy, dimly perceived things.

Anyway, here are some things I can say – even though they make my work sound more 'literary' than I hope and believe is the case. Most of *Salt Water* was written while I was researching my biography of John Keats, which will be published later this year, and my thoughts about Keats undoubtedly influenced me in several ways. I can see, for instance, that Keats's ideas about suffering and about the ways in which poets might function as healing truth-tellers, helped to shape some of the elegies I have included. I can also see that thinking about his context led me to reflect on certain historical figures – Napoleon and Goethe among them.

In the second part of the book, Keats's own life becomes part of my subject. It contains a prose journal and several poems written in the spring of 1995 while I retraced his final journey by sea from London to Italy. (He had been told by his doctors that the climate in Rome might help him recover from tuberculosis.) It was an extraordinary time for me – full of experiences that I had never had before, and never expect to repeat – and it told me a good deal about myself, as well as about 'my subject'.

My previous book, *The Price of Everything*, contained two long experimental poems in which prose and poetry were pulled close together. In *Salt Water* the separations are clear and the forms more familiar – but the underlying wish is similar. I have wanted to write in a way which combines lyric with narrative, the personal with the political, and which understands that 'axioms in philosophy are not axioms until they are proved upon our pulses'. I hope readers will enjoy it.

Salt Water 1997

Edwin Muir

Poems are written in enjoyment, or rather in a mixture of enjoyment and hard work. The reader should be exempted from the hard work. Some of these poems are 'personal', and came from some private feeling or actual happening. Others are shots at certain things which periodically trouble me, such as our origin and end, and the pattern of human life: perhaps I should call them return-shots, for the question must come from somewhere before one can make the response. From all I can learn, it is a common experience among poets to have some line occur to them spontaneously, almost capriciously, and this line, being a question, somehow or other then builds a poem round itself. About half the poems in this collection began in that way; the rest started from a general conception or subject which could be dealt with in a more systematic fashion. I imagine there is not much difference between the poems which began in these two separate ways, for the working on a poem seems to be what gives it character.

I have been asked to say something about poetry, and at the moment can think of nothing to say except that there can be no certain definition of poetry, and that if there were it would be of no conceivable use to anyone. One might as well demand a definition of mankind before setting out to become acquainted with people. We learn about poetry in much the same way as we learn about human beings, that is by coming to know it and them. There is this difference that in poetry enjoyment is the chief means of learning, as well as the reward for what we have learned. Judgement comes later, and it will probably come too soon: judgement is always something that has to be 'revised'; it is the uncertain factor in poetic matters, as in others, and it is not the most important. If our judgement of poetry goes against our instinctive feelings, out of respect for an accepted judgement or for some theory, it will be false for us, though it may be true for others. We learn mostly from our own errors of feeling, but fortunately poetry has this compensation that it insensibly changes our feelings; in time they become wiser and begin to distinguish more justly between the false and the true, both in poetry and, I think, as a delayed result, in life as well.

One Foot in Eden 1956

Paul Muldoon

I remember my father telling me that when he was a young man, in the 1930s, he determined to throw it all up; he would leave Ireland and emigrate to Australia. He arranged with a friend that they should meet at a crossroads somewhere in the wilds of Tyrone, from where they would make their way to Belfast and the boat. My father arrived at the appointed time. At noon, let's say. His friend was nowhere to be seen. He waited an hour. Two hours. Nothing doing. So he made an about-turn and went back home. It's an image that troubled me for ages, since it underlines the arbitrary nature of so many of the decisions we take, the disturbingly random quality of so many of our actions. I would speculate on my father's having led an entirely different life, in which, clearly, I would have played no part. And suddenly my poems were peopled by renegades, some of them bent on their idea of the future, some on their idea of the past. All bent, though. All errantly going about their errands.

I seem to remember my father telling me that he determined once to emigrate to Australia. Now he tells me it was a hen's yarn. Either he or I must have made it up.

Why Brownlee Left 1980

The title poem was sparked off by what I'd always taken to be a word passed on by my parents, a shibboleth of the kind that occurs in the private language of any family.

In 'The More a Man Has the More a Man Wants' I hoped

to purge myself of the very public vocabulary it employs, the kennings of the hourly news bulletin. In so far as it's about anything, the poem is about the use, or abuse, of the English language in Ireland. Indeed, one form of the name of the central character is 'English', though it may also be useful to remind oneself that 'Gallogly' is itself a corruption of a Gaelic name meaning 'foreign young warrior' – a mercenary.

In the aisling or 'dream-vision' which forms the middle section of the poem, Gallogly muses on his own mercenary past. He has made an abortive trip to the United States to buy arms, in the course of which he imagines himself to have killed a girl. That, for him, is the root cause of his present plight, the reason for his being pursued by an avenging Indian. The Indian, by the way, would seem to have a lot of time for the poems of Robert Frost – particularly 'For Once, Then, Something'.

If you will allow me to change course as dramatically as Gallogly shifts shape, I should mention that I wondered a long time about the etymology of this word 'quoof'. Did it come from Gaelic? From Elizabethan English, like so many of my father's words? According to him, he first heard it from us, his children.

Quoof 1983

The poems in this book were written over a period of four or five years and represent an attempt to get back to basics, to strip down the engine, lay it out on the front lawn, and rebuild it. The word 'attempt' suggests something willed. I try to leave the will out of writing poems, preferring to let them have their way. But I did have one or two demi-semi-conscious aims. I wanted to avoid longer poems as far as possible, though one poem seems to have found its way in, a piece called 'The Bangle (Slight Return)', which has to do with a 'muldoon' or stolen credit card. I also wanted to try to cut back on the wackier element in my work though, again, one poem seems to have found its way in, a piece called 'The Bangle (Slight Return)', which has to do with a 'muldoon' or stolen credit card. I also wanted to avoid repeating myself in a poem though, yet again, one seems to have found its way in, a piece called 'The Bangle (Slight Return)', which has to do with a 'muldoon' or stolen credit card.

Hay 1999

The poem which falls at the halfway mark of this collection, and which is the keystone in its arch, is 'The Stoic', its title a play on the Greek word *stoa*, the 'porch' or 'portico' under which the mighty Zeno held forth and after which a school of philosophy was named. The term 'stoic' is used in an everyday sense of 'one who practises repression of emotion', and is here used ironically of a circumstance in which the emotional charge is extremely high, since the subject of the poem is the loss of an unborn child.

'The Stoic' is set partly on the banks of the Delaware and Raritan Canal, in the New Jersey suburbs in which I live, and New Jersey is the setting of roughly half the poems in the book. I write 'setting', as if it were merely a backdrop, whereas I'm now deeply engaged by the place in which I've now spent so many years.

Not so many, of course, as I spent in Ireland, where roughly the other half of the poems are set. Perhaps it's a function of getting older, but I seem to have gone back to writing more and more about my childhood. The Northern Ireland of the 1950s in which I grew up was no less 'troubled' than that of the 1960s, 70s, 80s and 90s; it was simply less obviously so. Even then, there were army patrols, B-Specials on the roads, IRA activity that included the attack by Sean South on Brookeborough. One of Sean South's colleagues was named Patrick Regan, the name of one of my uncles who figures in several earlier poems such as 'The Sight-Seers' and 'Cauliflowers', which is why so much is made of that name in 'Unapproved Road'.

The emphasis in this book is less on my own family, though, than my wife's. She is of Russian and German Jewish extraction, and various members of her family figure in the last, longer poem in the book. I hesitate from mentioning this but, yet again, I've used a verse template which is carried across from other poems, including 'Incantata', 'Yarrow' and 'The Bangle (Slight Return)', for the channelling of this cataclysm of images describing the impact of Hurricane Floyd on the Delaware and Raritan Canal. These long poems take a bit of getting used to, of course, and I hope that readers will come to terms with the jagged edges of 'At the Sign of the Black Horse, September 1999' without doing themselves mortal hurt.

Some of that jaggedness stems from the elegaic nature of the subject matter, some from the necessity of modern poetry to reflect our increasingly jagged age. The combination of intractable material with intricate formal methods was a particular strength of W. B. Yeats and I'll draw attention to two poets much influenced by Yeats.

These are the Philip Larkin of *Collected Poems* and the Louis MacNeice of *The Burning Perch*, a collection which is still as commensurate to the moment as it was when first published, almost exactly forty years ago.

Moy Sand and Gravel 2002

Les Murray

Bunyah, where I now live with my family, is a small place, at least as far as the number of humans who live there is concerned. It's not even a village, but a valley and what is known in Australia as a district, and it lies about fifteen miles inland on the north coast of New South Wales. About half the district is heavy wet sclerophyll forest, in which my father worked for many years as a timber-getter and bullock driver. My mother was a nursing sister from the city, and when I was growing up we were dairy farmers. When I went to university in Sydney, I ran full on into a prejudice I'd only vaguely heard of before: I was said to be a peasant, a provincial, a hick from the sticks. I came to see this as one of the great weaknesses of Western civilisation, this attitude that had originated in ancient Athens and been passed down to us by Rome. As a worldwide thing, it still does enormous damage. Not all the millions of the rural poor whom it forces into vast modern cities wanted to go there, or obediently despise the regions they came from. I am one of those who managed to get home again. All of my books are full of a determination to bring sympathy and some truthful regard to those I had to leave in order to get an education and later a living, but *The Daylight Moon* contains the poems I wrote when it began to seem I would actually get home, and those I wrote after we moved there. In a way, I'm grateful to have run into that ancient prejudice; it taught me to be wary of received attitudes. From there, it was only a short step to opposing any and every Received Literary Sensibility. No one of those is ever commensurate with the whole truth. By no means all of the poems in the book are located in Bunyah, of course, but to the extent that place is important among its concerns, my home district is its centring focus.

The poems in the book were written between 1983 and 1987. During part of that time, I was doing my reading for *The New Oxford Book of Australian Verse*, which came out in 1986. This introduced me to the variety and vitality of poetry which used to get published in newspapers in the Australian colonies throughout the nineteenth century. This poetry, not all of it by any means good, got around the strictures of late Romantic high art verse by being regarded as 'light' verse, and so was able to catch the real speech and spirit, and the affection, of people all over the continent. I had long been trying to invent just such a style for myself, using the now very tired and always prolix Australian bush ballad as one source, but what I discovered while reading for the *Oxbook* (or *Ozbook*, as a friend at Oxford calls it) made me more daring and experimental, and helped me to put the storytelling culture I'd grown up in to literary use, in ways which I hope suit it. We hadn't had a Whitman at the genesis of our tradition, or not a literal one: we'd had a sort of collective one, and I could go on from that, while still using all I'd learned of poetry from other traditions and registers, including my beloved Celtic forebears, with their alternating masculine-feminine rhymes. I hope British readers won't find my many Australian references impenetrable. That would be ill-mannered of me, even if, from a global point of view, every place is now the centre of the world.

The Daylight Moon 1988

Norman Nicholson

After the publication in 1954 of my third book of verse, *The Pot Geranium*, I dried up as a poet. Until then my chief preoccupation had been with the Cumberland landscape seen as rock, with the little mining towns that came out of that rock, and with the dependence of even an urban and industrial society on the natural cycle of the seasons and the slower geological cycle of the rocks.

Then, one day, I began to think of my father and his family – of my grandmother, a gamekeeper's daughter from Westmorland, who came to Millom in 1867, of her fourteen sons, of their many occupations and the part they played in the life of the town. And, almost without premeditation, I found myself writing 'The Seventeenth of the Name'. I began to turn over my memories of the last fifty years – of the old mines, the boreholes, the little locomotives, the Dole Days of the twenties, the schoolboy friends of that time – letting my memories grow up into the present, just as the schoolboys have grown up in the houses and streets around me. I am still as concerned as ever with the problem of man and his environment, but, in these poems, I write less about man than about men – about my father, my uncles, friends and acquaintances from five generations in a small, self-contained and rather isolated community where you can hardly toss a penny into a crowd without hitting someone you are related to.

A Local Habitation **1974**

Up to the time when I published my last book of poems, *A Local Habitation*, the town of Millom and its immediate neighbourhood had provided nearly all the material I felt I needed for my poetry. It was a small, compact, in-grown community, where personal, family and class relationships were all clearly visible. It was also a mining and blast-furnace town, drawing its livelihood and purpose from the rock and surrounded by the bare, empty landscape of West Cumberland. Millom, for me, was human society in miniature, man in dependence on and struggling with his physical environment.

But round about the time when the poems in *A Local Habitation* were written, the mines were abandoned, the blast-furnaces closed down, and Millom ceased to be an industrial town in the old nineteenth-century sense of the word. Since then, though I can still walk through familiar streets and meet people I have known for sixty years, my poetry has become concerned less with the stability of a community rooted in a particular locality than with the many and varied processes of change – both the very quick and often unpredictable changes in the world of man and the immensely slow and inevitable changes in the world of nature.

It was for this reason, I fancy, that, in the middle seventies, I began once again to write what might be called 'nature poems' – poems such as 'Beck', 'Wall' and 'Shingle', which try to evoke some seemingly permanent aspect of landscape but without reference to any specific place. You can fill in the picture with your own beck or wall or seashore. 'Glacier' comes from a rather different impulse. Together with two or three other poems, it arises directly from a long visit to Norway. In Norway, I felt very much at home. It was partly because the landscape seemed very like a larger and starker version of the Cumbrian fells and dales; but it was more because I felt I was returning to the Scandinavian ancestry of the Cumbrian people. My own middle name, for instance, is clearly Norse in origin. In fact, wherever a poem of mine may start, whether in Norway or in the Western Highlands of Scotland, it tends to work round to Millom in the end. 'Home is where one starts from,' said Eliot. It seems to be where I finish.

Sea to the West 1981

Sean O'Brien

Like many poets and other unfortunates, I spend a good deal of time on trains. Recently this has meant a year of journeys between Brighton and Dundee, followed by a less arduous series between Dundee and Newcastle upon Tyne, not to mention innumerable one-off trips here and there along what seem to have become the back roads of Britain – to what the Spellcheck on the Amstrad (prose only: Luddites please note) encodes as Scurvy, Headless Bridge, Arboreta, Liquefaction, and beyond. I mention this not to advertise British Rail, with which I have the usual fraught relationship, but to suggest a part of *HMS Glasshouse* which is important to me. I'm fascinated by the years immediately before I was born, and the train offers a continual exposure of versions of England through the window, a contact of sorts with the past, with the Second World War, the Attlee government, and roads not taken, all of them evident in Britain's back yard.

At the same time, as the title suggests, maritime subjects are also prominent. Hull, my home town, is a port on an estuary, and I have almost always lived near the sea, as I do now in Newcastle. But stay on a train from anywhere long enough and you'll probably arrive at this ancient subject. In *HMS Glasshouse* it figures as both liberty and constraint, both empty and full of hardware, and the poems taking place inland often have it in the backs of their minds. As this mixed condition may imply, there is a familiar debate taking place in and behind the poems, between romanticism and obligation, the pleasures of the phenomenal world and the claims of history. There are also a number of poems about Scotland – the urban, nineteenth-century Scotland visible in Dundee, a different country entirely, which exerts its own effects on the imagination and sheds new light on its imperial neighbour.

It's hard to write about your own books without sounding omniscient. In fact the writing of *HMS Glasshouse* began in ignorance with a poem whose title stuck, and the book's shape only began to emerge fairly late. Its three broadly geographical sections are convenient rather than prescriptive or chronological. Stylistically, it tries to build on its predecessors. There are occasional rumblings these days to the effect that English poetry should escape its attachment to the concrete and particular. It's a course some may care to take; I couldn't agree less. The dense variety at our disposal seems to me a compelling basis for the imagination, however sceptical it may be, to work its revealing changes, given the chance.

HMS Glasshouse 1991

A *Selected Poems* is like a clock awarded by an affable but faintly impatient employer. It means it's later than you think. At fifty it means abandoning the illusion that you've only just started work and that there awaits a capacious afterwards in which to get it right. This book is what you've been up to for ages and what you will have to live with.

So what have these hundred-odd poems been talking about? Many of them spring from the sense of place – beginning in the half-bombed Victorian streets of Hull in the 1950s, taking in its hidden gardens, parks, railways and the vast presence of the Humber estuary.

When the time came to travel, I went by train. The train shows us the rear view of England. The train uses a nineteenth-century map rather than the latest AA update. On the train you can't avoid history – vast feats of railway architecture spanning rivers or delving into hills – or its multiple ambiguities. Industry, servitude, achievement, poverty, grotesqueries of exploitation, signs of rational hope, the brutal and the beautiful: their evidence abuts the railway everywhere, spray-canned with tags or poking out from fireweed and hawthorn, immune to nostalgia by virtue of showing a battle neither lost nor won. Writing about England and its condition means writing about history, not as an escape but a source of the possible. Fact and dream are neighbours there.

When I was young it was a truism that poetry and politics didn't mix: the one was too refined and other too befouled to permit their marriage. One served and the other denied the musicality of language. To me as to the poets who most inspired me, this was a lie. Poetry and politics are wedded unto death, and frequent English unease at this fact is another signpost into history, the realm of necessity from which we are always half hoping to get an afternoon off. Poetry too has a history – to be neither abandoned nor denied – and modernity is part of it, not its sole possessor.

At one time I might have supposed that a mythological dimension would have no place in the poems. Now, looking at the recent work, I'm not so sure. Such uncertainty tells me I haven't by any means finished. In fact, I've barely begun.

Cousin Coat 2002

Bernard O'Donoghue

I come from the borders of Cork and Kerry, from a country district called Sliah Luachra (meaning 'Rush Mountain') which is famous for traditional music and for poetry in Irish: two of the great names in Irish poetry since 1700, Aodhagan O Rathaille and Owen Rua Suilleabhain (both noted by Yeats) came from there. So did Fr Padraig Dinneen, the maker of the greatest Irish-language dictionary, whose reputation in local lore is equally exalted. Writing and the arts survive as popular and discussed issues there, and I grew up in a world of poetry, both formal and popular-satirical. Everyone there would know lines like Edward Walsh's mid nineteenth-century

I've the cold earth's dark odour
And I'm worn from the weather.

It is inevitable then, I suppose, that my model of poetry is a social, public one. Poetry, like traditional music, is a product of and a repayment to community. Such communal writing draws on the experiences and materials of a social group and states them back to it, as a kind of validating reinforcement. But poetry is not only addressed locally, of course. The writer also exploits the community and speaks over its head to the world at large. The title of my 1987 collection, *Poaching Rights*, is thinking of the poet as a licensed poacher, claiming a kind of ruthless poetic licence to draw on other people's experiences and stories. One of the best-known historical narratives of the Irish countryside concerns 'grabbers': families who used to bear the stigma that their nineteenth-century forebears were said to have taken the land of tenants evicted for non-payment of rent; in another poem, 'Donoghues the Grabbers', I see the poet as preying on the community in similar ways.

So what can the poet do for the community by way of repayment? I think some of the traditional bardic functions do survive: elegy is an obvious case. *Gunpowder*, like its predecessor *The Weakness*, is dominated by a handful of elegies to particular people, and they remain the poems that I feel most confident of. If this sounds bizarre, I think it reflects a paradox that is central to elegy: it is the most positive literary form because the way we can most powerfully declare attachment to being alive is to lament the loss of what Virgil calls a 'share of sweet life'. The 'weakness' of the title poem of my previous book was a fatal heart-attack; the whiff of gunpowder is potent through its evocation of the fragility of life.

Of course poetry is not only communal; it sends out exploratory linguistic tentacles in all directions. Gunpowder has an epigraph from André Maurois: 'We owe to the Middle Ages the two worst inventions of humanity: gunpowder and romantic love.' I chose this because it addresses, in its ironies, two of my three main subjects: the Irish countryside, death, and the Middle Ages. I am a teacher of medieval literature; my favourite poets are the storyteller Chaucer and the moralist Dante. But my ideal of the short poem (which is what I write) is the kind of 'wisdom' poetry represented by the Old English elegy. This is a mixture of universal emotion ('Where have the joys of company gone? Alas! the bright cup!') and the power of the half-stated (also attributed to classical Irish bardic poetry which has connections with the Old English). One beautiful Middle English poem has the rather baffling refrain:

The bailey beareth the bell away.
The lily, the lily the rose I lay.

But it ends with the wonderfully wistful and direct freedom-image, voiced by the apparent child-bride:

And through the glass window shines the sun.
How should I love and I so young?

What the form of these medieval poems exemplifies so well is how to convey feeling and even opinion without labouring them, which is the quality I most admire in modern poetry. The poems I like best are those where the meaning is left to dawn on the reader but is unmistakable once it has: Heaney's 'Clonmacnoise' poem, or Muldoon's 'Why Brownlee Left', or Austin Clarke's 'The Planter's Daughter' – all poems where privacies are set within strongly defined languages and locations.

Gunpowder 1995

Alice Oswald

I hope no one will read these poems who isn't brave enough to read aloud and beat the rhythm in the air; because the rhythm is the right level – the gauge of the feeling – and without it, you could mistake the book for something polished or earnest or quaint or nature-ish.

There is a way of reading which is a kind of falling – cadence – which is right for all those poems that are halfway to sleep, having mastered their object (and I like some of those) but my own position is dialectic – imagination and its object in argument – and it asks an alert rhythm, a rhythm switching and rising and with gaps.

So please read the poems very slowly, leaving enough time to turn right round between verses and to click the fingers between lines. Language has to balance. It has physical properties. I first recognised this in the sculpture-poems of Iain Hamilton Finlay, when I was being interviewed (in a rowing boat) to be his gardener.

I've been a gardener for nearly seven years, but I'm not a nature poet, though I do write about the special nature of what happens to exist. People are so delighted by the idea of gardening, but in the end it weathers you away. The inaccessibility of what you're working with becomes terrible. I do write about that.

On the subject of God, I don't like the facile distinction that is made between belief and non-belief. Those who don't believe are normally talking about a god they've invented; and for the rest of us, it doesn't feel like a question of belief, more like a slow process of experiencing what the terms really mean. There's a greater distance between the beginning and end of that process than there is between belief and non-belief. Christianity often entails living with contradiction, but I agree with Emerson that consistency is the hobgoblin of little minds. I want my next poems to reflect more of that kind of complexity, that criss-cross and open-endedness. Up to now, I've been using a dry-stone method: finding discrete blocks of words and jamming them together to make something unshakeable. But I need something more baroque and growing, more like hawthorn.

I'm sorry that the back of the book mentions Ovid, as I made a Latin mistake in one of the poems. If the worst comes to worst I could justify it. The other misprints – there are quite a few – I'm happy to leave as symbols of things being not quite right yet.

The Thing in the Gap-Stone Stile 1995

The river twice pointed out to me that water is greater than poetry. Ideally I'd create water, but I've had to make do with mimicking it – a rush of selves, a stronghold of other life-forms.

So the poem's full of voices. It's made of scraps of talk from people who live and work on the Dart. Not entirely by me at all. I wanted to give the poetic voice the slip, to get through to technical, unwritten accounts of water.

There are times in John Clare's poems when the mind has disappeared altogether and the world's going on as no human has ever thought it: '. . . and broad old cesspools glitter in the sun'. The idea of a map poem or song line (which is how I see *Dart*) is just that – the structure comes off the river, the transitions are geographical not rational.

And then at other times, all that water is only the map-symbol of a search for something else – for a language more opaque and fluid, fragmented, haphazard, instant, inspoken and breath-sensitive than is possible.

Dart 2002

Ruth Padel

I went to the asylum at Colney Hatch twice before it closed this spring. Empty 'Lunatick's Clothing' on show, 1870. Untearable sailcloth smocks.

I've been writing a book on Greek madness for two years, while poems were bombarding me from somewhere else: dreams, thrillers, film, anything. It was very freeing. What mattered was truth of whatever voice turned up, not proving by research and evidence. They came in weird personae and scenarios, sometimes with invented words. Separate poems; but I slowly began to see them also as different moments of a single persona. Mad clothes, for a mad girl; with another person in there watching, a sort of doctor. After a reading, someone told me this was a therapist, not doctor: 'doctors' dish out pills. But maybe he does that too, I don't know.

Where does meaning come from in a mask-to-mask thing like that? Whose is it, his or hers? *Angel* is about unknowability. She's an alien, on the sea-bed. No one really knows what hurts them, or why.

In my other work, I try to make alien ways of seeing violently real to people now, in a world (differently mad from ancient Greece) it could be mad not to go mad in. *Angel*'s getting at an unworkable innocence. The girl ducks behind caught voices: a mental nurse looking after a deluded starling, a corrupted GI at a war-crimes trial, a blind man's wife seduced by a witch. The 'real' world's outside with its madnesses (Gulf/Falklands War), political cruelties, real-life deaths. Her erotic fantasies, or maybe memories, are sometimes observed (that doctor, I suppose), sometimes spoken: in a voice whose true (or untrue) situation comes clear with a click at the end of each poem. The next section gives this a few mythic twists.

Finally the doctor winds things up, going for classic cure-by-childhood. Nothing's explained, but she's talking more open, and speaks the last poem to him. Maybe he could cure her; if he weren't so close an enemy. But this poem came also out of being in Israel, out of seeing – however superficially – two peoples, one land, mistrusting each other to the hilt. Political pain's in there too, inseparable from personal, and you can't cure that. Pinel painted *Freeing the Insane* in the Paris madhouse after the Revolution. In fact, the male lunatics got free first, but Pinel painted only the women. Blouses half off, wild and operatic, 'freed' to be exposed to the eyes of clothed men. Observers. The Norm. The world (or some version of it internalised, even by women) still tends to see women as basically or potentially mad. Or the mad as basically female, and curers/observers male. Though men often seem to have caused the madness in the first place. Madness is the preferred pain, when the real world's unendurable . . .

Oh well. My mad girl's not celebrating. She may have invented the doctor. (She says not.) Or he invented her, and it's all his. His casebook. His madness.

Nothing's knowable. But she does, in the end, find a voice that seems to be hers.

Angel 1993

One of the most important things behind this book was a kind of breaking of form. I felt I'd been imprisoned in three-liner poems. Did I 'naturally' think in that shape? Claustrophobia city. I complained about it to Matthew Sweeney, who said, 'You're hung up on it. Try something completely different.' So I did the most unnatural-feeling things I could, capital letters at the beginning of lines, indentation, complex internal rhymes. I began to find my mind was racing into formal patterns and relations ahead of me. One poem ('Don't Fence Me In') ends on the sound 'go'. It wasn't till I finished the first OK draft that I realised the poem had, on its own, prepared for that sound in every stanza all the way through – except one which pulled the o-sound into Joseph.

It was all amazingly freeing. I found I could get all sorts of things into a poem that I hadn't before, especially playfulness and humour. I found I could go over the top on the massed imagery that's always been one of my vices; and laugh at it from inside the poem. I also found I could expand into longer poems, which somehow suit me (all my books have contained one long one, but this has several) because mixing disparate things like humour and baroque imagery lets you vary tones and tensions. The poems somehow became closer to my own thinking voice, or freed it up, when I cracked a new formal whip at them. The Dickinson 'out of great pain a formal feeling comes' was in my mind a lot. Not the pain bit so much as a drive to put everything that matters into form. Thanks, Matthew.

Something else important to me was Colm Tóibín's preface to his collection of essays on Durcan, *The Kilfenora Tea-boy*, how Durcan stopped using 'like'. ('Paul, would you ever stop saying things are like things? They either are or they're not.') If metaphors were so important to me, if they were the things I think through, then they ought to be real.

Another big influence behind the book comes from writing alongside it a critical book about music and desire called *Just Like a Woman*, which I haven't finished yet. Listening to a lot of women's rock, and the ways of going at things I've been finding in P. J. Harvey, Tori Amos, Sinead O'Connor, Liz Phair, Michelle Shocked, Carole King, Laurie Anderson, has been a revelation. They have the same problems women poets have, but in a far more violent form: how the bulk of what's gone before has been made by the boys, you value the work but have to find yourself in reacting to it.

I gradually found I was writing love poems – a way of looking at a man which is modelled on but different from ways of looking at women in men's poems – in which love and sex become a new sort of springboard. For a way of describing the world which brought into combination ordinary life, objects, the media – CDs, faxes, *Esquire*, babygros, J-cloths, Xeroxes, Safeways, *Guardian* journalists, Spice Girls, Barclays Bank and the computer Deep Blue, tornado tourism – with other things which had always been important to me. History: the French Resistance, Cathars, Malory, Egyptian pots, Crusader swords. Science: the speed of light, periodic table, gravitational fields, atoms liquefying in a chrysalis. Myth: Pan, Echo, the Indian *Mahabharata*, a fascinating book by Frazer (author of *The Golden Bough*) called *Myths of the Origin of Fire*. Ecology: tigers, dolphins, polluted seas. Painting, and what I thought Rembrandt was up to, especially in the way he uses shadow. Literature: Peter Rabbit, Chrétien de Troyes, St Augustine, *The Horse Whisperer*, Yeats and my daughter's pony books. Music: Billie Holliday, Mary Black, pen songs, folk songs, Stravinsky.

The focus, obviously, is on female emotional things, things you'd call issues. Like going on the pill, deciding not to have another child, being a parent, putting children above anything. There's an implicit story-line and scenario with a moral question mark in it: a lot of the poems tangle with – or stalk through the shadowy undergrowth of – moral and political correctness questions of feminism and sex.

There's also the weird way love makes you think about death. Loving someone, you don't want them ever to stop being. This coincided with the way death and dying are around me in a lot of places just now. The last three poems in the book are all about dying.

There's a lot of exoticism: as if by going out, away, from your immediate culture (or sentence) into faraway places (or far-out imagery) you tackle central things. Like Durcan's Ireland in 'Going Home to Russia', or Muldoon in his poem about Mum washing his hair: 'Brazil' stands for the mystery of sex faced by a kid. For finally, I think my book's about imagination, generosity and risk. How creativity, like love, comes from being and staying vulnerable.

Rembrandt Would Have Loved You **1998**

Tom Paulin

Some of these poems are set in a society that hasn't been much written about (the best account is in Bernadette Devlin's autobiography). In the early and mid-1960s – which is as far back as my political memory can go – the North of Ireland had a placid, stagnant atmosphere. In those days I used to read Russian novels and various revolutionary texts, and I'd sometimes see Belfast through dim images of St Petersburg. Everyone was reading *Dr Zhivago*, the film was showing in the cinemas, and there was a storm of snowy paperbacks in the bookshops. Although I no longer have the political certainties I had then, I sometimes remember the atmosphere of that time – the political and literary enthusiasms some people shared as they walked about the streets of the capital of a remote province that dozed under a dull and corrupt oligarchy. I recall photographs of the Prime Minister, Lord Brookeborough, and see a face that is wrinkled and cracked in a cynically humorous smile. There is that thickened light and sickening stillness before a storm must break, or else there is a numbness, a flicker of images and a mysterious panic. Eliphaz's vision in Job perhaps describes this paralysing dream: 'In thoughts from the visions of the night, when deep sleep falleth on men, Fear came upon me, and trembling, which made all my bones to shake. Then a spirit passed before my face; the hair of my flesh stood up.'

Elsewhere there is another society which is more purely imaginary – I trace it sometimes in the west of Ireland, where a new cooperative factory, a housing estate, a Georgian house glimpsed across an estuary or an unapproved road seem like ideas set in a wild landscape. With this goes a sense of another way of life or living which I first began to appreciate on a visit to India some years ago. This is a kind of silky surface where ceremonies are performed, where life is a fated being, and dreams, mysteries and superstitions consort with all that is gracious and instinctive. In this community of warm feeling and self-delight no one discusses the meaning of life or art. I associate it with opera, oysters, spices and religious and erotic paintings, and its language contains no words for 'commitment', 'relevance', 'morality' or 'ideology'. It is the extreme opposite of that strenuous hyperborean society which insists on always meaning something and doing something. I suppose I flicker between these extremes, wanting sometimes to write a purely nonsensical poetry, at others to make a definite statement. Certainly I want to believe that it's possible to redeem historical fact, and I see this in terms of walking out of a social museum towards a more imaginary building. Some writers are compulsive mnemonists who dream of strolling in the gardens of forgetfulness.

The Strange Museum 1980

For many years I've carried around among the lines of poetry and phrases that litter my memory that line of MacDiarmid's – 'A watergaw wi' its chitterin' licht'. I remember the school anthology where I first read it, remember the black ink on the creamy page and the sense of recognition. A couplet of Hopkins goes with it – 'Degged with dew, dappled with dew, / Are the groins of the braes that the brook treads through.' When I first heard the phrase 'wind dog' it triggered memories of both poets – 'dag' I knew is one word among many in Donegal English for 'rain' so 'dog' must be a version of that word, nothing to do with the animal. I first heard the phrase in Donegal when I was out mackerel fishing with an old man, Jack Crabbe, who was a retired merchant sea captain from Islandmagee in Co. Antrim.

He spoke with a gently humorous Ulster Scots accent and his speech was strewn with dialect words. After a shower of rain, the sun came out and he looked up at the blue sky and said, 'D'you see thon wind dog?' It was a fragment of a new rainbow there in the intense blueness over the Gweebarra Bay. Later I looked up the term in Joseph Wright's great dialect dictionary and found there are a whole series of cognate terms.

With this goes a fascination I've had for a long time with primitive or naïf painting – there is a famous story of the English painter Derek Hill journeying to Tory Island off the coast of Donegal (Hill is a distinguished and sophisticated painter, not self-taught). One day, when he was out painting, a local fisherman, James Dixon, came past, looked at Hill's canvas and said, 'I could do as good as that.' 'Go ahead,' said Hill, and gave him some paint, brushes and a canvas. After that first attempt, Dixon used the colours scraped out of abandoned cans of paint thrown away after fishermen had finished repainting their boats. With this restricted palette, he painted wind and Atlantic weather with a unique power.

Dixon's paintings are now celebrated (he is the greatest self-taught painter to come out of Ireland) and as I write an exhibition of his and Alfred Wallis's paintings has just opened in Dublin. Two months ago I stood outside Alfred Wallis's house in St Ives and thought of both men, self-taught visionaries.

As well as memories of lines of poetry, like anyone else I carry about with me images of paintings – as well as Wallis and Dixon, I kept thinking over the time when I wrote these poems of Chagall. Obsessively the word 'shtetl' kept coming back, as I read about and watched on the news so many reports of rural violence in the North of Ireland – IRA punishment beatings, the burning down of ten Catholic churches, pipe and petrol bomb attacks and murders. I began to reflect on the subtle ways in which Chagall uses what in German is called – sinister word – '*volkisch*', how his Russian Jewishness puts it almost in inverted commas. It interests me that in Moscow in 1920 Chagall designed costumes and a set for a production of Synge's *Playboy of the Western World.* I can't paint, know only bits and pieces about art history, and I'm an indifferent linguist, so these poems have something to do with the shimmer of language and art being always somehow over there, just beyond the horizon.

The Wind Dog 1999

Sylvia Plath

In her earlier poems, Sylvia Plath composed very slowly, consulting her thesaurus and dictionary for almost every word, putting a slow, strong ring of ink around each word that attracted her. Her obsession with intricate rhyming and metrical schemes was part of the same process. Some of those early inventions of hers were almost perverse, with their bristling hurdles. But this is what she enjoyed. One of her most instinctive compulsions was to make patterns – vivid, bold, symmetrical patterns. She was fond of drawing – anything, a blade of grass, a tree, a stone, but preferably something complicated and chaotic, like a high heap of junk. On her paper this became inexorably ordered and powerful, like a marvellous piece of sculpture, and took on the look of her poems, everything clinging together like a family of living cells, where nothing can be alien or dead or arbitrary. The poems in *Ariel* are the fruits of that early labour. In them, she controls one of the widest and most subtly discriminating vocabularies in the modern poetry of our language, and these are poems written for the most part at great speed, as she might take dictation, where she ignores metre and rhyme for rhythm and momentum, the flight of her ideas and music. The words in these odd-looking verses are not only charged with terrific heat, pressure and clairvoyant precision, they are all deeply related within any poem, acknowledging each other and calling to each other in deep harmonic designs. It is this musical, almost mathematical hidden law which gives these explosions their immovable finality.

Behind these poems there is a fierce and uncompromising

nature. There is also a child desperately infatuated with the world. And there is a strange muse, bald, white and wild, in her 'hood of bone', floating over a landscape like that of the Primitive Painters, a burningly luminous vision of a Paradise. A Paradise which is at the same time eerily frightening, an unalterably spot-lit vision of death.

And behind them, too, is a long arduous preparation. She grew up in an atmosphere of tense intellectual competition and Germanic rigour. Her mother, first-generation American of Austrian stock, and her father, who was German-Polish, were both university teachers. Her father, whom she worshipped, died when she was nine, and thereafter her mother raised Sylvia and her brother single-handed. Whatever teaching methods were used, Sylvia was the perfect pupil; she did every lesson double. Her whole tremendous will was bent on excelling. Finally, she emerged like the survivor of an evolutionary ordeal: at no point could she let herself be negligent or inadequate. What she was most afraid of was that she might come to live outside her genius for love, which she also equated with courage, or 'guts', to use her word. This genius for love she certainly had, and not in the abstract. She didn't quite know how to manage it: it possessed her. It fastened her to cups, plants, creatures, vistas, people, in a steady ecstasy. As much of all that as she could, she hoarded into her poems, into those incredibly beautiful lines and hallucinatory evocations.

But the truly miraculous thing about her will remain the fact that in two years, while she was almost fully occupied with children and house-keeping, she underwent a poetic development that has hardly any equal on record, for suddenness and completeness. The birth of her first child seemed to start the process. All at once she could compose at top speed, and with her full weight. Her second child brought things a giant step forward. All the various voices of her gift came together, and for about six months, up to a day or two before her death, she wrote with the full power and music of her extraordinary nature.

Ariel is not easy poetry to criticise. It is not much like any other poetry. It is her. Everything she did was just like this, and this is just like her – but permanent.

– T. H.

Ariel 1965

Craig Raine

In spite of their evident variety, these poems have one thing in common. They were written after the birth of my daughter – a happy event, but one which, to my mind, accounts for the sombre overall tone. Few things bring mortality so vividly close as holding a perfect, vulnerable scrap of flesh in your arms. Especially if you happen also to be a heavy smoker. There is one poem, 'Sexual Couplets', which is intended as *jeu d'esprit*, but I would be disappointed if this was seized on by those critics who persist in describing my work as dandified. Wit is not incompatible with seriousness: when Donne writes, in 'The First Anniversary', 'How witty's ruine!', he means inventiveness, not facetiousness. Equally, I don't regard the use of metaphor and simile as unnatural or arty – either in Shakespeare's plays, ordinary conversation, or my own poetry. The equation (fashionable in the sixties) between sincerity and what Joyce called, as he repudiated it, 'a scrupulous meanness' of style now seems narrowly prescriptive: too often, unforced directness of expression declined into mere mannerism, widely copied because easily reproduced.

England has a tradition that emphasises the role of tone in poetry and rightly so. All the same, this frequently degenerates into something resembling caricature – a self-presentation that toadies to the reader and traps the writer, who introduces himself into his poems as unfailingly sensitive, modestly touched by venial guilt, but invariably charming. Berryman broke through this politesse by using himself as an anti-hero *in extremis*. I have deliberately chosen a neutral, objective tone which allows the images to speak for themselves – under authorial supervision, of course, but without overt moralising. I hope no one will be stupid enough to mistake this tone for lack of feeling.

Many critics are impressed by technical virtuosity – by which they mean the dead perfection of the sestina and other futile fifteen-finger exercises. The couplet I use is essentially a flexible instrument capable of accommodating a huge variety of subject matter. The sestina strikes me as the poetic equivalent of an instrument for removing Beluga caviar from horses' hooves – bizarrely impressive, but finally useless. The unrhymed couplet, on the other hand, is more like the tin-opener – so useful that one is inclined to overlook its cleverness.

A Martian Sends a Postcard Home 1979

The story so far: Craig Raine, aged twenty-five, sends out four poems to the *Listener*, *Encounter*, the *New Statesman* and the *Times Literary Supplement*. They are rejected, which buggers up his master-plan to follow the acclaim by total reticence, until the appearance of a full-length volume. Puzzled, he tries again. And again. Then seventy or eighty times more. After making a clay model of Derwent May into which he hammers nails, he decides that reviewing will provide a route to poetry publication. However, he mainly reviews for the *TLS*, which, it turns out, isn't the best way to make a name for yourself because in those days reviews were anonymous. After four years, though, the *TLS* do take a poem. On the strength of this, his poems are turned down for Faber's *Poetry Introduction 3*. He writes one of those letters: . . . one day . . . you'll see . . . Fortunately, a bit of reviewing for the *New Statesman* turns up and they start taking the odd poem. And so the poetry ekes out an existence as a parasite on the prose. Finally, at the age of thirty-four, his first book appears and in the meantime anonymity has worked in his favour: a few competition prizes. The book is not chosen or recommended by the Poetry Book Society, does not win the Somerset Maugham Award, nor the Alice Hunt Bartlett Award. After this string of successes, he is puzzled to learn from reviewers that the book is no good, though it has been highly praised. He would like to know where. With his second book, things begin to improve . . . Now read on . . .

This is only mildly exaggerated, though I don't expect anyone to believe that every poem in my first book was rejected at least once and most of them several times. About half the contents never appeared in magazines. Perhaps you have already rumbled me? Let me be candid. The role I'd like, if you could see your way to it, is to be one of those neglected figures who've had to struggle. You see, as far as I can make out, I'm perceived rather differently – disgustingly fertile, unserious, tediously clever, rhythmically inert, exclusively visual, repetitive, showy, and somehow instantly successful. But I could show you my passport. It's covered with stamps that show I've spent ages in the wilderness. The photo, taken in a booth on Darlington Station, shows a haggard little face, pale with provincial neglect. Is there no hope? Honest, I've done my time.

Rich 1984

Kathleen Raine

My view of poetry is that of tradition, and in absolute opposition to any poetic theories whose foundation is the positivist humanism so widespread at the present time. I would go so far as to say that the arts (normally the language of man's metaphysical and spiritual knowledge) are finally incompatible with these philosophies. I assent to Dante's definition of poetry as the writing of 'beautiful things truly', to Coomaraswamy's 'art is expression informed by ideal beauty'; to Blake's 'One thing alone makes a poet – Imagination, the Divine Vision'; to Yeats's 'Supreme art is a traditional statement of certain heroic and religious truths, passed on from age to age, modified by individual genius but never abandoned'; or indeed to Dom Bede Griffiths's belief that the function of the arts is 'to evoke the divine presence'; to Æ when he says, 'It is certain that metrics as a mode of speech correspond to something in the soul. But if we say this we are impelled to deny the fitness of verse utterance of any feeling, imagination or reverie which has not originated in the magic fountain'; to Plotinus's 'the soul itself acts immediately, affirming the Beautiful where it finds something accordant with the ideal form within itself. But let the soul fall in with the ugly and at once it shrinks within itself, denies the thing, turns away from it, not accordant, resenting it'; and in consequence, to the conclusion that 'one of the very first symptoms of the loss of the soul is the loss of the sense of beauty'.

I am in fact (in the tradition of Spenser, Vaughan and Traherne, Coleridge, Shelley, Yeats and all imaginative poets) a Platonist; and (in consequence, since that philosophy implies the concordance of visible with invisible forms) a symbolist. Among modern English poets I admire chiefly Yeats, Edwin Muir, Vernon Watkins and David Gascoyne. That the poems I have written will survive the test of these values I hesitate to hope; but if not, it is the poems and not the ground of poetry which are to be discarded.

The Hollow Hill 1965

Herbert Read

'Rum thing, painting,' said Turner; and 'Rum thing, poetry' is about all I feel inclined to say about the matter. My views about poetry have often been expressed, most recently in 'The True Voice of Filing'. Perhaps I might seize this occasion to offer a few words of personal advice to young poets – they are receipts for patience rather than for success:

1. Never lift your voice – modern poetry has an inaudible wavelength.

*

2. Never coax the Muse – she is as obstinate as a mule, and best approached from an oblique angle.

*

3. A poet, as Keats said, is the most unpoetical of any thing in existence. He does not know he is a poet until someone (the Secretary of the Poetry Book Society, for instance) tells him so.

*

4. Never write reviews of contemporary poetry – it makes you too conscious of being a poet yourself, and perhaps an inferior one.

*

5. Envy corrodes inspiration.

*

6. The best poets have been busy men – alas!

*

7. The only bad influences are those that are not poetic –

e.g. Rilke in translation, rhyming dictionaries, *Times* leader-writers, the universities.

*

8. The greatest poetry is probably the Chinese. Then the Greek. Then the English. It is probably better not to know too well any other language than your own. The best poets have had poor memories for words, but good visual memory. Poets are often tone-deaf: the music of poetry is not heard but imagined.

*

9. There is no hierarchy among poets. Poetry is outside history. We write its history and call it tradition. But in our hearts we know that it is a question of revelation.

*

10. A good poem is like a crystal – hard, compact, sparkling (but with light not wit!); and somewhere a hidden law of construction.

Moon's Farm and Poems, Mostly Elegiac 1955

Peter Reading

Autobiographer, please don't tell me the tale of your love-life:
much as it mattered to you, nothing could marvel me less.

In spite of the fact that the poems in *The Prison Cell and Barrel Mystery* are about love, I trust that I have been sensible, throughout the volume, of Auden's cautionary words, inasmuch as I have earnestly endeavoured to avoid the difficulties which attend this somewhat thorny topic. These difficulties are fairly obvious and probably the foremost of them is embarrassment, which is to be sedulously avoided, not only as far as the reader is concerned (because embarrassing sentiment is generally banality), but also I suppose that any writer is anxious to distance himself, through his writing, from matter which is rather too close for comfort and therefore a potential embarrassment to himself. At the same time, of course, as attempting to distance deeply personal matters (with the intention of transforming the purely personal into something of more general significance), one wishes to try and retain any originality of experience and convey any moving quality, poignancy and so on, which may have characterised the initial motivation. The crux is to get the balance right.

None of the poems in *The Prison Cell and Barrel Mystery*, I think, requires any explanatory note, with the possible exception of 'Trio', which, at a cursory glance, may perhaps appear to be rather curious in format, but is simply the concurrent treatment of three personae connected by overlapping amative interests, each character having his/her own column of three-syllabled lines throughout the poem (which continues, three being its basis, for nine pages).

To return to the de-personalising of motivation: one very simple way of achieving distance from an experience is to distort it – even to be a downright liar about it. So what is said in a poem is not necessarily journalistically accurate, though it aims, of course, at being a truth. Lying about people and events, then, can be a most useful poetic device (though it enrages and estranges acquaintances by the dozen), and it is the end product that is the concern of the reader – not the resemblance, or otherwise, of the poem to its stimulus. In the prose section '*Dichtung und Wahrheit*' of *Homage to Clio*, Auden remarks:

> I read a poem by someone else in which he bids a tearful farewell to his beloved: the poem is good (it moves me as other good poems do) and genuine (I recognise the poet's 'handwriting'). Then I learn from a biography that, at the time he wrote it, the poet was sick to death of the girl but pretended to weep in order to avoid hurt feelings and a scene. Does this information affect my appreciation of his poem? Not in the least: I never knew him personally and his private life is no business of mine.

The Prison Cell and Barrel Mystery **1976**

Peter Redgrove

The Nature of Cold Weather is a second selection from a vast number of poems that I've found myself writing during the past ten years or so. It contains some early poems, like 'For When . . .' and 'Basilisk', and much more recent ones, like 'The Gamut' and 'Ghosts'. I think, though, that many of both kinds show traces of a school and university training in science, not only, as occasionally, in their subject matter, but in the way they often seem to proceed from observation to hypothesis. 'The Stronghold', for instance, starts by picking out details about an old hollow tree and building up a picture of it, as real and concrete as possible, and then arrives at an idea of what the tree means to the person looking at it, as 'The shadow of my head cuts off the light'.

But I very much doubt whether, if I had gone on to make it my profession, I would ever have become a real scientist. I was, to be sure, fascinated by the insights the methods of science gave one into the physical world. I could see not only the creamy skull beneath the skin, but also the knitting of nerve-cell and fibre beneath the skull that enabled it to utter words. I observed not only the radiance of the moon, but the rocks that made up its mountainous surface, and their composition. I saw the X-ray diffraction pattern of the snowflake.

Like a good scientist I wanted to see things clearly and how they worked, but I was perhaps too ambitious about my subject matter. In due time, when I looked at an autumn forest, it wasn't the chemical reactions by which green chlorophyll was degraded into biologically useless red and brown pigments that

I wanted to understand more clearly, or that, I now found, had my allegiance. I wanted to penetrate further into and hold more firmly another kind of material which science probably wanted to deal with but had got nowhere near as yet: that sharp, bracing, melancholy tang that belongs to autumn and to nothing else, its mists, colours and smell. Hormones ceased to interest me as I fell in love. To be a good scientist I would have had to hold the two kinds of knowledge apart, and I could not. For a scientist, my observation was faulty: I saw not only things, but images and symbols.

And I found, or thought I found, that by writing about these things I could hold on to them, and penetrate further into them.

Poetry was a new sense. Literature, which recorded these things, was the textbook of the soul. Good writing was as exact as science, and went further. It was also more difficult and dangerous, for whereas I could have been perfectly sure that naming a new species of crayfish which abounded under rocks only on certain beaches would be useful to somebody somewhere somehow, how could I be certain that what seemed to me so splendid and important as I wrote it would in truth be memorable to another person? I had to rely on myself. And the words took charge. I couldn't help myself, though it looked like slow economic suicide to be spending so much time writing poetry. Nor could I falsify my material in the interests of a marketable product. I had to write as the poem wanted me to write, and the words wanted to be poems, not profit-making prose. For a long time I had to write prose of a kind for my living, but for me there was no truth in it.

There are, by the way, some prose-poems in *The Nature of Cold Weather*, and if anybody should say that a prose-poem is a contradiction in terms, I can only reply that the rhythm the poem asked for in each case was a prose-rhythm, and not that of any verse-line I knew or could invent, and though I gave the poems every opportunity to become verse, I eventually had to let them have their own way. In general I believe verse is the most flexible and expressive way of writing or speaking; but it just didn't happen to be the case with these seven poems.

To sum up, I think I keep enough of my scientific bent to be empirical, engaged on my own exploration of the world. On the other hand, the end-product of science is ideas – hypothesis, theory, natural law – and I think poetry is 'ideas in action'. So when I write about a fiercely jovial demiurge in 'I Stroll', camouflaged in imitated scraps of his world, with eyes green as the pools and hair grey as gossamer, arbitrarily dispensing various sorts of children to the lovers in the park whose trees recoil from him, I'm not trying to say that such a being actually exists – 'As flies to wanton boys are we to the gods.' Instead, if the poem is successful, I'm responding to and summing up some of those things in life that are menacing and perilous, by making up a being who is in charge of them. I believe it enhances the poem that it could also be the thoughts of a human madman: the God that is mad and the madman who thinks he is God have much the same feeling about them – how terrible if it's true, and can we be sure that it isn't? You may answer, 'Yes, we can be sure', but that is not the point of the poem; rather, this is what it might feel like if we weren't sure. It is a hypothesis tried on the pulses.

'I Stroll' is one kind of dramatic monologue; 'The Secretary' and 'Disguise' are another. In these, and in other poems like them in the book, people are facing themselves – as if they were suddenly given the ability to tell the truth, to understand and perhaps forgive themselves and others. I cannot hope to have gone so far in these poems, but it is as though the people in them were pleading at the bar of a judgement where all hearts are open and all things clear. That's what is, to me, behind the dramatic monologue, and what makes it so moving a form to me, and why I persist with it.

The Nature of Cold Weather 1961

A lot is said nowadays about the operation of the 'unconscious mind' in poetry. I would like to take a departure from the usual mode, and speak instead of the 'unconscious senses'. Aristotle assured us that we have only five senses: hearing, vision, smell, taste and touch. In fact we have many more: there are at least thirty different sense-qualities associated with touch alone; and it has been demonstrated recently that we can sense in some measure microwave emission (such as the Moon gives off in plenty) and electrostatic and geomagnetic fields. We can also react with extraordinary subtlety to what are called 'pheromones', which are a cross between perfumes and super-active hormones, and are emitted by all kinds of being, including trees, dogs, and our fellow humans. Now it is ourselves, what we usually call our 'conscious' minds, which are ordinarily unconscious of such influences, and which tend to relegate these gifts of sense to the supernatural ('vibes'), the animal (the 'mystery' of homing pigeons), the deprecated ('women's intuition'), or to poetic licence and the pathetic fallacy. There are also unacknowledged inner senses and effectors. If you tape a thermometer to your thumb, and imagine strongly that you have dipped the hand in hot water, the temperature of the thumb will rise, visibly. You have told your thumb, via your imagination, to notice its natural warmth, and by attending to it, to alter it.

This drawing upon capacities and sensory signals usually unnoticed is called biofeedback, and with its aid you can learn to control heart-rhythm, blood-pressure, brain-rhythms, etc., by means of imagined symbols and images. The act of imagination is a tuning-device that alerts one's inner senses to real but previously unnoticed signals. I think that this may all pertain to a new view of the function of poetry. It is currently held that a poem must arise out of experience. True enough, but only half the story. A poem must allow you an experience. It may be one of a kind that you have never had before – but that is no reason for turning on the poet and saying he hasn't had it either! By the exercise of imagination through entering into the images, symbols, diction, rhythms, fiction, thought of a poem, one notices and feels what one did not perceive before, both inwardly and outwardly. The poem is a tuning or feedback device which alters or adjusts our capacity to respond to the world.

I am very pleased that my book *The Apple Broadcast* is the Choice; not only for the book's sake, but because this may indicate a swing of interest towards a type of poetry which I favour and try to write: the kind that makes us imagine unexpectedly, which helps us value beings and events we thought below notice, and which provides us with images and symbols that, reimagined in this secular world, can help some of the energy and attention flow that used to be thought exclusively religious. Discussion of poetry along these lines has so far been infrequent in this country. It was an English author who proposed the idea of the Two Cultures,* and it is in England that Science and Art have been kept rigidly apart. Yet it is easy to see, particularly nowadays, how Science and Imagination must work together to give a modern account of the human universe. I myself believe that 'poetry, not abandoning itself to the unconscious, but seizing it and raising it as far as possible into consciousness . . . prefigures a final reconciliation of the two'.

The Apple Broadcast **1981**

* C. P. Snow

James Reeves

You have to distinguish between the desire, the need, and the ability to write poetry. With me, I think the need preceded the desire. Even when quite young – say, eleven years old – I experienced a need to communicate in words: to express a feeling, a longing, a discovery, an inner problem. To 'communicate' with whom? To 'express' for whom? For imaginary friends, or for myself alone. Those one thinks of later as one's 'readers' are imaginary friends. It seems to me to be useless to write poetry without a genuine need to do so – an inner compulsion.

Next comes the ability to write poetry. Poets are born, not made. The essential minimum is a certain inborn – or early-acquired – interest in words, analogous to the incipient artist's feeling for line, colour, shape. Words for their own sake: but it is never just for their own sake, it is for what they mean, and even more what they suggest, evoke, beyond their immediate meaning and immediate limits of the experience they describe. Some words are all right always, like Babylon; some are never right, like tapioca, which ought to mean not a savourless milk pudding but a quick light dance. Poetic ability is a complex tiling; it can be improved or developed, but it can't be assumed like a new suit or an accent. To each according to his need: if there is no real inner need, poetic ability will wither. If there is a real need, ability will reveal itself – perhaps only occasionally, perhaps only once. When it does so, it is unmistakable; it answers readily and spontaneously to the need. It can be helped, encouraged, induced by the reading of poetry, the writing of poetry, or simply doing nothing but letting words come into the mind: not words in isolation, but words in rhythm, words charged with an incantatory power. Rhythm means flow. It is the flow of words which marks poetic ability.

A discovery in oneself of poetic ability, however fitful, stimulates the desire to write poetry; that is something which, so far as I'm concerned, has to be resisted. It never leads to anything. The words won't come; there is no rhythmic power, no flow.

One writes one's poem as best one can, and they usually turn out quite different from what one imagines they will be like when one starts writing. It is as if they had a life of their own which they are determined to live in their own way. Yet they have to be encouraged; they are inevitably affected, if only indirectly, by one's idea of what a poem should be. The kinds of poem that stay in my mind are those which have a profound significance independently, as it were, of their literal meaning. What I value in a poem is what it expresses above and beyond its literal meaning. What matters about a poem, what gives it life, is its compulsive magic, its power of infinite expression or suggestion. Nothing else matters much.

Collected Poems 1929–1959 1960

Christopher Reid

There are two important ideals that, when I think of poetry, I like to keep in mind. The first of these found vivid expression in a letter Wallace Stevens wrote to Hi Simons in 1940. Stevens, who was baffled and stung by the apparent fact that no one understood or enjoyed his poems, spent a good deal of energy providing his correspondents with courteous explanations. The letter I refer to is as detailed and polite as any of the rest; but, in the middle of it, Stevens gives way to an impulse of short temper and lets the cat – a huge, blatant, bristling beast – out of the bag. 'People,' he tells Simons, 'ought to like poetry the way a child likes snow & they would if poets wrote it.'

Just so, I should like my readers simply to enjoy what I write. Most of my poems begin with enjoyment – a delight, say, in something perceived – and the poem will have lost everything unless that initial enjoyment is conveyed by the finished work. However, there is also the second ideal to reckon with.

In his essay 'Linguistics and Poetics', George Steiner speaks of 'what is, unquestionably, the most complex of all semantic phenomena, a poem, a major literary text . . .' And later, in a more anthropological vein, he remarks: 'Man is a primate who can lie, who can make "impossible" and counter-factual statements. What quality in the fabric of certain languages has translated this strange capacity into literature?' I cannot answer this; and neither, it seems, can Steiner, who is content, once he has started a hare, to let other dogs pursue it. At any rate, we can agree with his main point, adding our own observation that one of a poem's most intriguing qualities can be to tell a truth and a lie at the same time, without mutual exclusiveness.

I am thinking here of metaphor. My own poem 'H. Vernon' attempts to do something like this: a butcher's shop is described, with circumstantial detail and a degree of implausibility, as Paradise. Of course, this is not a verifiable statement, except in so far as the 'fabric' of the English language allows it to be proposed; and the irony involved is so harsh that it comes close to being sarcasm; but I have hoped in poems such as this to bring about a union of the two ideals I mentioned earlier.

The new breed of linguist-critic that George Steiner would like to put to work on poetical texts will have a hard time of it. The poet is luckier. He can simply rejoice, if he has any of the success that we now know Stevens to have achieved in abundance, in the happy ambiguity of being both as direct as a child's snowfall and as complex as the same snowfall when contemplated by an intelligent adult.

Arcadia 1979

Oliver Reynolds

Last July a satellite was launched on a nine-month journey that will take it into the heart of Halley's comet. The satellite is called Giotto after the quattrocento painter who included the comet in a *Nativity* of his. Incidentally, Giotto's own domestic experience of birth-scenes will have been extensive: one biographical dictionary tells us that he married a Donna Cuita di Lapo and they had eight children, 'remarkable, it is said, for their ugliness'.

This journey of a name across six centuries is an appealing one; so too, in a more accelerated fashion, is that of the satellite licking along at 150,000 m.p.h to its brief rendezvous next year on 13 March. (It won't be a Friday, but science still seems to be cocking a snook at superstition.) It's hoped that Giotto will have some four hours to transmit information back to Earth before burn-up begins and, quite possibly, consumes the satellite altogether: four hours of interstellar swan-song before metal flares to silence.

Now what (apart, perhaps, from the shared terminology of the 'launch') does any of this have to do with the publication of *Skevington's Daughter*? Nothing directly, but then the progress of poetry – like the orbit of a satellite – is often elliptic. The book's pay-load is diverse and includes the first editor of the *OED*, blood, Euclid having fun, sex in Suffolk, my Uncle George's red dicky-bow, how his cousins gave me my first name (and thus, perhaps, my interest in the circular), philosophy in Rhyll and such handy Welsh phrases as *Sui basech chi'n diffinio telesgop?* (How would you define a telescope?) The book's destination is obscure (nor is much known of whence it came), but the bright red of its cover plus the identity of Faber's poetry editor might suggest Mars. (The textually alert will spot two references to canals.)

Pope Benedict IX of Treviso, wanting proof of Giotto's skill, sent a courtier to Tuscany to ask 'for a little drawing for His Holiness'. Vasari's account of the painter's response is well known: 'Giotto, who was most courteous, took a paper and on that, with a brush dipped in red, holding his arm fast against his side in order to make a compass, with a turn of his hand he made a circle, so true in proportion and circumference that to behold it was a marvel.' This, in turn, led to a Tuscan proverb, applied to the slow-witted and punning on *tondo* which is used both for 'round' and 'stupid': *Tu sei piu tondo che l'O di Giotto!* (You're rounder than Giotto's circle.)

Skevington's Daughter lacks a dedicatee. For a brief spell next 13 March, I'm happy for it to have ten: Mr and Mrs Giotto and their eight ugly children.

Skevington's Daughter **1985**

Anne Ridler

Nadezhda Mandelstam records a conversation with Boris Pasternak in which he distinguished between a 'book' and a 'collection' of poems, saying that only once did it happen to him to write a book. Certainly, poems written over a number of years are unlikely to have the unity of inspiration implied in his definition, yet in so far as they reflect the 'fable' of an author's life – to use Edwin Muir's term – rather than its active surface, they must complement each other. The poems in *Some Time After* cover the last ten years or so of my life, a period in which I have also written drama, and have been interested in the problem of marrying words and music. They do not reflect the whole 'fable' of my life in that time, but as I re-read them I see that some themes recur, and that more poems than I was aware of are concerned with the mystery of human death.

Poetry is a way of discovering truth – this is one good reason for writing it; it is a discipline that helps one to face hard truths. The last poem in the book, written as a libretto, is an attempt to face the fact of death (whose bitterness is in parting from those we love) as something that has to be experienced fully, irrespective of any faith or lack of faith in immortality. Other poems are related to this, and the one quoted here, written about one of the superb concerts that Sir Thomas Beecham conducted at the very end of his life, sets two facts side by side: the blazing glory of his art and the darkness of extinction, two irreconcilable truths.

Some Time After **1972**

Maurice Riordan

I'm attracted to Frost's description of a poem as 'a momentary stay against confusion'. That more or less is how I experience the writing of poems – typically as a respite from reticence and unsureness. It must follow, I suppose, that I have little to add about them. They are what they say. I don't deliberately withhold anything! The best compliment I've had, so far, came from someone who, while disclaiming any expertise in the matter, said she liked my poems because she could follow them. And then, recollecting herself, added that of course she realised they might well contain all sorts of depths. I can only hope she was right on both counts.

I've been writing poems on and off for many years. But mostly off. The oldest poem in the collection, 'Nickname', dates from about 1984. I've an affection for it because it was written without effort. I 'found' it in a notebook where I'd been fooling around with snippets of childhood memory and, having typed it up, sent it to the *New Statesman,* where it was published. So a piece of oral family history unexpectedly acquired literary status.

But my writing didn't start to prosper until more recently. The key poem, I feel, was 'Flitcraft'. I'd long been intrigued by a passage in *The Maltese Falcon* where Sam Spade – Bogart, if you like – recounts the strange case of Charles Flitcraft to Brigid O'Shaughnessy. It's a conspicuous blot on an otherwise flawless narrative – and yet one returns to it. I came to think of it as the umbilicus of the novel: a technical eyesore, which nonetheless was Hammett's Donnée, the source of the story's darkness and misogyny, its obsession with facial expressions, physicality, all forms of counterfeit.

I'd only ever been able to write about personal things. But in 'Flitcraft' I saw I'd quite tucked away the connections with my own life. I realised what one could do – what many writers in fact do – is find fictional tangents to their own experiences. And so I began to write what might be called 'pseudo-confessional' poems.

This method served me well with the poem that opens the collection, 'Time Out'. It touches on matters I wouldn't dare write of directly. But due to a coincidence of circumstances (including exhaustion), some of my early experiences of childcare were shunted on to a siding and, before I could notice, found a downhill gradient. It struck me later how closely the poem repeats the rhetorical structure of 'Flitcraft'. It also occurred to me that I was finished with the pseudo-confessional, at least for the time being. But that month, May 1992, was a lucky one for my writing. That very day I'd finished what was to become the title poem of the book. Here the umbilicus is hard to locate. My work on the poem had been prolonged by the fact that my children had chicken-pox. It's hardly a serious disease but those spots remind one of smallpox; also it's never far from my mind that the brain survives at a few degrees below its maximum temperature. And chicken-pox, innocuous though it is, nonetheless narrows the gap. Perhaps such thoughts nourished the poem. I don't know.

In any case, I felt I'd activated an area of my mind which had been dormant hitherto so far as my poetry was concerned. For once I'd written something removed from my own experience; and, quite possibly, removed from everyone else's as well, since the poem is pseudo-anthropological (no classical author is more disarmingly named than the pseudo-Dionysius!). This is the way to go, I thought, and I set out to write speculative and, in a sense, more ambitious poems.

It has turned out not quite like that. My imagination has

remained fairly memory-bound. But, in assembling the collection (for which I thank my friend Matthew Sweeney for his help), I've hoped to build some sort of bridge between the 'original' village and a paradigmatic one. But I wouldn't want to press the point. I have no great faith in collections of poems as books – a book being perhaps no more than a convenient roost for poems, the best of which will prove both independent and flighty. They should crave the caress of the voice and the approval of the ear. I can think of no better outcome than that some of my poems find a perch in the memories of their readers.

A Word from the Loki 1995

'Nugget', one of the first poems I wrote for *Floods*, was based on an anecdote by Richard Feynman, who as a young scientist worked at Los Alamos on the Manhattan Project. I was struck by the playful innocence of that brief time in the presence of plutonium before the bomb was made. The material itself – truly the philosopher's stone – linked with other 'magical objects' I was carrying around in my head, like the lettuce in the poem of that name, and the unguarded crow I'd happened on, which appears in 'Badb' (the goddess of the battlefield in Irish myth).

And a sloe. This is the sloe that was found frozen, perfectly preserved, beside the body of a Stone Age man on an Austrian glacier in 1991. It is, I suppose, the oldest edible piece of fruit in the world. I thought I knew something about that sloe. My father, as we were fencing one September by the stream, plucked some from a blackthorn and said they were too sour for us to eat, but the frost when it came would sweeten them. And I'd read that sloes, or rather just their stones, are found in Neolithic graves. So I guessed (though with more scepticism than the speaker of the poem I eventually wrote) that the sloe was food for the soul.

That sloe I carried in my head but couldn't write about until the book was near its end. By then, I'd had my own losses. And with those came a confused experience of time. The linear sense one tries to make of life was erased. I couldn't often tell when, or indeed for whom, I'd come to grief.

And so, I expect, the poems here seem fractured, often more expressionistic and extreme than is right. I think I wanted to remove, or at least loosen, the struts from narrative language. And then I found a translation of Ferenc Juhasz's magnificent poem about the boy changed to a stag. This poem was greatly admired by Auden and was, I believe, translated (but is the translation lost?) by Ted Hughes. So, what I've done is perhaps unforgivable, since I've stolen a ride on its rhetoric and plundered its home-brew of myth and science and autobiography.

But I did try with the title poem to regain some composure. This too is a sort of translation. In antiquity several books were written about the Nile (nothing was a greater source of wonder) but all of them are lost, except part of a prose work by Seneca. And so I saw myself as 'translating' a lost book, written at the start of our era by a Roman colonist near Alexandria. I had the company of my poor broken-hearted, almost humourless Roman for a few months, as he drew on all his speculative reading – much wider than mine – to place his personal fate in an unmeasurable world.

Did he succeed? I can't say. But I knew with the last word of 'Floods' that my book was finished – though then I did write one more small poem. It is a return to a scale that is humanly bearable, to house and garden, to watching children play with water.

Floods 2000

THEODORE ROETHKE

The volume really consists of two books: earlier work and later. Since it is his last things which most interest a poet, let me dwell on these briefly.

I believe a book should reveal as many sides of a writer as is decent for him to show; that these aspects be brought together in some kind of coherent whole that is recognizable to the careful reader. This means that some poems will sometimes support other poems, either by being complements to them, or by providing contrasts. Thus, the first section of love poems in *Words for the Wind* contains pieces tender or highly romantic, others are 'witty', coarse and sensual. It is my hope that a reader will like both kinds of thing. Then, by way of contrast, there is a handful of light pieces and poems for children. These are rougher than what most children's editors prefer. The attempt – part of a larger effort – was to make poems which would please both child and parent, without insulting the intelligence or taste of either.

The third section of these later pieces consists of poems of terror, and running away – and the dissociation of personality that occurs in such attempts to escape reality. In these the protagonist is alive in space, almost against his will; his world is the cold and dark known to sub-human things.

There follows a series of poems dedicated to W. B. Yeats. Highly formal stylistically, these poems are related to the sixteenth century, with lines severely end-stopped, for the most part.

Finally comes a sequence of longish poems, 'Meditations of

an Old Woman'. The protagonist is modelled, in part, after my own mother, now dead, whose favourite reading was the Bible, Jane Austen, and Dostoevsky – in other words, a gentle, highly articulate old lady believing in the glories of the world, yet fully conscious of its evils. These poems use a technique of developing themes alternately, a method employed in 'Praise to the End!', an earlier sequence, a kind of spiritual autobiography beginning with the very small child. Of these last poems I have said: 'Much of the action is implied or, particularly in the case of erotic experience, rendered obliquely. The revelation of the identity of the speaker may itself be a part of the drama; or, in some instance, in a dream sequence, his identity may merge with someone else's, or be deliberately blurred.'* This struggle for spiritual identity is, of course, one of the perpetual recurrences. (This is not the same as the fight of the adolescent personality for recognition in the 'real' world.) Disassociation often precedes a new state of clarity.

Rhythmically, it's the spring and rush of the child I'm after – and Gammer Gurton's concision: *mutterchen's* wisdom. Most of the time the material seems to demand a varied short line. I believe that, in this kind of poem, the poet, in order to be true to what is most universal in himself, should not rely on allusion; should not comment or employ many judgment words; should not meditate (or maunder). He must scorn being 'mysterious' or loosely oracular, but be willing to face up to genuine mystery. His language must be compelling and immediate: he must create an actuality. He must be able to telescope image and symbol, if necessary, without relying on the obvious connectives: to speak in a kind of psychic shorthand when his protagonist is under great stress. He must be able to shift his rhythms rapidly, the 'tension'. He works intuitively, and the final form of his poem must be imaginatively right. If intensity has compressed the

* In *Midcentury American Poets*, edited by John Ciardi (Twayne Publishers, Boston, 1950).

language so it seems, on early reading, obscure, this obscurity should break open suddenly for the serious reader who can hear the language: the 'meaning' itself should come as a dramatic revelation, an excitement. The clues will be scattered richly – as life scatters them; the symbols will mean what they usually mean – and sometimes something more . . .

Words for the Wind opens with some very plain little bits of verse and descriptive pieces about a greenhouse I grew up in and around. But it is the longish pieces that really break the ground – if any ground is broken. And it is these that I hope the younger readers, in particular, will come to cherish.

I think of myself as a poet of love, a poet of praise. And I wish to be read aloud.

Words for the Wind 1957

Anne Rouse

Whether they describe a football hooligan, a cicada, or a secretary's retirement, poems need to be driven from within. Lacking a strong psychological impetus, however murky, poems become mere doodling, practice for the real thing. In a real poem, the words start up their own life and force both reader and writer to think freshly. Even my neighbourhood, the road I walk along every day, looks different through the intermediary of language.

The effect aimed for in writing, I believe, should be a chemical one: not the formula or record of an explosion, but the explosion itself. Achieving this is rarely a straightforward business. Letter-writing, getting ready for work (the work that pays the bills), the basic requirements of sociability – such duties can fall embarrassingly second to the demands of a given poem. Personal disorder increases as one tries to achieve its opposite on the page. After some while it becomes clear that the poem, or rather the poet, has failed, and that further tinkering won't help. Too bad: that's, as they say, the deal. I noticed in putting together *Sunset Grill* that the least honest phrases almost always sound wrong – tinny or infelicitous. These were the classic Freudian slips, the little spots of decay in syntax or grammar, the rhythmic hiccough, the excesses of discord, the metaphor turned to mud. Although there are innumerable ways of going astray in a poem, playing safe is no option. A safe poem is the postcard one mails to the office. Two ideas about poetry influenced me for many years. One was Pound's dictum that poetry is condensation. Reading that, I began to devise poems like Gordian knots, tightened to the point of unintelligibility.

Later, I was intrigued by an editorial comment of Ted Hughes, that the mature Sylvia Plath never discarded a poem. Both remarks encouraged me to work with material for longer periods than I had ever thought necessary. A generation of aspiring writers seemed to feel, after the Beat era, that we could simply 'let it flow'. The resulting poems were often dreary to read.

I've mentioned the personal and the formal, but of course poetry is also an engagement with the world. Although I've lived in north London many years, I'm still learning its accents and vocabularies. Jobs in the NHS and a mental health charity have made the culture progressively more intelligible and meaningful to me.

The Sunset Grill, a bar off a highway an ocean away, is meaningful too. For me it represents the rhythmic, romantic side of America, an oasis in the far suburbs. Having been raised nearby, I like to think that restless, polyglot Upper Holloway would approve of it. I've taken the poet's liberty of marrying them up.

Sunset Grill 1993

Carol Rumens

The first poem of mine to be published was in the *Daily Sketch.* This long-defunct tabloid had announced a search for English children poets, stimulated by (what else?) competition with France, which had Minou Drouet. I was shocked when I saw my effort in print – it had been submitted without my knowledge – and thus I've never forgotten it. 'Creative as the stars' seraphic host. / Words of great feeling from thy lips fall free. / Poet of the age, I love thee most, / Mortal, with thoughts of immortality.'

Edith Sitwell, the dedicatee, was the only poet I knew for sure was alive, because I'd seen her on the box. The grown-ups jeered at her, but I thought she was dashing. Would I look like her one day, if I became a poetess? I hoped so. I admired her poems, too, though I preferred Milton. The pages of my eleventh-birthday gift, *Golden Treasury*, always fell open at 'L'Allegro' and 'Il Pensoroso'. The more long words a poem had, the more glitter and colour and taste and smell, the better I liked it.

I didn't always aim for the seraphic heights. Around the same time I wrote a string of couplets in a more down-to-earth descriptive style, praising my favourite breakfast cereal. Cannily I sent it off to the manufacturers. I was nonetheless overwhelmed when, a few weeks later, a huge carton arrived, packed wall-to-wall with boxes of Sugar Puffs. No wonder I failed to give up scribbling, after a start like that.

It still goes on, the game of Seraphic Host v. Sugar Puffs. I want my poem to be emotionally true, always, and descriptively true, sometimes, but I'm not satisfied unless I get a bit of purely verbal sparkle onto the page. I hugely admire the Northern Irish, who seem so good at this – from W. R. Rodgers and Louis MacNeice to Ciaran Carson and (very differently) Medbh McGuckian. But my own personal muse tells me I must write closer to my voice – by which I mean the physical organ, its earliest, earthiest vocabularies and, above all, my own accent. As I now see it, such obligations are not confined to northerners.

I feel for my voice as a small wild animal, trapped long ago and trained to do all kinds of tricks. Language control was the dominant feature in a household unhappy with its class, hopeful of its upward mobility. I was constantly threatened as a child with the monster of 'being common' – which chiefly meant speaking like our upstairs neighbours, who said 'ain't'. Yet Grandma, our landlady, who went regularly to church in a flowery hat and gave posh teas, said 'in't it?' for 'isn't it?' and this was wrong too, more dangerously wrong because too close for criticism. I remember my mother being uncharacteristically silent and embarrassed when I pointed out (in private) this quirk of her mother's speech.

From time to time I've let my voice go wild for a bit, but having to give readings and do university residencies has always brought back the anxieties about speaking 'properly'. I can see, now, that as a younger woman I wrote too many poems in a would-be polite, fit-to-be-in-literary-company sort of accent. An authoritative middle-class English voice, male or female, still has the power to make me physically curl up and to produce, in reply, a voice like a poodle in a ruff.

In a Northern Irish journal not long ago there was an article on dialect words and idioms by the Belfast-born scholar John Wilson Foster. I found it a delightful piece of research, especially as I read it with so many jolts of recognition. Many of the 'sayings' had been around in the south London of my childhood. And when, recently, near where I live, I overheard an older woman remark to her friend, 'You see some sights when you haven't got your gun!' I was almost in the presence of my mother (who died three months ago, and to whom *Best China Sky* is dedicated). How she loved to vilify the dress-sense of friends and neighbours in those deliciously terrifying words. She probably said it about Edith Sitwell, come to think.

Maybe it's because I'm a Londoner in Belfast ('salt rebuff' answering to 'salt rebuff') that I want to let the animal out for a decent run in the fields and forests before we call it a day.

Best China Sky 1995

When I worked in Belfast, tuning into the live poetic conversation going on around me provided a wonderful source of energy and ideas, even if the notion that I was participating in it seems, retrospectively, a little optimistic. Now I'm in North Wales, where, though there are similarities, the emphases are altered. I'm not connected to the Anglo-Welsh poetry debate – it's just not audible on my side of the Bangor mountain, and I remain, perhaps complacently, ignorant of its passions and its themes. What I do know, from talking to Welsh poets, is that Welsh-language poetry, like Irish, is richly and joyously alive. Being more deeply woven into its social context, it remains closed to outsiders, however. For me, it's like living above an underground spring whose water is a distant rush of sound or over an intricate system of limestone caves that make an occasional hollow echo beneath my footfall. There is no well to be sunk, no pot-hole to be squeezed through, no way to access, as a non-Welsh speaker, this potent source.

Communities originating from Bardic societies sustain the public and social aspects of poetry. Welsh poets laugh at the idea of a separate category of Performance Poetry: isn't poetry always performance? People get together in each other's homes, as well as at Eisteddfods; amateur poets, unknown to the outside world, but valued in their communities, are in demand to compose verses for special occasions. As with the Bards, formal prerequisites smooth their way. To celebrate the birthday of a distant relative, for instance, and depend romantically on personal inspiration, would be a tall order, but if you are required to compose in a set form, the form to some degree finds not only the words but the pulse of feeling for you.

Even on the fringes of such communities, a poetic receiver perhaps can pick up one or two sound-waves. My love of the poetic forms, renewed in Belfast, continues to be refreshed through teaching. The usual suspects (sestina, villanelle, ballad, triolet, sonnet) line up in *Hex*. Some react to public events. Poetry's responsibility is response: to prise the mass-produced image from its frame and reinstate it in the real time of human feeling. I want my poems to mean as well as be. It's probably significant that the country which gave us those extreme distrusters of communication, the L=A=N=G=U=A=G=E poets, deals in such language-lies as War on Terrorism.

While writing my title poem, I succumbed to a sudden zest for riding the wave-crests of vowel sounds over the Anglo-Saxon pebble-beach of alliteration. Afterwards, I wondered if I'd caught a stray notion from that lovely Welsh form, the *cynghanedd*. The technique of writing harmony (which is what *cynghanedd* means) may form the next stage of my education. Luckily for haphazard autodidacts like myself, there's no poetic school-leaving age.

Hex 2002

Vernon Scannell

I find it very difficult to talk about my own verse because I'm afraid of sounding over-earnest and portentous, and it is one of my most firmly held beliefs that literary puritanism has, for a long time, done great damage in obfuscating the real purpose of reading or writing poetry. I believe that, above all, poetry must delight, though I must be careful here to say what I mean by delight. First, what I do not mean is that the poet should write about particularly delightful experiences in mellifluous language. I mean that he should aim at absolute honesty, total fidelity to the experience, whatever it may be, which has started his poem off, and, calling upon all his resources of technique, imagination, intelligence, vocabulary and memory, he should build a structure of words which, working upon both the conscious and unconscious instruments of reception in his reader, will thrill him in a way that no other art form can do. (We must remember here that thrill literally means to pierce, and that's the way I am using it.)

On looking through the verses I've written during the past few years I notice a growing preoccupation with the sense of mortality and also an uneasiness, a feeling, that has lately become almost an obsession, of anonymous menace. Of course, this may be at least partly explained in terms of the international situation and the great, flesh-eating fungus of the Bomb that looms at the boundaries, or maybe at the centre, of everybody's consciousness. But not entirely. For me it's something else: the chronic unease and fear are not caused by man's machines alone but by man himself. More and more I find myself appalled by man's inhumanity to man, by the ruthless, cannibalistic monster that he is, which means, of course, by the monster that I am. I begin to believe in the evil of man with an almost religious intensity, and then, in the miasmas of disgust and despair, I am suddenly cleansed and dazzled by an act of simple kindness, of tenderness or nobility, and hope comes up again like passion. It is this ambivalence towards the vile, comic and beautiful fact of existence that I've tried to get into the poems in *A Sense of Danger*.

A Sense of Danger 1962

Anne Sexton

What can I say? To apologise or advertise? To be read aloud or silently? To try to write one poem that is interesting just because you are tired of so much poetry that seems boring? To write words about life instead of seizing it with a camera? To explain what ought to be felt? I can't say. I can tell you that the poems are about insanity and recovery, the death of parents, lust and self-pity, an anger with God, a promise to a child. I hope they are not too cruel. I think maybe they are. And yet I don't want to disarm anyone with an afterthought of modesty or indifference. I care terribly. I always did.

What else is important? I am not sure. It is awkward for me to try to explain my work to you. Are they poems at all? All poets lie. Yet it is our function to try to tell the truth. The attempt to do this is what I call 'a poem'. As I said once in a poem, 'a writer is essentially a crook. With used furniture he makes a tree.' What I have tried to do is to make the non-verbal verbal; to make a section of my life an entity – a something on a page. These *Selected Poems* are only badly weeded poems from two books that cover the span of five years of writing; and by weeded I do mean that pulling out of the worst, the rankest amateur growth, and still leaving in some that are flagrant enough to seem embarrassing.

If you care about form, about half are in form of some sort. But form, for me, is a trick to deceive myself, not you but me. When I am finished with this trickery, I often hide it so that no one can see that I had my back to the wall at the time. Who, after all, wants to be caught doing an acrostic while they thought they were really telling all? What I mean to say is that some poems are too difficult to write without controls of some sort. An impossible syllabic count, an intricate rhyme scheme puts fear in its place. In the worst incidents of terror in my life I have found myself saying the child-lucky prayer, a rhyme such as 'one, two, buckle my shoe' or 'one for the penny, two for the show'. To count and rhyme as if God would listen. Numbers and sounds function for the last death-breath-twentieth-shibboleth. I use them when I hurt the most. I make up a cage that is strong enough to hold the poem in, as in the circus, as with the wild animal. Form acts like a superego, permitting this angry thing to enter the arena. The other poems are not so different. When I am lying best, I call them songs. They are no such thing. My cage was somewhere else, that's all.

Finally, I'd like to say that most of my poems tell stories. Many of them are true. Others are about lives I haven't led. Yet I keep thinking . . . Someone has to believe them! I hope someone will.

Selected Poems 1964

Jo Shapcott

I think of *My Life Asleep* as a quiet book. I can spot three distinct kinds of poem in it: a number of discursive and meditative pieces; some small lyrics, often in other voices, and often with animals at the centre; and a series of love poems based very loosely on Rilke's sequence *Les Roses.*

The discursive poems reflect on Englishness, gender and identity, and they feel big. I won't say more about them now. Poems like these are right at the heart of my current writing and I have the superstitious feeling – shared by many writers – that telling too much about them too early might stop me in my tracks.

The smaller lyrics allow for comedy – or, more often, tragi-comedy – and strangeness. They often involve animals. Someone once described the way animal characters weave through my poems as having the effect of marrying Jane Austen with Fred Quimby. It's not just me. Philosophers and artists from the earliest times have been fascinated with animals. They are the main subject of one of the first forms of human expression, cave painting, and we are still dependent on them for food, clothing, company and more. Many of the first riddles and poems in all languages are beast-based and animals have prowled their way through the canon ever since. In almost every case human characteristics are read into animal behaviour or appearance. There are some exceptions which are more about 'pure' observation, an admiration of nature and a belief in its fundamental separation from strictly human nature. I once met a poet of this school who genuinely believed that he could accurately and objectively depict reality in general and nature in particular. On reading one of my poems which featured a rather cartoon-like mischievous sheep, he rejected the whole thing, saying, correctly of course, 'But sheep simply wouldn't behave like that.'

But I am interested in transcendence as well as nature study. There is something compelling about the closeness of animals to us, as underlined by the links implicit in causing us to grant them their own kingdom and their own souls at all. Animals make us wonder how we can know them, how we can know anything 'other' at all, and how we can know ourselves. So it is that the many voices in *My Life Asleep*, particularly those of the animals, allow me to say more about politics, love, war – and now death – than I possibly could on my own.

For a while now, I've been obsessed with the poems Rilke wrote in French. This interest started with a sequence called 'The Windows', which went into *Phrase Book*. For the purposes of translation, or making versions, it's the French poems which interest me most, maybe because he's working in a language that's not his own. There's an appealing lightness, a frothiness, almost, that appears when he's away from the German. The French poems are not right at the centre of his work, though still fascinating, and offer a special freedom because of that. I can't imagine mucking around with the Elegies in quite the same way. In *My Life Asleep*, the Rilke sequence is called *Les Roses*. He wrote twenty-seven tiny rose poems and to him they represent, I think, twenty-seven different lovers or even twenty-seven different sets of female genitalia. He addresses the roses in his poems, calls them 'you' and 'O rose'. I've turned it round, given the rose – a traditional male image of the female – her own voice. Each one is, in its way, a small argument against the original Rilke version: 'No it's not like that, it's like this.' But they're still, above all, a sequence of love poems or, perhaps, one extended love poem.

My Life Asleep 1998

Penelope Shuttle

In our part of the world, Cornwall, peninsula, vulnerable, Atlantic-antiphonal, worm-warrened by mine-galleries almost all long abandoned, we have occasional minor earthquakes, one of which is described in my poem 'Snakes and Quakes', with its serpentineness – far, far down the earth zigzags like a snake. Only to be expected, then, that a number of the poems in *Adventures with My Horse* have to do with the other kind of 'when the earth moves'; as it is the erotic adventure that has occupied my thoughts a fair deal during the three years of writing these poems. More seriously, I share Engels's view (given in *The Origin of Family*) that the 'individual sexual love', as developed within the 'superior form of sexual relations that monogamy is', gives human beings 'the greatest moral progress'. In poems such as 'Overnight', 'The Fig Tree' and 'Lovers in a Picture', I have tried to speak of this morality in love.

What Horse? What other adventures? As I was writing, the heart of that energy of imagination, so close to sexual energy, needed, I found, to be given an actual personality, a physicality, and this turned out to be that of a Horse. The Horse is both a real horse, flesh and blood, and the animal force of imagination. The adventures are those of the sensual life and the Horse (curvetting, standing in wait, free as air, curbed or curbing) was the shape that the spirit of those Adventures took.

What's my job? Sometimes to be the rider? Yes. Sometimes to be the horse? Yes. Women have a huge dynamo of energy that is focused in our physical ability to conceive and bear children, but how many of us will want to have a great many children? We have one, or two, or three, and then what? Because the energy goes on, cycle after cycle after cycle. What's it for?

For me, it engendered a son of poetry. That force shoving us on and on to create more persons, confusing inner and outer needs, had to be channelled; this inward son (who appeared in poems in my earlier book *The Lion from Rio*) grew, became companion and prophet; he stayed as son in the poems 'Seventh Son' and 'Mother and Son', but he also became the Horse.

In the title poem of the book both Horse and boy appear. There's a boy who takes on the nature of a horse both to resist and yet to appeal to his mother, who is withdrawn and unloving. The boy makes himself into *another*, a horse, then makes himself a message. Only when the message reaches the mother, moving her to see him not as a troublesome child but as a creature with his own strong and animal innocence, a horse, can she love him as a child and become his mother. It is 'about' the way the perception of one person by another changes and the way that changed perception in turn alters the initiator of the process, in this instance of a vital emotional relationship.

There are other poems, other adventures with other animals – pig, cow, fox, snake; these animals either speak or are imagined in their secret studies. The voice of the pig speaks what she knows as well as any woman; the snake dreams. We desire to know our human feeling better. It is through these animals comprehending and reflecting back to us the full scope of their senses (especially the non-visual) that we gain fuller use of our own; of what perhaps we have forgotten, never knew, or are contemptuous of; by looking at, guessing at the animal's oblique yet relevant viewpoint, things move on, out of the darkness.

If feminist writing must exist, and if this is it, then it travels in my poems from and to a further place that is non-nihilist, non-sadistic, non-disposable.

Adventures with My Horse **1988**

Charles Simic

Didn't know I was doing it. Had the notion I was living a nice, quiet life patting the children on the head, going for a Sunday drive, in short, thriving. Useless words. My smile faded the day I found a man asleep on my steps. Why? I said stepping over him carefully. Spent the night on the other side of the door trying to hear him breathe. At daybreak, I made tea and took it to him, but he was gone, leaving a hat. Surely not far, I figured, walking out in robe and slippers into the snowy New York street, peeking in doorways. I even tried the locked church door. The cup and the hat in my hands made me seem even more daffy entering a dark alley. The sleepers woke, one or two poked their raw eyes out of their rags, puzzled. What did the other fellow look like, I wondered, backing out, distancing myself with a nod, while recalling the time an elderly, well-dressed man came up to me in the street to say I'm the spit and image of his long-dead brother. Well, what do you reply to that? I didn't. I just thought of a title for a book.

The book itself is made up of poems written as early as 1965 and as late as 1995. One longish sequence called 'White' is thoroughly revised; the rest I left alone. It cannot be regarded as a 'selected poems' since it doesn't include several books that made up *Frightening Toys*, my earlier Faber volume. I've always been a great believer and practitioner of collage, so this book was put together in that spirit. A book, then, like an American city, where intention and chance create many surprising and (hopefully!) satisfying juxtapositions.

My metaphysics: what a fearful man concocts in the dark of

gods and devils while his beloved is snoring away on the very same pillow. I find in myself two contradictory impulses: I'm a historical pessimist and a literary optimist. Armies tearing each other apart, bombed cities, prisons and concentration camps, orphan factories working around the clock, that's what this century has been all about. The chance that the future is going to be any different is slim in my view. On the other hand, I still have high hopes for poetry. Reality, truth, imagination – or whatever name you have for the genuine – can still be found in poems.

Looking for Trouble 1997

Burns Singer

I do not like writing poetry. It frightens me. I do everything I can to avoid it – trying to busy myself with all sorts of other occupations, many of them destructive to any small talent I may possess.

How, then, does it come about that, since the age of six, I have written continuously and, in so far as I can compute it, have scrawled down at least fifty thousand lines of verse? The best answer probably lies in a suggestion first made by Renan: if a man has a vocation for any particular activity it unfits him for all others. No matter how consistently he tries to escape, the external circumstances of his life will so arrange themselves that he is forced back into his original profession.

I, at any rate, have tried to be a school-teacher, a scientist, a book-seller, and so forth, but, by dint of an insane and abominable laziness, I have always landed back with a pen in my hand, face to face with the threatening whiteness of a virgin piece of paper. Even now, when I write books for a living, my mind continually wanders into the stricter fastnesses of the poetic responsibility.

It is this responsibility that frightens me. Most forms of composition can be achieved by an urbane and intelligent attachment to the facts of life and the rules of grammar. But, in poetry, grammar ceases to exist and the facts to matter. The poet is landed with the task of creating an autonomous system of rules parallel to those of grammar and of inter-related images that reflect, by an unknown process, both the facts and their transformation, through one another and beyond any of them, into the kind of meaning that used to be called spiritual.

I am sorry if this sounds complicated. Yet I hope it does, because poetry is complicated and a great deal of harm can be done by pretending it is simple. Milton, on the other hand, was right when he said that poetry should be simple – as *Paradise Lost* is simple – but this simplicity must be arrived at by a very devious route or it will not be poetry. On this route it is easy to get lost in an experimental and metaphysical jungle. And it is frightening to be lost. That is another reason why writing poetry frightens me. It is none the less necessary that somebody should arrive at a simple spiritual statement – and that is why I risk getting lost.

Still and All **1957**

Robin Skelton

My life does not matter. It has been very like everybody else's. Only its creativity matters – the way in which it has been given to it to express itself in poetry. Poems have entered it, altered it, possessed it almost as long as I can remember. I have tried for twenty years to let the poems come, to learn the craft of verse that they may not be born misshapen, and to understand something about the nature of poetry. I have even written a book about the poetic process. But however hard I work, however frequently I revise, amend, polish, and discard, I can never feel that I dare accept responsibility for the results. I am responsible for the mistakes, the clumsiness, but not for the successes – the extraordinary way in which the words form inevitable significances and images that my everyday mind, so much slower, colder, and more inhibited, can only wonder at. So if I write about my poems, I write either as a craftsman, whose job is really only that of a patcher and mender, and whose most ingenious devices are never as ingenious as the devices that happen without his help, or another reader. There are critics to talk about what craftsmanship these poems show, and you can read the poems yourselves without my leaning impertinently over your shoulder.

Of course I do have views about my own poetry. I sometimes even imagine that I know what I am trying to do, though mostly such opinions are mere deductions from past work, and a new poem very often shows them to be false. For example, I am at present under the impression that my work must more and more try to express perceptions of eternity. We dwell in eternity but perceive our dwelling place too rarely. Chained down by strong illusions of life as dominated by Time, Sequence, and Causality, we only occasionally see. What do we see when we escape? That is what I must allow my poems to tell me. And I must allow them also to adopt different voices, to look through different windows. I must not force them all into one mannered mould, but learn my craft well enough for them to have freedom to range. I must learn every form from lyric to epic – though I do not imagine that I will ever try to write an epic. I must study poetic drama in particular, for a play forced itself upon me only a little while ago, and, though completed, I think it has suffered because I don't know the craft of it well enough. But above all I must remain unsatisfied, and continually put poetry before all other things. Putting poetry first means not only writing it but teaching it, and, in trying to teach it, trying also to teach the truths it expresses.

It's a hefty programme, and I must confess that I doubt if I could ever have got as far as even these unequal beginnings without a tremendous lot of help. No words can express what I owe to the criticism, encouragement, and patience of my friends, while poetry itself falters before my debt to my wife. They have made these poems possible, and I am grateful for this opportunity to say thank you.

I am saying thank you for a great deal. In the act of creation the mind takes on a rare sensitivity, a triumphant clarity; the whole personality seems to operate as a unity, and with rapidity and passion. It seems that one has escaped from time into eternity, or returned to Eden, where there is nothing inanimate and all is significant of truth. Then one feels that man is indeed made in God's image and is essentially a creator; one has entered into a new fullness of being. It is impossible to describe the humility and the pride of that experience. People who help anyone to experience the creative act, to develop their creative powers and perceptions, are doing something of more importance than the poems, paintings, sonatas, or sculptures that result.

They are revealing the Kingdom of Heaven within us. It would be as well, also, to thank God.

Patmos and Other Poems 1955

Ian Crichton Smith

The first section of the book, the sequence 'The Village', was written some years ago when I came to live in the village of Taynuilt, in Argyll. It reflects my sense of wonder at the landscape, animals etc., after I had lived in a town for a long time. For I found myself in the presence of the perpetual activity of nature – flowers, trees, rabbits, weasels – in a way which I hadn't sensed so evidently before, though in fact I had been brought up in a village in Lewis. There was a luxuriance of vegetation which I hadn't encountered before. Also it was good to return to a real community where one was known and valued. The village too had a permanence which I set against the transient images of the town – old worn paths, cemetery, church. Its stories were traditional and often repetitive. The first poem in the sequence is a farewell to the town I had left but the rest are a celebration of the village.

The second section of the book is a miscellany of poems which deal with other places, other concerns, since in fact though I live in the village my imagination does not wholly remain there. Thus in the second section there is a poem about Belfast, a flawed community, which arose from a visit to that city. I have two poems about apartheid which I intensely hate, since again there we have artificially created communities set up for a supposedly inferior race.

My village therefore may be a central concern for me but beyond it there are echoes of war, injustices, violence, evil. It is a precious community but there are other areas of the world which are not so fortunate.

Nor of course do I forget that within that precious area there are also cruelties: e.g. from a human point of view the cruelties animals inflict on each other, emigration (in the past), some loneliness, the shadow of nuclear war which hangs over all of us. Nevertheless the village represents a home from which I can explore, and expatiate on that larger contemporary world.

The book as a whole represents my present position, as one who inhabits the village but also travels a great deal, and reflects on the other areas of the world. The concept of community is important to me, as one who grew up in one. It sometimes seems to me that the solution to much contemporary isolation, namelessness, violence, would be a return to community and that the graffiti scrawled over walls in cities are the cries of the anonymous ones to be recognised and named and valued. These often misspelt statements on the open blackboards of the world are an indictment of the fact that we have lost many of the values of community and that without retreating into a fabled paradise we can perhaps recover them again.

The Village 1989

Ken Smith

Wild root – a contradiction, a paradox, a species of tumbleweed, the name of a place far to the west, or maybe a woman's secret name for her lover that's no secret any more. Some years ago I invented a press whose only publication was the first version of my long poem 'Fox Running' and called it Rolling Moss. Same idea. An image of the tension between the desire to stay home with the one I love and grow tomatoes in my own neck of the neighbourhood, and the longing 'to goon' as Chaucer remarks 'on pilgrimages', usually in the spring – surely an ancient seasonal urge. 'Whan that Aprill with his shoores soote . . .' 'The winds of March that made my heart a dancer.'

For I love travelling, and I enjoy exploring strange cities, other people's countries, places where I haven't a clue in the language, and figuring it out. Or not, as the case may be. I dread departures: 'no man above mould . . . that before seafaring does not fear a little / whither the Lord will lead him in the end'. I love arrivals, and then moving on, but most I love coming home again with objects found along the way, tales to tell, characters to describe, new jokes, pages of my notebook covered in scribblings. Somehow I keep travelling further and further east, where lately I've been dumbstruck by the Carpathians and the Caucasus, wondering to which peak Prometheus was chained. In Tbilisi I heard a cock crowing, his call a distinct Cau-ca-si-an that he cried repeatedly to announce his identity. No self doubt there. And in the same dark marvellous mad city I talked with a woman called Medea who was from western Georgia – Greek Colchis – and whose hair was a silver rather than a golden fleece, and no, she had never murdered her children.

Neruda: 'I take great vacations outside of time.' And Dr Johnson, more soberly: 'The use of travel is to regulate imagination with reality.' I don't know that travel broadens the mind, but it surely whips things up in there. The fact is if I don't take long journeys and meet different strangers, I grow blunt and rusty like a knife left out in the rain. I think of the world as a great marketplace where I go hunter-gathering for images and words and ideas.

'Two hearts for fifty pence,' a woman calls on my local market. She's selling lettuces. And a white van goes by bearing the slogan 'Read the World'. That's what I'm doing, that's what I do. I'm an earwigger and an observer. I frequent railway stations and markets and the back of magistrates' courts, and nip in and out of guided tours, and anything that appeals to me in the way of words I'll snatch into my notebook, perhaps to appear later as the occasion of a poem or just a voice flitting through: 'Tarbert, this godforsaken hole: I've seen better on a card of buttons: waggontruss, windbrace; I was one chopstick short of a pot noodle.' I'm a word thief, and don't care what the sources are. For me there's no pecking order as to where the words come from: books, overheard in the pub or on a bus, glimpsed from the corner of an eye in a newspaper someone else is reading, machine language, graffiti: they're all interesting. Speaking of graffiti, here's one from the men's room of a bar in Cambridge, Mass.: 'The only time I ever refused a drink I misunderstood the question.'

And when I'm home there's still the tomatoes, and from time to time I make masks out of chicken wire and papier mâché. It distracts me, keeps my hands busy so my mind is free to wander, and sometimes when a face begins to form from the mess of paper and paste, questions swim up as to who this character is, and sometimes there's someone with a name and a history. Sometimes it may be just a line, or the start of something. And sometimes the whole poem. My methods are serendipity. I've been called a bricoleur, someone forever reassembling the broken bits of the world into new shapes. I thought the word, in Lévi-Strauss's term, meant beachcomber, but when I looked it up I found it defined as a do-it-yourselfer. I really don't mind; I'm easy with both definitions. Serendipity. I like lists. Fact is I'm a collector of junk, 'scavenger of skips' always on the look-out for surprises, hidden links, coincidences, images and phrases to be recycled. I collect postage stamps, signs, tickets, maps, books, sardine tins, shells, stones, feathers, buttons, leaves, bits of wood river-scrubbed into the faces of animals and birds, a compartmented box for a collection of toy legs found in the street, a board for the tacked-up gleanings of the beach at Guincho in Portugal, furthest point west of Europe, so they say. And a rare treasure, found abandoned in a hotel drawer, that felt addressed to me: *Catalogue d'objets introuvables*, by Jaques Carelamns, published by France Loisirs, Paris, 1969, a marvellous collection of drawings of impossible and therefore undiscoverable objects.

And borders, in all their manifestations, fascinate me, those tense edgy places of walls and fences and boundaries – borders political and geographic and psychological, transitions between one condition and the next: past and future, sanity and nonsense, life and death. Passing through them is to enter a place where the rules have changed, and are unknown, and this focuses my attention, so that I think in travelling I'm honing the edges of my hearing, sharpening the blades of words.

Words, words, words. And another collection, of visas and passport stamps. 'I am the Emperor, and I want noodles.'

Wild Root 1998

Pauline Stainer

I have always been grabbed by those glimpses which reassess the world: the small child scuffing leaves who turns up maggots working the breast of a bird; the great cats crossing the frozen moat into the public enclosure; the girl who, after eye surgery, sees women playing bowls in the hospital grounds transfigured into figures at an unidentified miracle; the X-ray of an embryo held to the light until the flesh glows into sacrament; wine waiters at a wedding glancing up through the gargoyles before a woman leaps from the tower; the monk who, coming upon a dead girl, is crazed by the sexuality of the drowned.

The image – and the moment. Perhaps for me they are indistinguishable, the poems slung from that glass hinge. Certainly much of my writing is inspired by art: Leonardo failing to divine the reciprocating pump of the heart; the cave painter taking up his handaxe to correct the engraved breast of a beast; the disturbing coolness with which Pilate's wife watches Christ from each impression of Rembrandt's etching plant; Saskia photographed in reflected light under the microscope, wearing Arcadian costume on a quartzite ground. Every now and then the Muse drops her domino mask, an owl strikes the windscreen, leaves its powdered image on the glass.

As I write this article, I am on holiday in West Africa. Alien territory gives a sharpness to the ambivalence of the image. The air is full of frequencies from an ivory coast – sea fog and dropping spices, the silent magnetism of cargo ships sliding into the haze; men paragliding over the slave routes. I touch the slow-burning fuse of the hibiscus – remember vermilion is quicksilver and sulphur. Poetry springs from such vicarious inspiritings. I hear the tapping hammer. The palm tapper is girdled to the trunk; he catches the sap in a gourd. Like me, he bleeds the source.

I am wary of explaining poetry. Metaphor is a dark and arterial currency. We sleepwalk into the well. What absorbs me is incarnating the image; finding the context where the scarlet particle jumps that free fall between writer and reader, and the sparking chamber ignites. The immediacy of paradise is things made whole. Magritte said, 'It is the power of enchantment which matters.' But it is more than that. I am driven to find a forgiving medium; to intinct the bread in the wine. Love is an infinite act.

Honeycomb **1989**

MATTHEW SWEENEY

Three things seem to me to have affected the writing of the poems in *Blue Shoes*. The first was the use of a house for the past six summers in the part of Donegal I come from. I have always written about my background, and being away gives such writing an objectivity that can be almost mythological in feel, but it can also become easily remembered. Going and living there again, even for one month a year, has brought back a necessary element of normality, and this has enabled me to find a way of writing about Donegal that is more consistent with the way I write about London, where I usually live. So although there are more Donegal-based pieces here than in my previous books, this is, I hope, more of a cohesive collection.

The second and most affecting thing was the death of two friends, one of them in shocking circumstances very early in the composition of the book. This disturbed me deeply and for a long period I could write nothing that wasn't prey to morbid fears. The most excessive of these efforts have been discarded, but there is still quite a high proportion of sombre pieces, certainly compared to my other collections. So much so that as I was reading the proofs, an extract from a review of a certain Julia Moore (1847–1920) came to mind: 'Julia is worse than a Gatling gun; I have counted twenty-one killed and nine wounded in the small volume she has given to the public.' I also noticed, however, that, as Louis MacNeice once put it, 'the grim elements are mixed with others' – chiefly a certain humour or offbeatness. Anyway, Julia's toll is safely out of reach.

Writing about death from a perspective of empathy, however,

meant I was also writing about life, and this brings me to the third thing – the discovery, or rediscovery in some cases, of a long list of American poets from Frost and Williams (W. C.) early in the century, through Plath and Lowell, to contemporary practitioners such as Dobyns and Williams (C. K.). (The influence of the American Studies Department on the library stock of East Anglia was a factor here.) The only common ground such Americans have, it seems to me, is an ability to find a new way of writing directly about the world they live in, when all possible new ways seem to have been used up. And a way that is not dependent on a showy use of language, but allows the poetry of the situation to reveal itself. This approach lets accessibility combine with subtlety, the public with the private – lets the poem crack open, suddenly or gradually, to reveal glimpses of the things that matter. I would hope to have learned something, in aspiration if not in execution, from writers like these.

Blue Shoes 1989

It is a poem just to mention driving into a strange barn to bide the passing of a thunderstorm, so wrote Robert Frost. And I take him literally. I don't like to explain. I don't think poetry should do this, though there are people out there who think differently. Another dead American, Robert Lowell, wrote that the author is an opportunist, and makes use of whatever comes to hand. I take him literally too. I have one poem that came from what a painter said – how if you took Donegal and cooked it in the oven you'd get Arizona. Another came from a notice in a Derry graveyard: 'Those who don't believe in life after death should be here after closing time.' A recipe for a stew of gazelle meat with Saharan truffles got another going. As did a streetlamp left permanently on; the sight of two children trying to plant a blown-off branch; an old man's gangrene-induced hallucinations in a hospital ward; a suicide story that was the talk of Donegal;

and a TV programme, years earlier, about a collection of bubble cars. In other words, the poems come from the world.

But the world, as glimpsed in the poems, can be distorted somewhat, the realism can be fractured. If this is more evident in this book than in any previous one, it is because of the influence of another book, a side-venture of mine, a book of poems for children, published earlier this year, called *The Flying Spring Onion*. These two books were written more or less simultaneously. I wouldn't know, when a poem was coming along, whether it would be an 'adult' poem or a 'children's' – although, in the writing, there would be no doubt whatsoever which category the poem would fall into.

Nevertheless, there was a clear cross-influence between the two books, and I remember a comment a friend of mine (a poet herself) made when I showed her the first of the children's poems – that they would be liberating for the other work. They were, and the main liberation was in the extension of the realism. Which, curiously, brings me back to my earliest attempts at writing in the seventies, when I hated realism, and was studying German, and my favourite writer was Kafka (still is). Which reminds me, I've always found Kafka's work hilarious (as he and his circle reportedly did), without taking away from the seriousness, for one minute. And that is an aim of mine too – to make the humorous and the serious coexist and enhance one another.

Cacti 1992

R. S. Thomas

I suppose that most poets dislike talking about their work. In my case it is not that I prefer not to, but that I don't know what to say. I never do discuss it; partly because I live a rather sequestered life, and rarely meet those who could or would talk about such things, and partly from a habit of non-introspection. If I were to begin speaking about poetry, or my sort of poetry, it would be a case of trying out a lot of phrases and statements, and realising in the end that one was only labouring a point, or discovering how unsatisfactory words were. Which would be to repeat clumsily in prose what Mr T. S. Eliot has already put more neatly in verse. Therefore I have preferred to make a contribution in verse myself. I am sorry not to be more helpful.

Tares 1961

I am a Welshman who has lived most of his life in Wales. I speak its language and know its problems, as well as its history and literature. These facts are responsible for some of the poems. As Welsh people form a very small proportion of the population of these islands, the appeal of such poems will be limited. A large majority of the people of the United Kingdom, Welsh or otherwise, is urban and participant in the scientific-technological revolution. Of what significance to them are the poetic statements of one who has deliberately kept to the backwaters of rural life, concerning himself with the things that are passing away? I am a priest of the Christian Church, another minority position, which will appear reactionary and functionless to most people. Yet all these facts about me have had some share in the production of the poems in this book.

I do not wish to isolate myself from my fellow poets. While each of us may be striving after some personal identity in his poetry, the difficulties of writing it are common to us all: the effort to marry the words and the tune; the struggle to keep the mind moving poetically; the concern to get right on paper what seemed right in the head; the task of avoiding propaganda, that is of exalting the message at the expense of the medium, or alternatively of perfecting the technique at the expense of the content.

Added to all this are the difficulties arising from the nature of contemporary society, transitional between the old one of the humanities and the new technological one. A poet is traditionally the custodian of language, as well as its renewer. In the age of the computer and the mass media, the proliferation of terms, the commercial inflation of adjectives, the encroachment of the novelist, can he still sustain his role? I do not wish to generalise a personal failure of talent. When the genius appears, he does easily what had seemed impossible. The poet of the new age may already have been hatched in some incubator or other. For myself I cannot boast even a guitar. I play on a small pipe, a little aside from the main road. But thank you for listening.

Not That He Brought Flowers 1968

It is heartening at this rather advanced stage of my life to find that the Poetry Book Society panel does not consider that the Muse has completely forsaken me, or that my work has lost relevance. Heartening also that they have not too frivolously dismissed these poems because they speak of Christianity to a generation that has largely turned its back on such. Or perhaps some consider that it is the Church rather than Christianity that is irrelevant. One has noticed the gradual shrinking of the clerical collar to what is little more than a white spot under the chin, as the clergy have lost their nerve or at least become increasingly embarrassed by their role. And it may be giving hostages to fortune to put a parson on the dust-jacket, as Bloodaxe did with my *Selected Poems*. However, being retired some years now I have discarded the dog-collar, so that any proselytising on my part is implicit rather than explicit.

Again it is to give hostages for a poet to try to explain his aims, if he has failed to achieve them in verse. One is reminded of Eleanora Duse: if I could express my meaning in words, why should I go to the immense trouble of dancing it? A poet has to use words, but let him at least restrict himself to poetry and not dilute his message to a prose trickle. That said, then, let me hope that the title of this book is self-explanatory. Perhaps one of the criticisms brought against the Church was that it was too glib, too pat. Yet to some of the greatest of its members like Pascal, Kierkegaard, Hopkins and Simone Weil, adherence to it meant mainly a bitter struggle against inner darkness and external misunderstanding.

In the late twentieth century in the wake of two terrible wars, in the shadow of the nuclear bomb and vis-à-vis the demonstrations by nuclear physicists of the contradictions of reality such as we know it, belief in God, immortality and spiritual values is more difficult than it has ever been. In my *Penguin Anthology of Religious Verse* of some years ago I tried to extend the boundaries of the adjective 'religious'. In the present sequence I have tried to face the fact that so many glib or conventional versions of the Christian message can be turned topsy-turvy by current thinking. Yet because that same thought invites the rejoinder that, if we cannot prove that God is, neither can we prove that he is not, I have tried to set up the counter-rhythm or counter-dialectic of poems which answer the dismissive or derisive ones with the suggestion: Perhaps there is SOMEONE. Perhaps there is something in it after all. I am haunted by the geometrical austerity of the Cross. Language is in crisis. Science predominates, not least, as in music, through its use of symbols. But in such an age I am astonished by the contemporaneity of the Cross. It is a valid and timeless symbol. It was heartening to read a while ago George Steiner's 'Real Presences', and to watch a fine mind surveying linguistics, philosophy and science in a civilised way and yet tentatively suggesting a not dissimilar conclusion. It is a somewhat neglected poet, Francis Thompson, who, ecologically ahead of his time, sang: 'The angels keep their ancient places, turn but a stone and start a wing.' So let me end by quoting one of the shortest of these present poems in the hope that by balancing the nihilistic and the destructive with the probing or trusting I may tentatively align myself with those whom I have mentioned:

I think that maybe
I will be a little surer
Of being a little nearer.
That's all. Eternity
Is in the understanding
That that little is more than enough.

Counterpoint **1990**

After a long life of writing poetry, one naturally has a certain facility. Yet the fact that writing poetry comes easily is no guarantee of quality. Being a lyric poet I have always sympathised with Keats's remark that if poetry does not come as easily as leaves to the tree, it were better that it did not come at all. I believe that the majority of my more successful poems have come easily. There is a natural suspicion of too much forced labour. And yet there is also the belief that contemporary verse has to be difficult. Can one achieve difficulty easily? Yeats's variorum sheets are a heartening reminder that good poetry can emerge from much hard work and many alterations.

I like to feel that the poet is the chief arbiter of his work. The writing of a poem is a continual act of self-criticism, of the choice of the right and the rejection of the wrong word; of the correction and control of the music and movement of the thing; of the finding of fresh and striking imagery and language, together with the over-all care that the poetic statement makes sense and is worth putting before other readers.

I am chary about writing about my poetry at all. I still remember Anna Pavlova's answer to the question as to what her dance meant: 'If I could tell you in words, do you think I would go to the immense trouble of dancing it?'

If a poem does not register of itself, no amount of talking or writing about it is going to make it a success. As I have grown old, I have become less sure of the worth of my poems, despite what I said earlier. Does one become more critical or is there really a falling-off? Because of the expertise acquired over a long writing career, I can produce poems, and they will not be bad. But how good are they? There is that damning sentence in John Berryman's 'Homage to Mistress Bradstreet': 'The proportioned, spiritless poems accumulate.' The penalty of being a lyric poet is the law of diminishing returns, the temptation to repeat oneself unconsciously or even consciously. The freshness fades, the effects are laboured far more than is good for the result. 'We poets in our youth begin in gladness, but thereof come in the end despondency and madness.' So there we are; malicious reviewers will point out with glee that good poetry cannot be made out of writing about the difficulty of writing it!

'The times are out of joint.' Was it always so? Without having lived in the different periods one cannot say. Does the fact that we are approaching the end of the second millennium have any effect? It is somewhat depressing to reflect that about this time at the end of the last century Yeats, Eliot and Joyce were incubating their fine work. Are there comparable writers waiting in the wings now? The English language, despite being the world language, is jaded; a flexible medium for commercial and technological purpose, but for new, major poetry . . .? In discussions I have often been asked why good poetry cannot be made about machines and other ingredients of contemporary society. The answer is surely, 'Why not?' But following hard on the heels of that comes the question, 'But where are the poems?' It has been said that the opposite of poetry is not prose but science. I would agree, if by science is meant applied and not pure science. In so far as pure science is an attempt to contemplate and understand the mystery of creation, it can evoke the wonder from which poetry also can arise. It is the other, in alliance with a cash nexus, which creates a climate inimical to poetry. In that climate religion cannot flourish. In that of technology and big business there is no place for God.

The large themes the high values, remain as part of the human make-up. 'Thou hast made us for eternity.' said Augustine, 'and our hearts are restless until they repose in Thee.' To many today those words come from a dead past. Is God dead? The very mention of his name and of prayer in a poem now arouses the derision of jobbing reviewers. Generally speaking, contemporary English poetry is cheap and shallow as a result. The mark of liveliness and significance is to be able to deploy four-letter words passim. Then if the poet manages to come up with an image of trite tenderness, that is taken as a sign of major status. Poetry is no longer repaired to for inspiration in facing the great issues of life and hearing the deep organ notes of humanity. It is sought for minor titillation, for little flashes of verbal facility and slickness. There has been a kind of inverted treason of the clerks. The intelligentsia, if it reads contemporary verse at all, reads it for the above reasons and not because it is willing to have its material values and beliefs disturbed. I suppose this in its way has been an apologia for my own beliefs and the sort of poetry I try to write. I believe with past writers on the subject that metaphor is the supreme sign of poetic ability.

Without this gift a lyric seems to me to be generally speaking dull. That is why I find so much of contemporary poetry dull and trite. But modern reviewers have decided that metaphor is out of fashion, so I give hostages to fortune by resorting to it. I am a believer, so in dealing with God, prayer and eternity I am again out of fashion. In attempting the larger themes I give the same hostages.

Despite my earlier statements I realise that technology is an inseparable part of our lives, and that to ignore it in poetry is to risk having nothing relevant to say to one's contemporaries. So some of my more recent work is an attempt to come to terms with this situation by using words from science and technology and seeing whether poetry can be made in this way.

No Truce with the Furies 1995

Charles Tomlinson

The poems in *A Peopled Landscape* span a various field: some of them were composed in the United States, others in Somerset and Gloucestershire, two in the industrial Midlands, another from memories of living in Liguria. I mention these localities because most of my poems seem to grow out of very definite places and even in the 'Ode to Arnold Schoenberg', which celebrates a discovery international in application, namely the twelve-tone system, Gloucestershire church bells and cockcrows insist on being heard in the piece. In my last volume, *Seeing is Believing*, humanity was present by implication in the buildings, landscapes and artefacts contained in the poems and there was, of course, the human mind of the poet as it dealt with these impingements. In *A Peopled Landscape* there are both animals and people, perhaps more numerously than before, and I was glad when, in 'Over Brooklyn Bridge', I was able to persuade one of my characters to talk with a voice not my own.

Unlike most of my English contemporaries, I owe much to American poetry. The Americans have given a good deal of attention over the past forty years to getting the full semantic richness out of their words by dint of matching them abruptly against surrounding silences, by running them with measured swiftness through typographic space. The device of the three-ply lines in a number of these poems attempts to do precisely this. Commenting on a similar attitude to line in William Carlos Williams, Alan Stephens, the American poet and critic, has brilliantly summed up what is at stake here:

> The general principle is this: a line is a line because, relative to neighboring lines, it contains that which makes it in its own right a unit of the attention; and it is as precisely various in its way as are the shadings that play about the abstract norm of the metrical foot, for it too has a norm against which it almost constantly varies, allowing for feats of focusing on values that would be otherwise indistinguishable.

Perhaps I should add that the short lines of these poems are not to be read staccato: they are intended to be full of the rubato of daily speech, to be kept in flowing movement like a melody and, like a melody, to be felt out against their accompanying silence.

It was no accident that *A Peopled Landscape* closes with the Schoenberg ode. From Schoenberg, and even more so from Webern, our awareness of the value of the single note, and its concomitant silence, has brought about a parallel extension to that which American poetry offers us. I further believe that the poet must consciously try to make up on his own behalf for the great divorce which has come about between poetry and music.

A Peopled Landscape 1963

Rosemary Tonks

My foremost preoccupation at the moment is the search for an idiom which is individual, contemporary and musical. And one that has sufficient authority to bear the full weight of whatever passion I would wish to lay upon it.

Every poet who has been confined – at the mercy of form when he has come of age emotionally – and has found half the things he wants to say well out of his poem's range, knows the immensity of the task. And I am not speaking here of metrical skills, but of absolute freshness and authenticity in handling diction.

What I write about must develop from my life and times. I am especially conscious of the great natural forces which bring modern life up to date. My concern here is with exact emotional proportions – proportions as they are now current for me. Ideally, whatever is heightened should be justified both by art and by life; while the poet remains vulnerable to those moments when a poem suddenly makes its own terms – and with an overwhelming force that is self-justifying. For this reason certain poetic ideas have little validity when lifted out of context. I am consequently uneasy when discussing the logic of a poem with those whose intellectual equipment is purely mathematical. If you say that the English have a love of order which is puritanical, and the French a love of order which is imaginative, that does not make one more orderly than the other. The progress of feeling in a poem may be no less logical than the development of argument.

Telling the truth about feeling requires prodigious integrity.

Most people can describe a chest of drawers, but a state of mind is more resistant. A hackneyed metaphor is the first sign of a compromise with intention; your reader damns you instantly, and though he may read on with his senses, you have lost his heart. Some poets do manage to converge on their inner life by generating emotion from an inspired visual imagery; in this instance the images exist in their own right, but may be thought to be in a weaker position as the raw material of the emotion, in preference to a larger existence as illustration of it.

Notes on Cafés and Bedrooms 1963

C. A. Trypanis

I should try, perhaps, and explain how it is that a Greek, who grew up in Greece and was educated in Greece and Germany, comes to be writing English verse. My parents had a deep admiration for English culture and saw to it that their children grew up practically bilingual, employing English governesses for that purpose. So it came about that, till I was twelve, I spoke Greek and English with equal facility. Ever since I can remember, I have been haunted by the music of the English language, by the cadence and variety of its vowels – in modern Greek all vowels are pronounced short and rather abruptly. At the same time, from a very early age, poetry itself has always fascinated me, and in particular English poetry, much of which I was made to learn by heart. Later, of course, it was ancient Greek poetry that captivated me, and especially the *Iliad.* Since I was twelve, I hardly think there has been a single day during which I haven't read some part of the *Iliad*, and that was the only book I took with me when I joined the Greek army in 1940. If I were asked the famous and preposterous question, 'Which book would you like to survive, if all the books on earth were to be destroyed?' I would undoubtedly answer, 'The *Iliad*.' The balanced beauty, the power and the wisdom of that epic have always overwhelmed me, and as time went on I became intimate with a number of its minor characters, some of which appear as central figures in my 'Homeric Sequence' in *The Stones of Troy.*

The imagery of my poetry – such as it is – owes a great deal to the early and happy years I spent in Chios. It is the hard Mediterranean light that still dances before my eyes and the haunted corners of that island with its vines and pines clinging to the stingy earth over the glass-blue water. Moreover, an island society is in a sense 'a whole world', and so I became acquainted with a number of human problems in their 'eternal kernel', so to speak, in a natural and simple way that no complex Western city can ever give you. For in large cities the details and the side-issues are so many that the basic human truths often evade you.

Many of my younger friends have asked me, 'How do you set out to write a poem? What makes you want to write it in the first place?' I am afraid I cannot answer their question, because I really don't know. Often it is an image that floats before my eyes, and draws to it a great number of other half-forgotten, or fully present, elements, and so builds itself up into a poem. Sometimes it is the bare rhythm of some forgotten poem – I mean whose words I no longer remember – or a line or a phrase of a poem I am actually reading that sets the whole process moving, and drags into it what appears to be incoherent and disjointed material; or it can be a landscape, a face, a limb, practically anything I should say. Such is my experience. Of course what actually happens when this stimulant is given, I cannot tell. Nor can anybody, I suppose; but by some psychological process the poem is completed, and often very swiftly. 'Is it an agony, or a pleasure?' I have been asked again and again. I think I can honestly answer this: 'It is both.' Sometimes the one is more prevalent than the other, but both are always present, together with an odd fascination, a grip the poem gets on you, that will continue, until you complete it and are thus released from its overwhelming 'mood'.

I suppose Aristotle is right when he says that first of all 'man by nature desires to learn', to find out about the nature of things, and that this is one of his primary pleasures. Poetry to my mind is one more means of approaching 'truth', or as much of it as is available to man. For the rationalist it is the intellect, for the mystic the emotions that bring us as near to truth as possible.

But poetry, a fusion of intellect and emotion – the one being heightened by the other – is perhaps the highest form of truth that man can aspire to. Undoubtedly this lyrical truth can be enjoyed on more than one plane. Undoubtedly too there is an element of ambiguity in it; but it remains all that man, infirm and transitory as he is, can aspire to.

The Stones of Troy 1957

John Wain

Both as reader and as writer, I have always enjoyed poetry and responded to it more deeply than to prose. There never was a time when my most fascinated and absorbed reading was not 'poetry' of one kind or another, starting from nursery rhymes and graduating to 'real' poetry by the recognised route-school, Shakespeare, Gray's *Elegy*, bits of French romantic verse suddenly perceived, amid the boredom of the classroom, to be about something. I was seventeen before it struck me that I myself might be a poet, but this I attribute to growing up in a milieu in which – for all its good points – one just didn't think of being a poet; that wasn't the kind of thing that happened.

It was Oxford that taught me that poetry was something that actually did get itself written, now, here, by people one might conceivably meet in the street. I began to write verse in 1943, but it was not until 1951 that any of my poems got into print (except, naturally, in the undergraduate papers in which everyone publishes). In that year, the University of Reading put out 120 copies of an elegant paper-bound book, *Mixed Feelings*, containing nineteen poems. Nineteen poems ready for publication after eight years of writing verse? What kind of poet is this man? The answer is, a slow one. I noticed, early in life, that poets who write very copiously are usually either (a) no good at all or (b) very fine in a few of their poems and repetitive or uninspired in the rest. The best thing to aim at, in my opinion, was to write the few good poems and skip the many bad ones.

In this, I have naturally not succeeded. Although I have written a very small body of poetry (not more than fifty in my life that I 'wish to preserve'), quite a high proportion of it is bad. To write a good poem one needs a very special combination of energy, finesse, vividness of mood, directness of response to life, the right time, the right place, no distractions, and a lot of luck. If all those come together, and if one is a poet (which is not a profession but a condition), the bell rings. I have heard that bell ring precious few times in my life (those who dislike my poetry would say, of course, that I have never heard it), and I would rather have that feeling than any other I have known.

For the rest, I believe that being a poet is a matter of avoiding two pitfalls. One is complacency, the kind that decides on an easy formula for being in the right (such as Identifying With the Working Class, or being religious, or not liking the hydrogen bomb, or knowing Latin and Greek) and then turns out verse to this formula, confident of its being good because it is founded on superior attitudes. Most of our self-conscious 'rebels' are bad poets of this kind.

The other pitfall is intellectual laziness, which results in shoddy, imprecise writing. If one avoids these, and was born with the seeds of a poetic gift, there is always hope.

I haven't said anything about what my poems say – what kind of subject matter I write about – because the poems themselves take care of that; and if they don't, we might as well not take this any further.

Weep Before God 1961

VERNON WATKINS

I prefer my poems to speak for themselves, but I have been asked to supply a note about the poems and also about my method of composition.

I began writing when I was very young. I collected the English poets one by one, starting at the age of seven. My imagination was stirred by lyric poetry more than by any other kind of reading. Twenty years later I became aware that writers of poetry are of two kinds, those who write to an instrument and those who neglect the instrument for the sake of action, leaving it, as it were, in the next room. My own poems all belong to the first category. I believe that the freedom offered to a lyric poet is not offered on easy terms; he must refuse rhetoric, and be attentive to the possibility of freedom within the restraint of the poem, a freedom much greater and more rewarding to the imagination than any other. The poet who makes fifty drafts for the sake of one knows this, and he understands that the poet who neglects the instrument has chosen an easier freedom because he has not the patience or perseverance to listen. Poetry is the interest of many, but the vocation of very few.

I have been told that the occasional expositions of my poems which I have read on the air are more obscure than the poems themselves, and perhaps this is inevitable. A poet is able to throw light on the source of a poem, but he cannot simplify it; he can only make it more difficult. The true simplicity of a good poem is always intricate and difficult, and the false simplicity of a prose paraphrase is bound to render it inaccessible. The most one can do is to state the theme.

Perhaps I should go no further until I have quoted an example. Here is a note I made stating the theme of one of the poems in this book, 'Egyptian Burial, Resurrection in Wales':

> In ancient Egypt the mummified body of a queen was commonly swathed in masterpieces of art written upon papyrus. Wine-vessels, money, and ears of corn were laid close at hand as they would be needed on the soul's journey. These were for sustenance and the manuscript for protection. The mummy and the tomb were themselves works of art in which every detail was important. The rarefied nature of the dead would carry with it all that was richest and purest in life, and only that.
>
> The first three verses of the poem show the confidence of the workmen in the power of art to overcome all evil spirits. They are possessed by the faith that the dead life is enriched in the measure in which they have enriched its tomb.
>
> In the last three verses of the poem the confidence of the workmen is shaken by the soul's experience, and the mummy herself now knows that the widow who cast her two mites into the treasury, which was all that she had, had made the right preparation for death. Egyptian burial represents pre-Christian exaltation; resurrection in Wales represents Christian humility. Emerging from one into the other, the mummy has died, and is born.

I should say something also about my ballads. The ballad form is, of course, as old as poetry itself, and one of the laws attaching to it seems to be that it must be hammered and beaten and knocked into shape until it is as hard and anonymous as a pebble on the shore.

My own ballads have a great deal in common with those of tradition. They are all rhythmical and intended to be read aloud;

and in some I use a refrain. They are not in any sense private poems. Yet here the likeness ends. These ballads are elemental and they belong to myth, but they do not belong to history. In these it is not the narrative but the metaphysical situation that counts, and the symbols surrounding the situation.

The Death Bell 1954

Peter Whigam

Poetry (Auden on Yeats) is a mouth. Unfortunately, when we want to talk about poetry we have to talk about what the poem says: there is little that can be said about a mouth. If poetry is what disappears in paraphrase, or is present when no distinction can be made between form and content, how can we talk of it? We shall always find we are talking about something else: the effect the poem had on us, whether we approve of the poet's politics, admire his taste in women, or deplore his use of the pathetic fallacy. There is also a relation between the impulse to write about poetry and the state of poetry at a given time. When the impulse is strong, poetry as a viable social medium is likely to be in a bad way.

Then there is poetics. Mirror on mirror is all the show. There is a sense in which we are condemned to mirror ourselves forever in surfaces. In the poetic synthesis form disappears into content and content into form. Means are ends. But except to the initiate – yes, 'poetry can be understood only by poets'; in our age this is almost true – purely technical analysis is as remote from the experience of the poem as gossip about a poet's opinions. The desideratum is a development of poetic sensibility, and this will be achieved only through a long succession of poetic experiences, preferably of a communal nature.

Speech is not a private activity. We have to recapture the sense of language as experience. We had this sense in childhood. All primitive people retain it. Which is why in the cave there is no art. Art appears only under centrifugal pressures of tribal break-up and the formation of castes. The tribal dance is both religious and patriotic, but it has never been a substitute for either religion or tribal loyalty. Art, our long-descended degenerate of ritual, nearly always is – with the results we see today.

I believe the so-called fine arts are finished, because the social conditions that gave rise to them either have passed or are about to pass. The Israeli kibbutzim and the Chinese communes are indicative of the new forms of tribal living shaping up for us. Man is not only a person, with his private quirks of character etc., but also an individual, an item of individuated humanity. In the West, since the Renaissance, he has lived almost exclusively as the former. Gary Snyder has written a far-seeing essay on this subject in his book *Earth House Hold*.

Poetry will become increasingly tribally oriented. There will be nothing you mightn't have picked out of the bottom of a trash can, or found scrawled on the back of an envelope under a pile of children's toys in a corner of the living room. The analytic and descriptive uses of language, so necessary in times of disintegration, will be at a discount: not the separate-ness of things – name/object, image/thought, man/woman, ambience/act – but their identity will be our base. Nourished in communal experience, 'art' will once more become a communal expression. Poetry will again tap its mantic roots, and words-as-experience, rescued from the limbo of childhood, speak beyond themselves. I can foresee a time when poetry as we have known it will, like the Marxist state, wither away, and only poets be left.

The Blue Winged Bee 1969

C. K. Williams

Poems are not written merely to be read, as novels are. A poem is meant to be read and read again and again, to be run through the mind until it is part of the mind, until the mind recites it as it recites itself. We tell poems to ourselves until their rhythms, their forms, and their meanings find, or perhaps create, a place in our voices, rather than in our minds. So we find sometimes we have memorized passages of poems without having tried to. Poetry shares with music this astonishing quality of moving through our perceptions and our mind to a place in us beyond either, a place which participates concretely in both consciousness and sense.

Mind becomes doubled in its dealings with the formal arts. We aren't satisfied to 'know' a poem, a painting, or a piece of music by being able to describe it to ourselves, to paraphrase it. There has to be the incorporation of the actual object, of the precise notes in a piece of music or the precise words in a poem, so that we hear the music or the poem when we think it, so that we hear our own actual voice, the voice we speak our own lives with, drawn into and fused with its melodies and rhythms.

Of course poems offer material for moral reflection just as novels do. They have to deal with the same themes because there are not, for human beings, all that many themes. Poems seem to deal with issues less comprehensively, less exhaustively, than novels, but this is deceptive. Because what a poem might have to sacrifice in the accumulation of details of surface subtlety, it more than makes up for in the intensification the form of the poem effects. It is one of the more profound mysteries of the mind that the struggle with form, which we have seen is defined by seemingly arbitrary necessities, actually enriches the expression and effect of content. The double movement of willing consciousness towards form and expression enacts a struggle beyond anything that is happening in the matter of the poem, and the capacity of mind for self-distancing, for standing aside from itself and regarding itself, is obliterated by the force of this struggle.

It is also our sense of this struggle that attaches us to the poet, as much as to what a poem is saying. When we read a novel, our sense of its author manipulating from behind the scenes drifts in and out of our awareness; we can be curious about why the author's character may have generated such and such manifestations of itself, but, unless we know the novelist, this is quite incidental. This is not the case with a poet. In the struggle toward form, what happened to the poet in the creation of the poem happens again in the here and now of our reading of the poem; the impulse toward form, our feeling of its successful attainment, is absolutely critical to the experience of reading poetry. What the poet has undergone in the contending with form is not something that happens to the poem's content; rather it is the poet's actual self, his or her ultimate reality, which is the material of the poem's artifice. There is a self-making involved in this struggle, but it is of a radically different sort from that which afflicts the characters, and, as we have seen, possibly the readers, of novels.

Poetry induces the mind into involving itself entirely in an awareness of its formal striving, and in doing so, it demands that the mind realize as much as it can its own entire nature, not only its intellectual or moral capacity. The poem offers the mind – the soul, we could probably say now – a way to experience itself objectively, by participating in something which both draws it beyond its own spiritual capabilities and still refers in the most concrete way to these capabilities.

These involvements, these intensities, these movements of

the poem into the voice of consciousness help explain why, to those who are attached to it, poetry is an implement of the moral imagination every bit as efficient as the novel, and whose potential effects are even more, and fortifies the impulse toward resolution, toward definitiveness, in our spiritual reflections.

The beauty which the poem devises, enacts, elicits in us, is essential to our moral nature simply because it cannot be contained in any ethical system or moral code: it certifies to us that there is something within our potential which goes beyond our ability simply to think about things, to reason our way through our experience; beauty proves to us that there are ways out of the circularities through which we reasonably examine our narratives, and narratively try to comprehend our self-reasoning.

New and Selected Poems 1995

After I finish a book, I often forget how I wrote the poems in the book. I even seem to forget how I wrote any poem, ever. By this stage, I suppose, I should anticipate that post-partum madness, but it still leaves me helpless. To try to speak about poems I can't imagine having written is absurd, but I can say for certain that many of the poems in the book deal with various extremities: issues of morality, and mortality, other people's, my own, the world's; issues of love, lost love, love insufficient; there's even a poem about money. Are such questions ever resolved in a definitive way, even in poems? And might one dare to believe that such resolutions, were they feasible, might change anything: human nature, or the world, even a little? I wonder whether my poems are still driven by those wistful ambitions. In the meantime, I do know, that is I can remember, that when I was writing *The Vigil* I was looking for a denser, more self-consciously evident music than I usually used in the past: I wanted to intensify the kind of finely grained attention which I seem to value more and more lately. Of course in poetry necessities of form are generative factors, and take us places we wouldn't be able to go otherwise: it's form which allows us to move into the unique kind of consciousness poetry inspires, to be a bit possessed, or at least surprised, by what our minds bring forth. Besides the music in *The Vigil*, I realize that I was surprisingly taken in some of the poems by such seemingly incidental matters as syntax and tone. The poem 'The Neighbor' is composed almost entirely of noun-phrases rather than sentences, which seemed to allow me to organize some rather painful memories.

(One of the women in 'The Neighbor', an old sweetheart I haven't seen since I was nineteen, sent me a letter care of the magazine in which it was published. On the envelope was written, 'I'm the woman in the poem!' She seemed to have forgiven my ancient cruelties.)

But sometimes the formal necessities we come up with for poems can surprise us in less agreeable ways. 'Insight' took me some twenty years to get right. Although I'd as soon have let its subject matter drop, I was driven by the intuition that the poem would be longish, one-sentence stanzas of a certain unmercifully emotional-analytic tone: it took that much time to get it all to jibe. So perhaps at least some of our amnesia serves the function of permitting ourselves to keep on with this.

The Vigil 1997

Glancing back over my work a few years ago, I was struck by how much of my life, how much of what have been the most crucial experiences and perceptions of my time in the world, I was able to find evidence for in the poems I'd written. I certainly hadn't set out to account systematically for my experience that way, but there it was: I felt pleased, albeit a little shy to behold myself quite like that. At the same time, though, I also recognized that there were still emotions, events, ideas, even images and sounds that I'd taken note of, even written a few lines of, but had put off trying to make into or get into poems. My hesitation sometimes seemed to have come from feeling that those initial glimmers weren't mature enough in me to be expressed, and sometimes I thought I must have felt I wasn't competent enough in my craft (yet, I hoped) to deal with them in the way I thought they had to be dealt with. If there's anything I can say with any confidence about *Repair*, it's that during the time I was composing it, I did manage to find the patience, or the courage, or the wherewithal, whatever it represented, to outwit my diffidence, or my equivocation, so that I finally figured out ways to get at least some of those pressing or rankling beginnings into structures which could contain them. It wasn't always easy: some of the poems in the book took an absurdly long time between their impetus and their completion – almost thirty years in several cases. It occurs to me to wonder as I write this now whether I miss having those uncertain inchoate whispers in the eroded folders on my desk rather than captured unequivocally between covers. I think not – there still seems enough as yet unresolved in the various realities I've endured or enjoyed to keep me out of retirement for now.

On the other hand, some of the poems in the book came easily, as poems thank goodness sometimes will, as though of their own accord, embodying movements and acquisitions of the imagination I hadn't considered seriously before. The composition of those sorts of poems, that groping but gratifying propulsion into states of mind one had no notion one had access to; those inspirations – there's no other word for them – which arrive so unexpectedly, one certainly can't help but long for: the poems which are their result can feel less like evidence of imaginative vigilance than the residue of unlikely and often unrecapturable felicities. And yet those poems too, in a more surprising and even more gratifying way, reveal links between the work and experience.

But then, being suspended between unrealized responsibility and unrecognized possibility seem to be the coordinates of the life of poetry; one can never quite be sure what one has earned, and what's been given, probably despite yourself; either will do.

Repair **1999**

Hugo Williams

One of my themes is the war between objects and people. For instance, I'm a prospective sugar daddy. I want to buy everyone and everything. I try to buy my two-year-old daughter. I buy a garish humming top and climb into her pen like an ape and pump it till it screeches for her, hungry for thanks. But she just bawls. She'll learn like the rest of us, I suppose, but when they're young they're dumb. All they want is love. They don't know when they're on to a good thing. They have this maddening immunity to the magic of money. We don't understand at all so we throw pennies at them as they slowly superannuate us. From *Easy Rider*: 'It's awful hard to be free when you are bought and sold in the marketplace.' From *Hair*: 'She was busted for her beauty.'

The poems move from detached bachelordom – a somewhat still-life: 'I stare out through my tent-flaps like a squaw' at things like sports cars, scaffolding joints, mauvish masonry blocks and detectives. Other urban scares from the Paddington area are followed by a painterly series on the Australian aborigine and colour bar. Then come the birthpangs and pleasures of commitment, as well as a baby girl, a home and a motorbike: 'I lust strangely after a new alternator.' The poems get shorter. There is (temporarily) a pram in the hall.

> The poet who succeeds in writing a short poem is like a man who has found his way through a stone wall into a valley miles long, where he lives. He walks back up the valley, and opens a door in the wall for an instant to show

> you where the entrance is. The more imaginative readers are able to slip through in the twenty or thirty seconds it takes to read the poem. Those who expect the poet to give them ideas see only a vague movement on the side of the mountain. Before they have turned all the way round to face the poem, the door is closed.
>
> – Robert Bly

The only ideas in these poems are the poems themselves. Though many started descriptively and quite long, they nearly all ended up short, factual, but at all costs hopefully more than the sum of what is left. I think the writer has to be in the experience rather than the colour of the ink. This has left no room for texture or poetics. There are very few lines that couldn't have been spoken in – not necessarily rational – conversation. So they have a found quality about them which is supposed to make them seem inevitable. I greatly admire the technique of certain English light comedy actors who can weigh lines on a scales inside their heads which tells them the exact tone of voice with which to drop them cold, or otherwise. It's the aureole, the echo, the haze of a line which counts, not its specific gravity.

In keeping with fashion rather than strict honesty, I put the poems to do with unhappiness and searching at the end of the book, but the wheel has gone round often since then and most people read slim volumes backwards.

Sugar Daddy 1970

The interest of the past lies in its absurdity. All our lives we are looking down on a mock pastoral with teddy bears and teacups, wondering how to get back there. Usually we have taken a wrong turning somewhere and got lost during an ill-advised venture into the future. Hunger has set in. Homesickness and depression.

Workaholism. We needn't have worried. They won't start without us. They know we are on our way.

Certain primitive tribes believe that the past lies in front of us, being before our mind's eye; the future behind our backs, being invisible. It seems clear that we are heading backwards through our lives, like white hunters striding through elephant grass. If we stop to ask the way, friendly tribesmen set us on the right track with a little smile. The past is a writing more than a shooting land. 'A great yellow ball rolls back through a hoop / To rest at the head of a mallet held in the hands of a child' (Louis MacNeice). 'I come on walking offstage backwards' (Robert Lowell). I imagine him fencing his way back through swishing curtains like Stewart Granger in *The Prisoner of Zenda*, except that poets are obliged to lose their duel, alas. Prevent the past!

'Memory is a form of the past that was never present,' said Jacques Derrida. So that when we say our adolescence was like drawing a gun in slow motion over and over again, we don't mean it literally, since we don't know what adolescence feels like any more, being dead by adolescent standards. However, we know what drawing a gun is. We have somewhere to start from. We buckle on our jewelled holster and swagger about like one of Andy Warhol's gay cowpokes in *Lonesome Cowboys*, chatting about hairstyles and cross-draws. It keeps us happy for a while, but there are drawbacks. 'You can't put your arms round a memory,' as Johnny Thunders says, so poetry does the next best thing by putting clothes on abstractions and giving them things to do, 'pieces of action', 'bits of business', like striking a pose or making a pass at a girl, 'my inspiration dressed in red'. My own poems are best described as self-satires.

My father, who stands opposite me most of the time in *Writing Home*, was an actor; a handsome, hedonistic character who slowly turned himself into a first-rate light comedian and later, when things started to go wrong for him, a successful playwright. Ours was a hazardous, changeable background in which surfaces were the consistent element. Appearances were not a disguise, but a belief, a virtue in themselves. Though countrified, it was a dandified world where wit, clothes and looks took precedence over the worthier values and a joke was the only possible excuse for being late or wrong. My brother and I dressed up to go tracking. We practised our cross-draw. We discovered that stage-falls begin at the knee, then pitch forward, twisting in mid-air. We imagined that acting was raising an eyebrow at ourselves in the mirror. And of course we wanted to be actors.

Our father's favourite period was the Regency. He played Mr Darcy with his hair curled. His favourite character was Beau Brummell. His family feeling, however, was Edwardian. When he ate a sour grape his children's teeth were set on edge. I reacted in the traditional manner by going bohemian: long hair, jazz, road-books, poetry. Until he died. It seems to me now that the dandy is the truer poet. Clothes, make-up, hair ('You should be with someone a full minute before you realise they're well dressed'), these things seem closer to poetry than deep stuff because they have bypassed thought and presented themselves instinctively to the world. They have the integrity and sexuality of their own existence. They have a head start. They are like women. They are already poetry. 'In the amorous realm,' said Roland Barthes, 'the most painful wounds are inflicted more often by what one sees than by what one knows.'

In the theatrical world, timing as well as what is seen is of the essence. Timing is what actors talk about when they talk about acting. It is what they admire in other actors. It is what I admire in poems: pace, weight, balance. In *Writing Home*, which is about acting as much as writing, it was natural talk, the throwaway rather than the iambic line, that I was interested in. This is an elusive, dry-fly thing, a matter of wrist rather than feet. On stage, it collaborates with an audience's expectations, weighing them in its hand and leading them on rather than overwhelming them with effects. 'To make verse speak the language of prose without being prosaic, to marshal the words of it in such an order as they might naturally take in falling from the lips of an extemporary speaker, is one of the most arduous tasks a poet can undertake' (William Cowper).

Writing Home 1985

It seems to be half-time already. Someone is coming on to the field with lemon slices. I pucker my lips. A few years ago I was desperate to have a *Selected Poems* out, but now the lid is coming down on thirty years' production I find myself gasping for air. Give me one more year and I'll get it right! Perhaps it is no big deal to put a few slim volumes back into circulation, but one cannot help remembering how few poets have improved much after forty if indeed they didn't get a lot worse. Is the mould set or can one still shrug free? Something tells me you really have to go for it in the second half just to stay on the same spot.

I had thought of calling my life's work *A Slight Improvement*, after my most favourable school report. The concept of improvement runs deep. We need it to come to terms with time: 'Every day in every way I am getting better and better.' Art, love, truth, fame, even good looks and talent are within our grasp if only . . . but then fate pipes up, reminding the Olympic hopeful that he has a wooden leg. 'And a wooden leg is no excuse for wooden verse,' as Kingsley Martin once reminded an agent.

Looking back over thirty years' work, it is easy to see the various shifts, though whether these are my own or everyone else's is harder to say. One is away from metaphor and towards speech, another is away from the page and towards humour, the *Review*'s cleansing minimalism and the rise of the poetry reading acting as a hinge for both. I wonder were they movements away from poetry in the dubious search for a voice? You start with no voice, but no stifling awareness of the fact. If you do acquire one, it may be accompanied by a hobbling self-consciousness.

Awareness of this is the difficult card called 'maturity'. Give me two new cards!

It is easy to patronise one's younger self; the struggle out of it leaves one strangely impervious to its charm. One early poem of mine about a pick-up has a mix 'n' match metaphor which raises a smile today: 'Both know they walk / Tightropes like duellists and to gore / The enemy is to fall on one's sword.' I had to fight my right hand not to slim that down to something like 'Both knew / They walk tightropes through air / And into each other's eyes.' But feeling is the one unfakeable part, the one unreproachable element. And thereby hang my doubts about the upward mobility of it all.

Mercifully, the true state of affairs is hidden from us most of the time, though one does occasionally see through a chink in the safety curtain of friends and white lies that surrounds one. 'There was a moment in the seventies when you looked like being the next thing,' said John Ryle once when he saw me off on the last tube from Notting Hill Gate, 'but somehow it never happened, why was that?' A number of possible excuses flashed through my head, but I had to catch my train. The fact I wasn't willing to miss it in my defence was a sort of answer: caution, tidiness, self-preservation. (It is a consolation to my lack of wildness now that I was never wild then.)

My habit of containment and limitation may be in for just the kind of jolt one needs at half-time: a field trip to Central America to do one of the BBC's *Great Journeys*. The world is divided up into different types of TV programmes – Turkey is holidays, Norway is wildlife, etc. – and the BBC thought it would be amusing to send a non-current affairs man into a current affairs area and see what happened. Who knows, perhaps this is how one becomes an expert.

Selected Poems **1989**

I thought I was doing so well at my reading in Pitshanger Manor, Ealing. But I undermined my good work with my very last word. At the end of the reading, when there was no more time for debate, I was asked a simple question which needed either a 'yes' or a 'no'. I had the chance to say the right thing and I blew it.

For the first half, I ran through my back-catalogue. Then it was downstairs for refreshments, book sales, signings and those brief respectful conversations which in my case so often turn out to be about my brother, who made a lasting impression in the seventies TV series *Upstairs, Downstairs*, our respective looks etc. One woman had seen the film *One of Our Aircraft is Missing*, which my father was in, six times. The bottom half of my face was quite like his, she said, cutting it off with her hand and narrowing her eyes, but not the top half. I gave my best stiff-upper-lip smile at this piece of bad news and prepared to go over the top again for the second half.

This was the half I had been dreading, because I had decided to read some of the poems from my new book, which I hadn't read from before and which I had a feeling weren't as audience-friendly as my old stuff, being without the jokiness favoured at readings, the 'Don't worry, we're only here for the beer' ingredient. I had tried to build a disclaimer into the book with the lines 'Re-reading what I have written up till now / I am conscious only of what is not being said, / the mirror history running underneath all this / self-pitying nonsense . . .' but this only seemed to draw attention to what was lacking.

Having been almost debonair in the first half, in the second I turned sinister. As it says in the blurb, 'the poems trace the course of a love affair, now ended', but was this an appropriate subject to be showing off about to a crowd of mostly elderly strangers, given that I still seemed to be married? My wife, who is French, lives in France; I live in London; we visit one another on Eurostar. As the blurb goes on, the author 'divides his time between London and France', and what a world is contained in that airy euphemism 'divides his time'. I produced a proof copy of the book the other day and gave it to my wife to read. She read through the book in about half an hour, pausing only once to laugh at the line 'But no, I couldn't go through all that again, / not without my wife being there . . .' and made some comment about the wife being the deus ex machina of the piece. Then she closed the book and said, 'Five years' work?' as if she thought I'd been slacking somewhat.

Years ago, at a poetry reading in America, I forgot to read out the titles of my then even more minimalist poems. After the reading someone came up to me and said, 'Congratulations, I think you've cracked the long form.' The poems in this new book aren't so uniformly brief, but they do add up to a sort of story, a novelette really, on the page as in life, so I thought I would read through the best of them in the same way and see what happened. During the question and answer session that followed, one person said he thought the book read like dialogue, which was interesting seeing that only one person speaks. It was said enthusiastically, so I understood that he meant it was like a film, which seemed OK. Then, just a minute before the end, someone came up with the question that floored me. 'Would you publish a poem if it was going to hurt someone?' Swallowing an instinctive 'Well, it all depends . . .', I hardened my heart and said, 'Yes.'

Billy's Rain **1999**

John Hartley Williams

Péret a introduit dans la poésie une qualité supersonique.
– Robert Benayoun

This book began as an act of homage to the French surrealist writer Benjamin Péret. The third section of *Canada* was written with his instructions for writing a poem in mind:

> . . . forget you're married, that yr child has whooping cough, forget you're a Catholic, you're a shopkeeper, bankruptcy looms . . . forget about literature . . . You don't want to know anything except what you're about to be told . . . Write as fast as possible so you lose none of the secrets about yourself being confided in you, above all don't re-read anything. If by chance you find you've suddenly stopped, don't hesitate to force the door of the unconscious and write the first letter of the alphabet for example. The letter 'A' is as good as any other. Ariadne's thread will come back by itself . . .

Automatic writing gets a bad press in English-speaking countries, so when I began to write I certainly didn't have anything as grand as publication in view. I cd already hear the protesting screech, 'O no! Not surrealism!' followed, of course, by those confident tones, 'No, we don't know and we don't want to know what it is, who its poets were, what they wrote, whether the movement still goes on, or what the whole thing was about, but as we're all surrealists now, why shd we? It's about not making sense, isn't it? Monty Python and so forth. Thank God we have our sense of humour.'

Listening to English writers talking about surrealism is about as fruitful as listening to Frenchmen discussing a cricket match.

When I began my venture into automatic writing, I also had in mind André Breton's notion of automatism as a technique for releasing what lies buried deep in the unconscious. Surrealism is, after all, a psycho-revolutionary strategy designed to bring about the total liberation of humanity thru the identification and plenification of unrealised wishes and desires. No less. When I now read – from a recent review – 'It is, perhaps, no more than surrealism deserves that the technique of arbitrary juxtapositions has become the stock-in-trade of commercial advertising,' I grit my teeth, enraged.

It goes without saying that 'arbitrary juxtapositions' is precisely not what surrealism is about. If the highly manipulative juxtapositions of advertising seem 'surreal' to bystanders, this simply indicates how casually the word is now used. Moreover, surrealism certainly doesn't 'deserve' to become the stock-in-trade of hype. From the surrealist viewpoint, any kind of propaganda/advertising is death to the human soul. In 1945, Péret (who was exiled in Mexico at the time) published an article called 'The Dishonour of the Poets', furiously attacking an anthology of poems produced by French writers during the Nazi occupation to which they had given the title *The Honour of the Poets.* This was, as you may imagine, a highly patriotic work. (Paul Eluard, unfortunately, was its editor.) With virulent asperity, Péret observed:

> It's rather significant that most of these texts strictly associate Christianity and nationalism as if they wished to demonstrate that religious dogma and nationalist dogma have a common origin and an identical social function. The pamphlet's very title, *The Honour of the Poets*, considered in regard to its content, takes on a sense foreign to all poetry.

> In short, the honour of these 'poets' consists of ceasing to be poets in order to become advertising agents.

He went on: 'As long as the malevolent phantoms of religion and fatherland, in whatever disguise, buffet the intellectual and social air, no freedom is conceivable . . . From every authentic poem, on the other hand, issues a breath of absolute and active freedom, even if this freedom is not evoked in its political or social aspect . . .'

No poet, in other words, can be a propagandist, not even for a righteous cause. As for literature . . . that too is a highly suspect project: 'Not one of these "poems",' commented Péret, 'surpasses the level of pharmaceutical advertising, and it is not by chance that the great majority of their authors has believed it necessary to return to classical rhyme and alexandrines.'

What I love & admire in Benjamin Péret, apart from the exuberant, unstoppable invention of his poetry, is his refusal to play the game of literature, his absolute independence from fashion, his anarchic, exfoliating humour, his child-like enjoyment of the good things in life, his contempt for religion, his political & artistic idealism. Perhaps, for English taste, this makes him too much of a Jacobin (albeit a benevolent one). He wrote his poems anywhere, on café table mats, odd envelopes, bits of paper. Later, when his friends read them back to him, he had no recollection of having written them. He was entirely without literary ambition in the career sense. This must be very puzzling to poetasters.

Georges Ribemont-Dessaignes said, 'In the end, the best position probably consists in accepting the universe, and not accepting oneself, and laughing at the comic effects produced by this tragic dialogue.' The poems of *Canada* were all written with this in mind. If there is humour here, I hope that, rather than the laughter which greets a farce, it may evoke that ghostly laughter which echoes the withdrawal of the gods. Humour without tragedy is a ghastly rictus – the canned laughter of a television audience. I have tried, in *Canada*, to let myself be influenced by Péret's sublime cackle.

Canada 1997

Gerard Woodward

These poems were written between March 1987 and October 1990. Nearly half of them were written in a house in Manchester which we occupied between the owner dying and the children selling. Fourteen poems were written in a miserable ground-floor council flat in Gravesend where the old woman upstairs sang, and hoovered her carpets every morning at half past five. Spiteful children fought outside the windows. I worked nights in a pizza restaurant and fought with drunken sailors and was spat at by their girlfriends.

The earliest poems were written in a flat overlooking the harbour at Falmouth, where we ate our breakfast in such sunlight we were blinded by our eggs. The most recent poems were written in this house in one of the Medway towns which we now occupy. The title poem was written in a house we shared in Gravesend with two nurses and three Scottish labourers who were digging the Channel Tunnel, who wept at night on the phone to their distant wives, and who came home drunk with bloody noses and had to be let in by me when they forgot their keys. Our room smelt of pizzas and oranges. Mainly oranges.

It is not that my poems are all about places, but they are all about things. Objects. My poems are made to be touched, smelt, seen, heard, tasted. I write a lot about food because food is important. It is what we make ourselves with. I write about kitchens, because it is in those places that we stop ourselves withering away. Kettles know about this because they are forever going through this process of death and resurrection, of coming to the boil and cooling down. That is what 'The Kettle's Story' is about.

I also like to write about dirt. *Householder*'s cover is a Stanley Spencer painting of a dustman's resurrection. The gifts offered at this event are, appropriately, rubbish – an old tin can, a broken teapot, cabbage leaves. Thereby dirt is also resurrected and finds its proper place in the world. Some of my poems attempt to rescue from the class of abominations those objects we don't know what to do with. 'The Invisible Pet Shop' celebrates that class of animals we do not permit into our lives, superimposed on the class we do, the fluffy class of kittens, mice and puppies. Elsewhere I try to make use of disorder, whether it be an 'Unmade Bed' or 'Rough Sea'. It seems that untidiness and activity must go together. Poems are controlled chaos, always on the point of vanishing, collapsing, dissolving, like the house in 'Suffolk Interior' which, I've just realised, mentions three people, my mother, my father and my brother, all of whom are now dead. My father died just three weeks before this book appeared. That is sad, because he was excited about it and was quite happy and it was nice weather. One day we'll know how to die properly, and what to do with the dead. That is partly what 'Forbidden Food' is about. I am not suggesting that we eat the dead, but allow them into the living sphere, let them come to the dinner table. In Paradise everything becomes food.

Householder 1991

Soundings

Fleur Adcock. I've never relished the idea of being readily identifiable: 'That's a typical Adcock poem' is not a phrase I wish to hear. I'd rather be unpredictable. Probably this is an unnatural and pointless ambition; after all, poets are usually *praised* for 'finding their own voice', and if vocal parallels are anything to go by I'm often recognised on the telephone before I've said any more than 'Hello'. But I can try. *Time Zones*, 1991

Michael Baldwin. There's always a danger if you try to work through an area of experience in a hurry that you'll mix poem with poem, or have to falsify a line because you can't afford the time to wait and see what it is. Worse, and every poet knows this danger, is the risk that you'll dig up fragments of somebody else's poetry, and there it is, after the cement has dried, a monstrous hybrid, its head sculpted by Graves, its limbs undeniably Hughes, its belly all Barker, and only its backside indisputably your own. In the past reviewers have found my work violent. All I can say is that it must be. The world is.

Death on a Live Wire and *On Stepping from a Sixth-Storey Window*, 1962

Wayne Brown. The truth is, I think, I write verse because of a persistent sense of the limitations of the kinds of 'reality' offered us by historian, economist or ideologue. People, when they recognise others (and themselves) as individuals in thrall to the living world, and not merely as flesh of a political or societal theory, suffer many marvellous, half-grasped encounters, to which they respond with terror or joy, hope or abandon; and it is that sense of marvel or wonder, like the wonder of metaphor, to which, whatever the theme of each individual poem, I have tried to be true. Poetry, however, remains for me essentially a religious exercise, calling for the suspension of the ego – Keats and his sparrow . . . *On the Coast*, 1972

ALAN BROWNJOHN. Myth, magic and mysticism are out; or if they are referred to, the references are not serious or reverential. Things like that are often excuses for moral irresponsibility.
A Night in the Gazebo, 1980

JOHN BURNSIDE. I am under no illusion that my own, recurrent concern with community is rooted in anything other than need. Something is lost, or lacking. While it is easy to classify the lyric as private, and therefore apolitical, a case could be made – an essentially ecological case – for saying that we need the lyric, to celebrate and to elegise, in order to reaffirm the land in its full mystery and richness. A similar case can be made for folk myths and fairy tales, for the preservation of old recipes and cures, spells, songs, invocations, weather charms, cultivars, forms, sub-species. It is the case for the irrational, the case against every kind of reductionism – behaviourism, positivism, materialism.
The Myth of the Twin, 1994

CIARAN CARSON. I began to think of the poems as woodcuts populated by stark interrogating figures. Indeed, our assumed rights are often questionable. I was brought up between the Irish and English languages, and still wonder about the way to say a thing. Poetry does not offer any answers.
The Twelfth of Never, 1999

CHARLES CAUSLEY. My aim, at all events, has been always to realise an experience, a place, a situation, in terms of its human associations. Whether the book reveals something I think essential to a collection of verse – a genuine sense of unity – is, of course, not for me to say. All I am moderately certain of in the present context is the truth of a remark by Martin Buber: 'All journeys have secret destinations of which the traveller is unaware.' *Secret Destinations*, 1984

Barry Cole. I have a great fear of dying and leaving behind me nothing but bones; my poetry is an attempt, in part, to outlast, to cheat time, to convince me (and you) that my (our) death(s) is (are) more than the end product of birth.

Moonsearch, 1968

David Constantine. A poem takes me a long time to write, but once I have done it as well as I can, I let it be. I understand composition as the attempt to tell the truth about a particular poetic occasion. That occasion itself lapses once I have done my best to realise it in words. To revise a poem I should have to revive the whole occasion, and though that *might* happen, I can't command it. My usual condition as a writer of poetry is inability; when I have the ability its occasion or event is most often a new one, not an old one come back. *Selected Poems*, 1991

Patric Dickinson. Poems are what they say; which is not always what the poet intended. I have explored to the essence of many poems in a way that a reader *need* not, have got near to what the poet aimed to communicate. I have always felt, in so working on a poem in order to offer it to others, that I was the first reader of it – always therefore exhilarated and excited, and chastened into some disciplined delight; contriving to have the poem say all it said and imply all the poet meant to say, perhaps failed to. These self-imposed identifications with poets, often antipathetic, but of inviolable worth, have given me an objective insight and a strict catholicity which I know has brought my own work to whatever value it has to others.

Poetry is not the addition and subtraction of its critics. It is the multiplication and division of those who like it.

This Cold Universe, 1964

DOUGLAS DUNN. When I first wrote poems, the concept of 'tradition' was completely unknown to me. Now I feel bedraggled by it. 'Tradition' may have been an idea which actually produced active poems through the confrontation of poets with it. To me, it looms, an inhibition. A poem should live for the day. Posterity is for libraries to look after. I admit and court the political implications of this assumption. To be counted as truly contemporary in a country where all things are measured by a past (itself tampered with and redesigned according to the expediencies of the present) is what I would like for myself. The most urgent responsibility is towards one's own time. To feel oneself contemporary is perhaps also the best way to avoid pessimism. Though not necessarily, it might also lead to delivering a strong political insult to a stale and jaded present time, though not hopelessly, not with disregard for one's fellow citizens in all classes, not without concern for possibilities and the future.

Love or Nothing, 1974

PAUL DURCAN. All I can say about *Greetings to Our Friends in Brazil* is that I spent six years writing it; that it is my anthology of the 1990s; that, in the course of the writing of it, I felt that it might well be my last book of poems. Whether or not it does prove my last, I think it is my best. To myself I call it my Book of the Affections. *Greetings to Our Friends in Brazil*, 1999

U. A. FANTHORPE. I've been conscious, as usual, of the tug between the accessible and the opaque, between poems that an audience can follow and poems that are really only intelligible on the page; conscious, too, of the way in which certain poems need a particular kind of voice to make them work. This is my problem, dear reader, not yours. But I should like you to know that I realise what you have to put up with. *Consequences*, 2000

PAUL FARLEY. Footnotes, notes to readers, explanations . . . they all seem to be getting longer and longer. Like 'slim' volumes in fact. In the past, when an opportunity like this has arisen, I've tended to shirk it. I'm useless at trying to explain what my poems are 'about', and loath to start joining the dots or identifying themes for the reader.

The Boy from the Chemist is Here to See You, 1998

ROY FISHER. Where there is an 'I' in one of my poems it is likely to be a character wholly given up to the sorting of his perceptions, and certainly not the empirical Roy Fisher, for whom this is only an occasional luxury. The poems are to do with getting about in the mind, and I tackle that in any way I can. *Matrix*, 1971

ROY FULLER. It would be difficult to overstress the value of the poet's irony. Without it he tends to be a solemn show-off and his 'life-long ambition to amuse' (as my title poem puts it) as trying as some noisy life and soul of the party. For me, the sense of the ludicrous may counterpoint even the most poignant of human affairs; as, in reverse, prosodic regularity helps to authorise the trivial or informal in content and language.

From the Joke Shop, 1975

PHILIP GROSS. I've given up envying poets who produce tight slim volumes in which every line breathes *their* voice, *their* purpose. I suspect my English teachers misled me when they talked about 'finding your voice'; it seems all I can do, like Pooh, is stand in the right place and hope the voices find *me*.

Cat's Whisker, 1987

HARRY GUEST. I don't know why or how I write poetry and suspect that if I knew I wouldn't be able to any more. Defiantly and perhaps unfashionably, I believe poetry is a different language from prose, one that solves and poses its own problems and in doing so paradoxically shows itself to be piercingly relevant to the lives we lead. The poets I admire create a fourth dimension while remaining passionately concerned with the texture of the other three, displaying familiar and unknown objects as under starlight with their own elegance and mystery.

A House Against the Night, 1976

GEOFFREY HILL. Although a poet must put a great deal of himself into his work, I have never been able to agree with those who say that poetry is 'self-expression'. When I was twenty I thought that Eliot, at the end of the second section of 'Tradition and the Individual Talent', was absolutely right; and at forty-six, having been taught to be broad-minded and wary, I still think that he was more right than wrong. *Tenebrae*, 1978

SELIMA HILL. Sometimes I think it might puzzle people less if I were a painter or musician, like most of my family are. I don't *want* to be obtuse. My readers are my allies, and I feel a sort of conspiratorialness between us I am grateful for. A sense of being subversive, like the coolest monk, of being true to whatever it is we know we want to be true to.

Trembling Hearts in the Bodies of Dogs, 1994

—————. . . . what I do know is that these poems are love poems. I believe all poems are. You don't have to like it, whatever it is, but you do have to love it. That may sound nonsense, but that's why I'm a poet. It's a kind of surrender to something until, paradoxically, the subject itself is no longer what it's about. The world of the poem, if nothing is rejected or resented or regretted, acquires, for the writer, its own robust comeliness. I'm like both its queen and its victim. It's hard to explain. *Violet*, 1997

MICHAEL HOFMANN. At a time when a great many activities are suspect or disreputable, poetry, which is both, suddenly seems to be neither. A friend of mine took a picture of some poets grouped together under an advertising hoarding: *The Mild Ones.* Of course, a poem is furious concentration, excitement, invention – but all in the service of nothing and no one else. There is a little sketch by the German writer Kurt Tucholsky of three steps, ascending *ad astra*: 'Speech. Writing. Silence.' This attraction of poetry – its blamelessness – applies generally.

Nights in the Iron Hotel, 1983

CHRISTOPHER LOGUE. I am afraid when I sit down to write. Sometimes the sweat runs out of me. If you work regularly, every day, as I try to do, the fear subsides. But it is never far away. Self expression is no reason for writing. The task is to make a work of art and, in so doing, to say something. Pity for poets who have no subject save themselves. *The Husbands*, 1994

GEORGE MACBETH. To be a connoisseur of disaster . . . to relish the working of the worm in the wild apple, is a fault often laid at the door of those doomed by a classical education. I plead guilty to the flaws of this, not least in an itch – growing worse with time – to write in strict and traditional forms.

The Long Darkness, 1983

GLYN MAXWELL. I'm sure established and aspiring poets alike are all wearily familiar with the phrase 'finding one's voice'. It's the cheapest polite way of binning a manuscript: 'You haven't quite found your voice.' In fact, I don't know why some publishers don't go the whole pig and print it as a form letter, filling in the names and so on. It's not, though. Often the publisher is saying, 'You haven't found *my* voice yet', or 'Your voice hasn't found my ears.' Why should a poet settle for one voice? You can get inured to one voice, you will cease to hear it, it will lose its power. *Rest for the Wicked*, 1995

CHRISTOPHER MIDDLETON. . . . A poem can read the spell of experience backwards, so that a configuration appears, in motion, dark like a shoal of fish beneath a sea surface. Motion as configuration – *configuration du mouvant* is the meaning Emile Benveniste assigned to *rhuthmos* in his analysis of the Ionian etymology. At play in that rush of sound and movement there is a logic which the human voice can convert into a cosmos of its own making. Poetic space – necessary as the air in and out of which speech comes to be, and volatile among vast mutations as the logic of the shoal. In ways particular to their erotic impulses, poems enact transformations of this kind in *figures*.

What configures in a poem? Not opinion but idea, not sentiment but sentience (for want of a more tenuous word). A poem can also cross unspeakable distances, as ghost speech . . .

Carminalenia, 1979

EDWIN MORGAN. I do not share what is sometimes called the current disillusion with science and technology. I count myself lucky to have lived at a time of discoveries of such far-reaching potential as space travel must be. The poet, I think, is entitled to set up his camp on other worlds than this, and to bring back what he can in the way of human relevance.

From Glasgow to Saturn, 1973

SEAN O'BRIEN. I'm aware of so many exceptions and reservations that it's hard for me to write confidently or accurately about my own work. The poetry I value is that which gives the reader access to the interior of the imaginative experience, re-creating the present tense with the benefit of hindsight as well as the original innocence, and this is what I would like to be able to do. Failing that, I try to make the models accurate. With honourable and obvious exceptions, I feel that a vital element of poetry is currently neglected: the effort to extend the half-life of our vocabulary. Should this tendency persist, it seems to me that the bulk of what is now contemporary will seem etiolated and flatly subtle to the reader- and writership now resident in our infant schools. *The Indoor Park*, 1983

Peter Porter. I have always thought that serious and light can mix in the one poem. I don't believe in a form of apartheid where a serious poet occasionally condescends to write light verse (as Eliot did) or the sort of ambidexterity which uses the right hand for serious poems and the left for satirical ones (Robert Graves's method). But the Muses are watching and are quick to point out each other's defects. *The Last of England*, 1970

_______________. After Auschwitz, they say, all art must be existential and at the edge of desperation. I am sure that the opposite is the case. It is the duty of art to make palatable somehow the real tragedy of the world. It must tell the truth about the facts of that tragedy at the same time. This is a tall order but one which poets have to face up to. One way of doing so, I believe, is to question the machinery of language, to try to test the worth of the words we use to describe our feelings. I don't mean games with words, but a constant awareness of the shapes language makes of itself. Such questioning means that poetry can never hope to be very popular. Yet its feelings should be universal.

The Cost of Seriousness, 1978

Peter Reading. I have been attracted to the idea of trying to draw forth responses to entirely synthetic stimuli – to see whether the quite artificial fabrication of an event, a situation, an emotional state, could be as effective in producing a desired reaction from a reader as the faithfully rendered Genuinely Felt Poetic Experience is said often to be. Conversely I have sometimes tried to fictionalise an actual experience until it is beyond the recognition of its original participants (thus parrying embarrassment, legal action, actual bodily harm) and yet retain something of it which is able to move the reader.

Tom o'Bedlam's Beauties, 1981

Oliver Reynolds. It might be thought that the poem is born through the unaided labours of the poet. This elevates the poet to the status of 'onlie begetter' of immaculately conceived offspring. It is just as plausible, though, to think of the poems as the result of more promiscuous goings-on involving a greater number of participants. (Fortunately, this makes writing poetry sound, at the very least, rather jolly.) Language plays a vigorous part in the proceedings and, though a singular noun, it is a teemingly plural reality. Language is where structure meets chaos (a meeting at which the poem is an interested onlooker).

The Oslo Tram, 1991

Vernon Scannell. I find it difficult to talk about my own writing: the likelihood of seeming absurdly pompous and self-aggrandising is the first gag to try to rip off and then this is at once replaced by the equally inhibiting one of sounding a note, no less offensive, of facetious and phoney self-disparagement . . . For me, chat about poetry only becomes really interesting when it gets away from vague generalisations and down to the mechanics of the craft itself, and I am embarrassed by writers – usually of concussingly boring work – who say things like, 'The informing spirit of the poetry of my middle period is essentially neo-pantheistic. . . .' that sort of thing. *The Loving Game*, 1975

Peter Scupham. I would like my poems to be windows, not mirrors. A window frames a scene which has its own strong and independent life; the personality of the poet both shapes that scene and is subordinate to it. The frame, however, is important. A window cuts a shape, and I am fascinated by structure, harmony, balance – all those qualities which give definition to the view which the window elects to show.

The Hinterland, 1977

Penelope Shuttle. Poetry is an antidote to the poison level at which we often consent to live. We are, many of us, amnesiacs.

We forget the amazing things that happen to us. Poetry remembers them. Also, what is given shared articulation can never hurt so much as whatever remains unuttered. *Selected Poems*, 1998

Iain Crichton Smith. On the whole my new poetry book is about loneliness, though the poems do not flower so much from a common centre as I would wish. I have been concerned with this theme for a long time now and there is nothing new in it as far as I am concerned. I think it is an eternal and central human theme. I am perhaps not as interested in the poem as an aesthetic artefact as I used to be, though I don't much like talking about poetry anyway.

The Notebooks of Robinson Crusoe, 1975

Charles Tomlinson. A fisherman comes to know the ways of water and negotiates a mode of living with it. The poet, also faced by a water world – a world, that is, where, in the old formulation, everything flows – must also discover his way through that given reality, using craft, knowledge, experience.

Written on Water, 1972

Chase Twichell. To me, one of the durable mysteries of writing is the inconstancy of access I have to my own work. When a poem (or in this case, a whole book) is finished, its surface closes over. My memory of how it was written begins to erode almost immediately. In the end, I come to see the poems as artefacts of the adventure I had. They are the containers of whatever it was I learned, the only residue. I hope that the poems in *Perdido* briefly hold open for readers, as they do for me, windows in the mystery that death makes of love.

Perdido, 1992

Kit Wright. I regard humour and irony as indispensable to rendering a poetic account of life and make no apology for the various comic modes employed in the book. Seriousness, despite the rival claims of currently warring schools of poetry, is the absolute prerogative of no individual aesthetic and it informs the work of different poets in different ways. The punch-line poem, the pun, the banana-skin reversal are all proper and available methods of exposing the world and the psyche. They fail when the wit's flat and the feeling's dead.

The Bear Looked over the Mountain, 1977

LOUIS ZUKOFSKY. *'A' 1–12* is part of a long poem, begun in 1927 and to be completed in twenty-four movements. In a sense the poem is autobiography, as I believe all poems are, revealing the life through their words.

Looking back, *'A'* is another of my 'found objects'. With the years the personal prescriptions for one's work recede, thankfully, before an interest that *nature as creator* had more of a hand in it than one was aware. The work then owns perhaps something of the look of *found objects* in late exhibits – which arrange themselves, as it were, one object near another – roots that have become sculpture, wood that appears talisman, and so on: charms, amulets maybe, but never really such things since the struggles, so to speak, that made them do not seem to have been human trials and evils – they appear entirely *natural.* Their chronology is of interest only to those who analyse carbon fractions etc., who love historicity – and since they too, considering *nature as creator*, are no doubt right in their curiosity in – and one has never wished to offend anyone – the dates of composition of the parts.

'A' 1–12, 1966

Acknowledgements

With thanks to all contributing poets and to the estates of the following for permission to reprint pieces originally published in the Poetry Book Society Bulletin: George Barker, Frances Cornford, Gavin Ewart, W. S. Graham, Roy Fuller, Peter Levi, Peter Whigham, Norman MacCaig, Barry MacSweeney, Kathleen Raine, James Reeves, Anne Ridler, R. S. Thomas.

The excerpt by Kingsley Amis on *A Case of Samples* appears courtesy of Jonathan Clowes Ltd.

Excerpts from pieces by John Ash on *The Goodbyes*; Iain Crichton Smith on *Collected Poems*; Donald Davie on *Selected Poems*; Robert Graves on *Collected Poems*; Dom Moraes on *Poems* and Burns Singer on *Still And All* are all reproduced by permission of Carcanet Press.

John Betjeman's piece on *Summoned by Bells* reproduced with permission of John Murray (Publishers) Ltd.

Pieces by Charles Causley (*Underneath the Water*); Geoffrey Grigson (*Ingestion of Ice-Cream*); John Heath-Stubbs (*Selected Poems*); Elizabeth Jennings (*Song for a Birth or a Death* and *A Way of Looking*); Louis MacNeice (*Solstices* and *The Burning Perch*); Norman Nicholson (*A Local Habitation* and *Sea to the West*) and Herbert Read (*Moon's Farm*) reproduced with permission of David Higham Associates.

Austin Clarke on *Old-Fashioned Pilgrimage* reproduced with permission of R. Dardis Clarke.

Frances Cornford on her *Collected Poems* printed with the permission of the Trustees of the Mrs Frances Cornford Deceased Will Trust.

Lawrence Durrell's piece on *The Tree of Idleness* reproduced with permission of Curtis Brown Ltd, London, on behalf of the Estate of Lawrence Durrell.

D. J. Enright on *Sad Ires and Others* reproduced with permission of Watson, Little Ltd.

James Fenton on *Out of Danger* and *The Memory of War* reprinted by permission of PFD on behalf of James Fenton. P. J. Kavanagh on *One and One* and *Selected Poems* and Anne Sexton on *Selected Poems* reproduced by permission of PFD on behalf of the estates of P. J. Kavanagh and Anne Sexton respectively.

Ted Hughes's pieces on *The Hawk in the Rain*, *Wolfwatching* and *Ariel* by Sylvia Plath reproduced with permission of the Estate of Ted Hughes.

Philip Larkin on *The Whitsun Weddings* reproduced with permission of The Society of Authors.

George Macbeth on *Selected Poems* and Rosemary Tonks on *Notes on Cafés and Bedrooms* reproduced with permission of Sheil Land Associates.

Edwin Muir's piece on *One Foot in Eden* reproduced with permission of Faber and Faber Ltd.